AF601526

Praise for *Honolulu Blues*

"What a heartwarming book about a man and his crappy football team. Over the decades, the Detroit Lions epitomized NFL awfulness for its legions (dozens?) of fans. Yet somehow, all those setbacks brought meaning—and redemption—to Joel Walkowski. Forget Barry Sanders; forget Calvin Johnson; forget Jeff Komlo and Stephen Boyd. After reading this gem, you'll associate Motown City gridiron with one name: Walkowski."

—Jeff Pearlman, New York Times Bestselling Author, *The Last Folk Hero*, *Showtime*, and *The Bad Guys Won!*

"Unfortunately, for Joel, the poor guy grew up a Lions fan. Lucky for you, this book is so sharp, funny, and entertaining, even a Packers or Bears fan would begrudgingly love it."

—Sam Morrill, Comedian and Podcast Host, *We Might Be Drunk*

"Makes the losing make sense, beautiful even. I read this the morning after the Bills lost another playoff game and it helped. Joel wrote a great Rust Belt book that will make you say 'screw the Super Bowl, I just want to experience some disappointing football with my loved ones.'"

—Joe Pera, Comedian and Star of *Joe Pera Talks With You* on Adult Swim

"I will never watch another Detroit Lions game without thinking of Joel Walkowski, who has authored a one-of-a-kind football memoir connecting his searing life story with the enduring misery of his beloved Lions. Alternately heartbreaking and heartwarming, tearfully sad and laugh-out-loud funny, *Honolulu Blues* deserves an audience. Highly recommended."

—John Eisenberg, Sports Writer and Author, *The League*

"*Honolulu Blues* is a poignant, endearing story about fathers and sons, love, heartbreak, resilience, redemption, and the Detroit Lions. On these pages, Joel Walkowski cuts like Sanders, charms like Fontes, and shows the grit and fight of Dan Campbell. He's worth reading."

—Tom Stanton, *New York Times* Bestselling Author, *Terror in the City of Champions* and *The Final Season*

"Reminiscent of Frederick Exley's *A Fan's Notes*, Joel Walkowski dares to be an unabashed follower of the Detroit Lions. In following that long, hard road, he gained insights and lessons that any true sports fan can hold dear."

—Tim Wendl, Author, *Summer of '68*

"As a lifelong Boston sports fan who's known his fair share of personal heartbreak and dysfunction (before all those championships), reading *Honolulu Blues* felt like an autobiography from a different fanbase's perspective. Walkowski's incredible ability to weave his own struggles with that of his favorite football team with immense humor and heart is a brilliant narrative construct that leaves you both rooting for him and, miraculously, the Detroit Lions as well.

"In *Honolulu Blues*, Joel Walkowski brilliantly takes the idea of suffering alongside your favorite sports team to a place no fan may have gone before. And that's a good thing, since being a Detroit Lions fan can be so deleterious to your health. That Joel's path mirrors that of the Lions is uncanny, as is his way of weaving personal and painful anecdotes in and out the history of the team. That it leaves you feeling for him, the team, and the fanbase, all while laughing hysterically, is a testament to his talent."

— Nick Stevens, Boston Sports Personality

"I learned how to read for this book."

— Chris Waelti, Local Bar Fly

HONOLULU BLUES

HONOLULU BLUES

HOW LOVING A LOSING TEAM CREATED A WINNING MAN

JOEL WALKOWSKI

Matt Holt Books
An Imprint of BenBella Books, Inc.
Dallas, TX

DISCLAIMER. This book reflects the author's memories, impressions, and personal perspective on events and conversations over time. Some names, characteristics, and identifying details have been changed, combined, or fictionalized to protect privacy. While the author has made every effort to present events truthfully as remembered, others may recall them differently. Certain events have been compressed or reordered for clarity. The essence of the story—and the feelings and emotions it conveys—are intended as an accurate representation of the author's lived experience.

Matt Holt is an imprint of BenBella Books, Inc.
8080 N. Central Expressway
Suite 1700
Dallas, TX 75206
benbellabooks.com
Send feedback to feedback@benbellabooks.com

BenBella and *Matt Holt* are federally registered trademarks.

Printed in the United States of America
10 9 8 7 6 5 4 3 2 1

Library of Congress Control Number: 2026000721
ISBN 9781637749043 (hardcover)
ISBN 9781637749050 (electronic)

Editing by Katie Dickman
Copyediting by Scott Calamar
Proofreading by Sarah Vostok and Martha Gallant
Text design and composition by PerfecType, Nashville, TN
Cover design by Paul McCarthy
Cover image © Adobe Stock / Nikola
Printed by Lake Book Manufacturing

For Liam

We always shared a story. Why would this one be any different?

CONTENTS

GAME 1

THE LOSS IS THE WIN

• 2017 •

Most godfathers get the job at a christening; I became a godfather at a funeral.

I accepted the position in a parking lot in Remus, Michigan—a forgotten Rust Belt town with the bare minimum of everything: one stoplight, one gas station, two dollar stores.

★ ★ ★

Thirty-six hours earlier.

I shuffle through security at a Brooklyn Nets game. The phone rings. Uncle Joe is dead. Anguish is chased by two realizations: 1) There will be no flights until morning and 2) the game hasn't started.

I watch the game, sneaking behind the visiting Clippers' bench and failing to access emotions. Chris Paul cries after every call, making me jealous. I can't muster a single tear.

Since gaining cognition, sports have helped me process emotions. Decades of addiction, failure, angst toward a father who couldn't help but come up short, more addiction. It's surprising so few men view games this way. Any of these issues could have—and probably should have—done me in, but I found a coping mechanism: Turn on the game and reflect on existence.

If the process works? I get a life lesson. If the process fails? I'm simply watching sports. It's a win-win proposition.

I developed this practice watching the Detroit Lions. My beloved "Motor City Kitties" are the prism through which I understand the world. They also happen to be the worst team in American sports. I've seen winless seasons and legends retire early, but remain undeterred. I never miss a game.

Being a Lions fan is like being a musician on the *Titanic*. Each Sunday arrives with a choice, and each week I choose to play music on the deck of a sinking ship.

Decades, generations, *eons* of mismanagement have made this team synonymous with failure. The Lions belong to people like me but are owned by the Ford family. Henry Ford may have built our city and the auto industry, but his lineage can't build a winning team.

A new Lions squad unfurls each autumn, as I announce to anyone who will listen that "This year's different. The Lions will finally be good."

I've done this every year of my life and have never been right.[1]

We have exclusively failed since 1957. That's a wide-ranging "we"—the Lions, my city, and my family have all floundered since our last championship. This is how things go for Detroit. Failures made our town a punch line. It's easy for the world to laugh. It's much harder acknowledging our fate as a plausible outcome.

There's a reason why sports fans say "we." *We* are the team. At a foundational level, I am the Lions. I am not a success. I usually come up short. But we win another way: by greeting each day with enthusiasm.

---

1. Spoiler alert: We get good. Turns out all it took to turn around the Detroit Lions was writing an experimental memoir prominently featuring the team. Take note, Browns fans. 😀

Life is not about winning. This story is about how learning to derive joy from even the biggest losers—the Detroit Lions—reshaped my inner life. I hope our intertwined failure speaks some greater truth about adversity. The Lions rarely provide a good Sunday, but I have a good one every week by adjusting my expectations.

Fandom is illogical. Fans of winning teams tie happiness to outcomes. Doing this with the Lions only creates disappointment. Accepting losing protects against high hopes and aligns with life's disappointing nature. Only one team exits an NFL season as the winner. Why not plan accordingly?

Men struggle with emotions. Given the time investment the average man dedicates to sports, it's wasteful not to channel that energy toward self-improvement. Watching the Lions is what I do *for fun*. To be a fan of *this* team is to preemptively search for (Honolulu Blue, our team color, and) silver linings.

Two things are true simultaneously: 1) My biggest dream is seeing the Lions in the Super Bowl and 2) I would not alter franchise history. This dissonance is a chasm, but I accept this team fully. They are perfect to me.

Other fans savor Super Bowls. The Lions gave me something more sustaining: low expectations. Learning how to love something certain to let me down is the best lesson I could've received. Watching this team lose *and lose and lose* has dramatically improved my life. I don't think many Patriots fans can say that.

★ ★ ★

My departed uncle demonstrated that life is what happens between chugging coffee, popping pills, and scrounging nicotine. Life—in whatever form it takes—is there to be loved. Chat up the clerk at Meijer just enough to sneak a candy bar in your pocket but still enjoy the conversation.

It's not a bad way to live.

We mourn in a shabby little house, proving "dirt poor" to be a literal definition.

Joe lived here with his wife, his daughter Kayleigh, and her seven-year-old son, Julion—whose dad isn't in the picture. Joe was the man in his life. Family consensus deems me the second coming of my departed uncle. By that logic, Julion will take after me. He's too big to be coordinated, too smart for his surroundings, too addled with ADD to follow directions. *I get it, kid.*

We spend the funeral fucking around. We play tag on the lawn, and he tails me to the gas station where I unsuccessfully show him how to steal.

I'm leaving the funeral to rush back to New York when Kayleigh pulls me aside. She's the sweetest person I know, struggling with her weight but afraid to take up space. Her grabbing my attention means it's important.

"Thanks for playing with Julion."

"He's awesome."

"Will you be his godfather?"

"I don't believe in God."

"That's okay. He just needs a guy."

I can be a guy. It's more than I had.

I have a dad. That dad isn't a typical father. He's Banjo Bob, a tiny Polish man with autism who usually dresses like a cowboy. He won't give fatherly advice but will speak for hours about leather and banjos to anyone who will listen. Even though most people tune him out within minutes.

I'm the light of Banjo Bob's life, but he can't express this truth. This is trauma's impact. The Walkowskis bear the generational albatross of abuse. Banjo Bob was molested. A lot.

It's difficult to be a damaged man's son. He'll growl if I bring up an emotional topic—*literally* making the aggrieved squeals of cornered animals—before shrinking away for one of 80 daily cigarettes. That's how Walkowski men deal with emotions.

I can do better.

I accept the position as godfather.

I consider the boy. What will help him grow? What will show him the way? What will make him kind and confident and whole? I rack my brain, trying to pinpoint what *actually* supported me on my journey to becoming "a guy" he just might need.

It's the Detroit Lions.

WEEK 3: SEPTEMBER 24, 2017. ATLANTA FALCONS (2-0) V DETROIT LIONS (2-0). FORD FIELD, DETROIT, MI.

Nine months after Joe's passing. I drive from Brooklyn to Detroit in a 1998 Mitsubishi Mirage, purchased for $400. Like modern Fred Flintstone, I watch the blur of the highway tick by through holes in the floorboards.

I stop at Meijer, buy Julion a Calvin Johnson T-shirt, and chat up the cashier while pocketing a Twix. Calvin doesn't play anymore, but the true mark of a Lion legend is retiring early. What we lose gets lionized. We understand failure's frustration and appreciate these players more for walking away. Heck, half the fan base probably works for Ford and wishes they could quit too.

Julion is unimpressed with Ford Field, our stadium. He has no interest in sports or my understanding of male bonding. His rambunctious nature makes it difficult to focus or control his body enough to participate. *I get it, kid.*

I was the same boy. Grueling physical therapy taught me basic skills like using straws and tying shoes. Severe doses of speed were prescribed at a young age. Intended to make me fit in, speed ultimately ramps up the intensity of thought patterns and makes life's most meaningful aspects occur in my mind. I became a 6'3" ball of muscle who can't attend a football game without being asked about nonexistent playing days, but my core remains this irrepressible boy.

We enter the stadium, greeted by the vista of a lush, green faux field. I whisper to Julion in mythologies: "No championships since 1957, no playoff wins since 1991, no problem."

The Lions do nothing but lose, often in progressively innovative ways that make failure an art form. The Super Bowl has existed for 57 years. We've never won, never been, and only won a single playoff game in that span.[2]

I watched the 1991 playoff win with my family. It was the first time I picked an activity for us to do together. The clan came together to watch the game, but what they were really doing was supporting me. Five-year-old Joel expressed his needs; loved ones rallied around them. It was easy to accept the Lions as full-fledged family members. They're losers like the rest of us.

This year, *like all other years*, will be different. A 2–0 record sends hopeful vibes through a city that renders these feelings moot. Sun shines in our domed stadium.

Julion and I perch over the end zone in the upper bowl. Banjo Bob once advised, "these are the best seats because you can track receiver's routes." Now that I'm the one paying, I know they're the cheapest. Still, nosebleeds allow a clearer view of the big picture. Julion experiences 65,000 people crammed together to feel the same things: anticipation, belonging, desire. It's an ideal scenario to share.

Detroit promptly shits the bed. Atlanta strikes first, and second, and third.

Matthew Stafford keeps getting shown on the jumbotron. Julion asks, "Who's that?"

I am unable to truthfully answer. I can't explain that my adult life has coincided with Stafford's reign as Lions quarterback or that I've adopted him as my concept of *what a man should be.* Nor can I impart a franchise quarterback's value or explain how the Lions mirror life's struggles.

The answer I settle on is: "He throws the football."[3]

---

2. Spoiler Alert:

3. I imagine this is the same answer Matthew Stafford gives when a therapist asks, "So who's the real Matthew Stafford?"

Anyone who visits Detroit or watches the Lions develops a singular sentiment: *Things were so much better before.* The "before" hangs in the air. No explanation is offered because so many things fit in the gap. Before the race riots, population decline, urban decay, systemic failure, corruption, bungling ownership. Barry Sanders retiring, Matt Millen, Calvin leaving, and many other reasons. It's best to sigh, appreciate the past, and avoid getting smothered by nostalgia for an era you weren't alive for.

Growing up in Detroit means accepting things as imperfect and broken but no big deal. If heartbreak is inevitable, why not cling to the moments before that happens?

An errant Falcons pass caroms into the waiting arms of Glover Quin. He races the interception into the Atlanta end zone, reigniting all possibilities. The Lions will start 3–0! I will be a good godfather!

Julion does not know what transpired. I tell him to "be happy" as the stadium breaks into "Gridiron Heroes," our commercial jingle-y fight song. The tune has embarrassing lyrics, a terrible melody, and is devastatingly perfect.

Stafford wields control, tying the game. Nothing holds us back from a bold new future except a weighty history of certain failure.

For region and self, accepting lifelong also-ran status is psyche defining. Juxtapositions of internalized low self-worth are hypercomplex and locally specific but perfectly defined by three little words: *Same. Old. Lions.*

This adage is a reminder to never expect anything good—an omniscient warning forged by the sands of time. I warn Julion of the curse I'm bestowing as Atlanta turns a six-yard completion into a 75-yard touchdown. Maddeningly and repetitively, *Same Old Lions* strikes again.

The Lions offense—which is technically a Ford product—predictably stalls. Stafford's gunslinging mentality is perfect when heroics are needed but unnecessary in positive circumstances. You don't need to swing for the fences with the wind at your back.

Back-to-back punts have fans filing for the exits. If Banjo Bob were here—and in a way he is—he'd hiss "real fans don't leave early." I always follow Bob's rule and steadfastly remain until the final buzzer, but I understand others' exodus. Anyone dedicating a lifetime of Sundays to this team deserves to recoup as much investment as possible.

The Falcons need one first down to run out the clock. They fail.

Fourth Quarter; Atlanta 30, Detroit 26

Stafford is placed where he does his best work: with his back against the wall.

A pass interference advances the ball to the precipice of victory. All the Lions must do is punch it in. A 3–0 start will fill Detroit with joy as opposed to techno music fans and urban explorers.

0:12, Third and Goal

We are inches from the promised land. A childhood habit of burying my head in my father's sleeve during stressful plays stays with me. When the team faces dire outcomes, I find the closest loved one and cling. I pick up Julion, hoping our embrace will shift the city's karma.

Zero remaining timeouts limit Detroit to passing packages. Stafford takes the snap and finds Golden Tate at the one. Atlanta's secondary converges but not quickly enough to stop him from breaking the plane. *TOUCHDOWN LIONS!*

Ford Field explodes with rare exuberance. We'll spill from the stadium on a bright September afternoon, discovering a city redefined. The Lions have won.

Julion does not contextually understand this moment but processes the feeling as pretty friggin' good. Formally beginning our relationship like this will create a Pavlovian response between his perception of me and happy memories.

These thoughts occur in a matter of seconds. It's enough time to imagine the Lions becoming a winner and the boy as a confident man—all thanks to me!

It's argued that the most beautiful phrase in the English language is "cellar door." Unpacking this phrase's meaning reveals numerous positive connotations. It's a way out of the darkness, our language's clearest distillation of hope. The opposite—a most devastating phrase—also exists. It's about to be uttered, shattering rosy visions of the future and forever fastening us to this underwhelming reality.

"The previous play is under review."

Verification is unnerving, but the jumbotron shows Tate crossing the goal line. Even a reversal leaves enough time to run one play, maybe even two.

The referee emerges from his cute little video review tent like a horror film axe murderer stalking a coed. I've always resented authority due to the Lions' relationship with referees.

"Upon further review, the runner was stopped short of the goal line."

Boos descend. Julion joins the jeering. I've never been prouder.

"The result of the play is a ten-second runoff," the referee states before cataclysmically continuing, "this is the end of the game."

The Lions lose. Not to Atlanta but to bureaucratic machinations. An elite athletic contest is decided by a rule book footnote.[4]

"What happened?"

"The Lions lost."

"Why?"

"Because that's what they do."

Some entities aren't supposed to succeed. Regardless of strategy or execution, they're bound to predetermined fates. Detroit has an abundance of mind-bending defeats, but truthfully? The Lions losing is universal order. Crushing defeats accord with Mother Nature.

There are two photos of Julion and me from this game. They're taken within 60 seconds but occur lifetimes apart. In one, we are joyful, electrified to our cores by the intensity of happiness. In the other we are emotionless, painfully aware of struggles within the world and ourselves.

---

4. Imagine if this made your team lose.

We aren't supposed to win. Golden Tate found the end zone, but authorities buzzed in from New York. "Overturn the play. A young man is in dire risk of having a positive outlook."

The loss serves Julion well. I do not give him a positive memory but an emphatic illustration of the way things are.

You will lose. It will be unfair. Yet somehow, you will enjoy it.

★ ★ ★

Unwaveringly rooting for a hopeless team reinforces the emotional muscles that articulate unconditional love. Lions fandom improved my relationship with my father and, more importantly, myself. This team, this family? They tell the same story.

Fandom is not rational. The team's importance to my psyche is surely a defect, but I can't call it unhealthy when it's served me so well. Why does continued disappointment cause love to grow? Because sifting through failure for the positives made me who I am. Long ago, when I was Julion's age, the decision was made. *This* is what I love. Why would I let their performance change that?

Intermingling team and personal history is the only way to reach out to my father. He's lying in a shack surrounded by team media guides, moving toward death as fast as a senior citizen with heart failure can go. This is me telling him our story in the only way he'll understand.

He gave me addiction, generational trauma, a love of this team, and hundreds of switchblades. Well, Banjo Bob. This is yours. Know that the net result of what you passed down is a positive. This is a story of fathers and sons, of how the things we love change us, and of the wins that accompany losing. This is the story of the Detroit Lions and their fans.

Banjo Bob has read almost all this work. He agreed with everything that was written and generally enjoys it.

He doesn't get to read the ending.

He dies at the end.

We're alone when it happens. The Lions choke away the Super Bowl, but we celebrate (almost) winning. I'm whispering to him about the team, but talking about myself, when he quietly slips away.

I put a Lions jersey on his lifeless body. The number is 1. The nameplate reads "Before I Die." Almost, Banjo Bob. Almost.

The coroner wheels him away but he's still with me. I sit on the bed, buried by an avalanche of emotions suppressed for generations, figuring out what to do next. I know where to go.

Forward Down the Field!

GAME 2

THE CENTER OF THE WORLD

• 1934–1962 •

Four NFL Championships, One Happy Fan Base

2024

The NFL draft is in Detroit. The city's bright and clean, pulsating with fandom. A chipper populace crowds the streets, dazzling in waves of Honolulu Blue. Julion and I burst through the crowds, drawn toward the NFL draft, tractor-beam style, like famished cartoons sniffing delicious aromas. Spilled beer, Coney dog, and football fan sweat. Gridiron by Calvin Klein.

Real men don't pay for parking. It's part of our patriarchal duties. We park too far away. Julion won't complain. My bullshit's gospel to his now fourteen-year-old ears. It inspires him to lift weights, make eye contact, and make conversation with girls. There's no curriculum; I simply exist in proximity to the boy.

I point out Detroit's many changes. What was populated became abandoned and now bustles again. Cities have their own circle of life.

"Will you two slow down?!?" pleads Kayleigh from behind. We roll our eyes, slow our pace, and approach the NFL draft as a makeshift family.

"What's the NFL draft?" Julion asks.

"Names get called. Like your teacher taking attendance."

"Why do people care?"

"It's a spectacle. And the spectacle's in Detroit."

Approaching security, Julion grows anxious, eyeing the metal detectors.

"What's wrong?"

"I have a switchblade."

Kayleigh clears her throat. "I also have a switchblade."

I don't ask why. I know why. We all have switchblades. Banjo Bob spent the past decade compulsively giving switchblades away.[1] To friends, to family, to strangers. Kayleigh and Julion bring their knives everywhere but I don't. I carry enough of him with me as it is.

I've parked too far away. "Just bring them in."

I breeze through security, gazing back at Julion, who is now boiling with fear. The metal detector *beeps.* Guards repeat the process. Detectors *beep* once more but security waves him on. Pausing in contrition, Julion announces, "I have a knife."

Security sighs. "Welcome to Detroit." We enter.

Detroit's on display, showcased to our oligarch's specifications. Suburban chatter and national media identically exclaim: "Detroit is back!"

Detroit's not back. Detroit never left. It's always been here, keeping the beat for America's story through good times and bad.

1934–1962

Our industry, our manufacturing acumen. It changed the world. Detroit was a hybrid of Silicon Valley and Wall Street with the vital exception that it actually built something.

You've heard of boomtowns. Industry sprouts up and a functional city blooms. It's all well and good until *POP!* Opportunity springs elsewhere and populations redistribute, clustering alongside the next big thing. Detroit is a boom city.

---

1. And every Social Security check.

Henry Ford did it. The dream of internal combustion vehicles was globally pursued, but Ford did it best. He produced the car cheaply and repeatedly, each decision aligning with the vision of scaled-up operations. Success didn't come from the invention but from making it available to the masses.

In 1908, Henry Ford made the first Model T. By 1917, the Ford Motor Company produced over half a million annually.

The assembly line made it possible. Workers handled one specific task by design. Tighten a bolt, place an axle, repeat until retirement. Detroit's industrial breakthrough was Ford understanding how treating labor fairly could catalyze growth.

Ford became the world's richest man. The sum of money generated and people tied to it will shape Detroit as long as it exists. Posh existences aren't necessarily easy. Being born with a silver spoon in one's mouth is great until it's time to cry out and express your needs. His scions, his company, and the team they'd govern would struggle to bloom in his shadow.

Assembly-line work made Detroit the world's fastest-growing city and a uniquely promising place to build a life. Employees received five dollars a day, work-life balance, vacation homes up north, and a Model T to tool around in. Sure, Ford's goons might rough you up if you stepped out of line, but the trade-off was worth it.

The core feeling of life in our pleasant peninsula is derived from working the lines and driving home in a car you built. But *aha!* Blue-collar boys need to blow off steam.

Football was growing. The sport stiff-armed a potential ban from Teddy Roosevelt,[2] proliferating across college campuses before ascending to the professional ranks in the form of barnstormers and exhibition games. A nascent NFL gained a Midwestern foothold but had yet to be optimized for ideal markets and concentrated populations. That was about to change.

The Portsmouth Spartans were a talented team but a horribly run business. They'd routinely beat rivals but were so poorly marketed that more

2. Surprising given how easy it is to imagine ol' Teddy in a leather helmet.

fans attended practices than games. Even their finances were bungled. Team accounts were overdrawn so often it was not unusual for a player to receive team stock instead of a check.

In 1934, George A. Richards, owner of WJR radio—a local institution on par with Vernors ginger ale—bought the team and relocated them to Detroit. The name was changed to "Lions," an attempt at manifesting their rule over the NFL like their namesake ruled the jungle.

Walkowski men bought the first batch of season tickets. They weren't football fans but considered games "a great place to drink beer and fight." They drank and gambled to excess, allowing vices to limit their lives. This is not unique to my family. This happens to many men. My family is this story's subject, but we represent the emotionally stunted, masculine many.

Detroit hosted the inaugural Thanksgiving game during its first NFL season. In light of the holiday's genocidal origins, the Lions playing is arguably the better reason to celebrate.

The Lions won the NFL championship in 1935. This magical year saw Detroit win the crown in the NFL, MLB, and NHL. It made sense. We were the only city capable of producing enough cars for all the championship parades.

World War II shifted Detroit's priorities from local affluence to global security. Industrial competencies pivoted toward war efforts well before the United States' involvement. "The Arsenal of Democracy," as FDR called Detroit, possessed unmatched manufacturing abilities integral to the Allies' victory.

Many automakers had contracts with Nazi regimes. Only Ford stood with the ideology, publishing periodicals demonizing the Jewish people and cultivating a fawning relationship with Hitler.[3] Adolf hung Henry's portrait at headquarters and awarded him the Grand Cross of the German Eagle, the highest honor available to non-Germans.

3. Ford should also be credited with creating Reddit's predecessor, i.e., a written concentration of extreme opinions.

Ford's Rouge plant, the man-made marvel and Henry's personal crown jewel, produced vital artillery. As someone who supported Matt Millen but eventually protested for his ouster, I cannot help but relate.

Allied victory pushed Detroit into the spotlight, ushering in a hard-earned golden era. The Lions led the charge, establishing a symbiotic relationship with the city that continues to this day.

The Lions were purchased by a symposium of local businessmen and governed democratically. Key decisions were made at spaghetti banquets hosting the various owners. This manner of civic investment served the city well.

All Detroit did was build dynasties. Automakers turned the American Dream into a product, Motown Records manufactured hit singles with assembly-line efficiency, and Detroit revolutionized culture.

The Lions followed suit, heralding modern fandom. Ravenous support pushed forward in-arena experience, television broadcasting,[4] and holiday celebrations. On-field product further channeled civic enthusiasm into excellence. We ran the first two-minute drill and made crowd noise specifically to disrupt opponents.

The 1950s Lions won three championships. The cocktail of team success and collective support created a dynasty and a high we've been chasing ever since.

Imagine that you're a 1950s Detroiter. You work at a globally important company, listen to local music that'll influence pop radio for the foreseeable future, and root for a team actualizing the bond between city and football team. It's good to be king of the jungle.

Banjo Bob was born in July 1952 with radio broadcasts of back-to-back championships floating from the living room and into his crib. My father will not speak of his upbringing. If he does it's about Bobby Layne.

Bobby Layne was a Lions legend and pop culture crossover, establishing ideas of what a gridiron hero should be. Layne barked orders, improvised,

---

4. These Lions teams were the first squad with prime-time broadcasts and to shift their schedule to maximize viewership.

and was the sort of man who lets you know that you, too, have what it takes, because why else would you be in the trenches with him? The swashbuckling quarterback could run, pass, command huddles, and win championships hungover.

It's unfair to call Bobby Layne my father's childhood hero. He never graduated from the position. Banjo Bob would sit on his deathbed, arguing he was named after Bobby Layne. I do the math. July 1952. A family wouldn't name their son after a journeyman with a handful of career starts. I don't correct him. Keep your myth, Pops.

Bobby Layne—like many central figures in this tale—was a drunk. Layne's on-field exploits are only rivaled by Herculean efforts in Detroit barrooms. Apart from three championships and supernaturally haunting the team, Layne's known for his relationship with alcohol.

Layne was a legendary drinker, lauded for keeping jazz clubs open by throwing $100 bills into saxophones and blaming a championship loss on *not* drinking the night before. He even got out of a DUI with the explanation that, as a thick-accented Texan, he always sounded drunk. I can only imagine how poorly one had to drive to get pulled over as the star player of a beloved team in the 1950s Midwest.[5]

Layne was traded to the Pittsburgh Steelers early in the 1958 season.

Rumors abounded. Layne had a bar fight with replacement Tobin Rote or was implicated in a point-shaving scandal—as it was well known that players intermingled with gamblers.

Facts remain. Trading Layne was mutually beneficial. The Lions moved forward with Rote, the only man to quarterback championship teams in both the AFL and NFL, and reunited Layne with Buddy Parker, his long-time coach in Detroit.

News reached Layne while picking up a relative at a nearby airfield. Circumstances of discovery incensed Layne, believing he'd earned a more

---

5. Similar to wondering how vile Detroit Tigers star Ty Cobb must've been to be considered racist during his 1910s playing days.

graceful exit. The Lions avoided having Layne learn of the trade over the radio, but there's ultimately no good way to learn devastating news.

Furious, Layne cursed the franchise, vowing that "the Lions would not win for fifty years." Bobby Layne was sacred to the city. Getting rid of him betrayed his devotees. The curse came true. We haven't won a championship since trading Bobby Layne. It is the most enduring hex in sports.

There were more bad omens, more dark plagues. Layne was not alone lingering in the rearview mirror as the team sped toward oblivion. There was also William "Moon" Baker.

Moon was the dynasty's greatest fan. Baker was a true supporter, revolving his life around impacting Briggs Stadium games. Desire to improve game-day atmosphere was coupled with Detroit ingenuity as Baker produced a 25-pound Lion costume he started wearing to games. Baker was present at every contest, ascending to the role of official mascot.

It was a Friday. Baker was running pre-game errands when he went missing. A panicked search found him dead on a sidewalk at 3 AM. The man who gave the Lions a mascot became a cut-covered corpse adorned with a meticulously placed pair of eyeglasses. The coroner ruled it a heart attack. The team represented the city and Detroit was an organized-crime town.

Covering up the murder of a self-made team mascot doesn't have the on-field impact as trading the best player but strips away as much of the franchise's soul. Curses are illogical, but if the football gods exist,[6] these gestures were unlikely to curry favor.

In these times the Walkowskis are the Lions. The autoworking family enjoys their lot, cruising through halcyon days in a cloud of drinking and carousing. They don't know this is the peak. They don't appreciate what's sacred and callously discard it. Short-term desires create generational wounds. Neither team nor family ever recover.

My grandmother was a pedophile. My father was the target. Molestation went on for years but, true to this type of trauma, damage lasted a lifetime.

---

6. They do.

It started in 1958, the same year as our curse. My grandfather Harvey—a heroic figure on multiple accounts—found out and put a stop to it. He protected his son where he could.

Little Bob was enrolled in a well-regarded Catholic school and did everything right. Got good grades, became an altar boy, and a priest resumed the torment. Some are born victims; Banjo Bob was made one by predators acting as protectors.

Early moments ensured that Bob would only see the world through traumatized eyes. Development was stunted, forever suspending Bob in a childlike state, a Jurassic-era mosquito eternally encased in amber. Unable to progress through life's milestones, he grows comfortable in his interior world.

The Layne trade, sexual abuse in my family. Events echo through time, shaping modernity. It's not fun to think of your father's sexual abuse or how trauma occurring decades before your birth shaped you. This is how it goes. The first thing Detroiters learn is that the world was much better when we weren't in it. How do we get back to *before*?

Men learn worldviews from their fathers. It's natural to assume we're normal, that everyone's just like us. I'm no different, learning from my father without realizing he's Banjo Bob. He's a scared child just like me, still existing in 1958, sublimating true feelings and turning conversation to football.

2024

I am my father's caretaker, flying from New York to rural Indiana each month. I enter Bob's shack, tiptoeing past decades of garbage. Every Walkowski hoards.[7] Emotions are not the only thing never unpacked to determine whether they're worth keeping. There are thousands of books, literal

7. Everything is kept for potential value that never comes to fruition. The sole exception is that my fifth-grade class is assigned to build seismographs. I take 50 old Pringles cans from the house, bringing this bounty to school like a conquering hero.

tons of leather, and every emotion. Heap them in a corner and ignore them until life's accumulation becomes someone else's problem. Mine.

Some families pass down heirlooms or properties. Purposeful planning builds wealth and bond. That's not our way. We only pass down the team, our trauma, and—if we're being completely honest—17 banjos we've grown to resent.

Banjo Bob has a sister. Aunt Jackie's crippled by rheumatoid arthritis at a young age. There's no interference or intervention. Affliction's magnified and submitted to. Her skeleton twists into cartoonishly cruel shapes, but living's made more difficult by being a hoarder. It's hard to maneuver a broken body, harder still to contort around mountains of Happy Meal toys "that'll be valuable someday." The potential value of McDonald's toys is worth more than an easier life. Nothing's of value, yet nothing can be discarded. The Walkowskis are tethered to everything that has ever happened to them. To break free from the binds would mean dealing with the impact.

Bobby Layne's *Time* magazine cover is tacked above Bob's ratty bed. My father's bedroom today looks like a six-year-old's bedroom in 1958 Detroit. He's in his seventies on a technicality. He might have a senior citizen's bald head and medication-laden bloodstream but projects a child's wondrous aura.

I'll drag Bob to social functions and bring him toward others, noticing his eyes take on a bewildered, frantic look. He rattles about banjos, switchblades, leather, the Lions, expounding on obsessions until others sidle away. He excuses himself for five cigarettes. He constantly smokes but never inhales. He simply needs to live in the fog.

Other issues plague Banjo Bob. Alcoholism, autism, depression, poverty—but other calamities are water off a duck's back for a man who was never truly there.

If I ask an emotional question he drops his voice, grumbling until the moment passes.

If I insist, making eye contact and repeating the question, he'll deflect with humor.

"What was the worst thing to happen to you?"

"Former quarterback Greg Landry."

If he answers, he'll phrase it like a reference book, hiding perceptions and personhood behind a guise of primary sources.

No one paid attention to spectrum-specific quirks during his childhood. "I was a good kid. I got good grades. I didn't bother anyone, so no one bothered with me." This is the way. No one's parented. Lives are simply lived in the Walkowski context long enough to become one.

"Do you think life would be different if you grew up during a time when autism was addressed?"

"I think so."

Every time I see him, I can't help harboring hope for cathartic conversations that never come. Grumbles are all I get. There will be no breakthrough conversation. This is my dad.

I love him because he paired me with the team that trained me to strain to see the positives. It's also the only way to love him. It's accidental but more than enough. I might be pathologically wired to only love what disappoints me, but this kind of love is full and true. It's unconditional.

Molestation didn't just change him. It changed me too. I self-inventory. Where did this shame and low self-worth come from? With no explicit cause it's fair to conclude it's in the DNA.

Banjo Bob is a deeply kind man equipped with a studious nature. My grandfather Harvey was a war hero. During World War II, the one Detroit helped win, he was a paratrooper for the 101st Airborne and went missing over enemy lines. Months passed. Harvey was presumed dead only to reappear, alive and well, save for a missing finger.

He took his story to the grave. Who has time to explain their trauma when there's whiskey to swill and football to bet on?

My dad, a decent historian, spent years researching these events. A favorite activity is visiting libraries, studiously examining archives trying to answer vital questions like "what happened to my dad?" and "how did it affect me?"

Here I sit doing the same damn thing. I need to know what shaped my father in order to figure out what shaped me. We lose because events occurring decades earlier still stubbornly define *everything.*

Like Banjo Bob, I must find my own answers. Unlike him, I'm breaking the chain. The spectrum-adjacent string of Rust Belt men ends with me reaching across the generations, announcing to the bloodline, "Our shit can be fixed!"

I give my dad a copy of *The Body Keeps the Score*. He loves it like one of the dog-eared media guides piled high enough to eclipse the sun. I engage, begging him to write down his traumas. He can't do it. I sit him at the computer, begging him to type. His fingers, wonderfully dexterous sausages that expertly pluck instruments and bind leather, suddenly stop working.

We travel to the longed-for era. The golden period *before it happened.* We're champions and the world belongs to us. Our love of a team brings glory and evolves the league. Detroit's fandom grows the game. It's the banquets. There's untold power in people coming together, pinpointing issues, and finding solutions. Caring builds dynasties. At least it did in Detroit. Details are analyzed, synergistically pieced together to produce wins.

August 8, 1958. The future's bright. How could it not be when the present gleams so preposterously? Bobby Layne is traded.

This is the crossroads, the moment that changes everything. One bad move is all it takes. A dynasty becomes a doormat; a growing boy becomes a shell of a man. Ramifications are still felt decades later. It's hard to face what happened. It's much easier to say we're cursed.

The Lions trading Bobby Layne has an impact similar to my father's molestation on my own life. They aren't the same but they are, forcing us to trace the current situation to one singular event, wondering, *just how much did that set us back?*

I ask these questions. My father grumbles gibberish and slinks away for a cigarette, leaving me alone to search for my own answers.

GAME 3

FAILURE IS IN THE FOUNDATION

• 1963–1988 •

Zero Playoff Wins

APRIL 2023

The season won't start for five months. The Lions still lose.

Jameson Williams and three other players are suspended for gambling. Jamo functions as the team's deep threat and lightning rod for criticism. If there's a problem with the team or scheme or even game day traffic, surely Jamo's to blame. He's the scapegoat. Human beings tend to blame people or things they love.

"Irresponsible! There's no place for gambling!" the fan base cries.

Incorrect. There's space for gambling on this team. Gambling made us who we are. Betting on football is a player's cardinal sin, worse than arrests, steroids, or replicating the opening scene of *The Last Boy Scout* but . . . betting on football is a vital part of Lions lore.

APRIL 1963

Walkowski men gamble, only deriving enjoyment from betting on football. Love of the juice, not the game, draws these men to Briggs Stadium. "A great place to drink beer and fight" is repeated so often that a Walkowski family crest would feature the phrase over a tapestry of my grandmother assaulting my dad. Walkowski men bet so much and lose so often, only one gains the financial stability to move out of their childhood bedroom.

Sunday's for religious activities, specifically betting and carousing at the Lindell AC, the city's first sports bar and front for underworld activities. The Lindell AC allowed everyday residents—which is what Lions players were at the time—to gamble and intermingle with Detroit's power players. The relationship between bar and citizens catalyzed the Lions' extended decline but "we bet at the same bar as Alex Karras" remains a familial boast.

Alex Karras was designed in a laboratory for my father to love. Before starring in Mel Brooks movies and syndicated sitcoms, Alex Karras was a Lions defensive tackle. Appearing in the film adaptation of George Plimpton's *Paper Lion* made Karras one of the first athletes to move on to greater fame by monetizing charisma.[1]

Karras was a Lindell AC regular caught riding home from a road game in the bar's conspicuous Honolulu-Blue-and-silver party bus. The FBI tailed Karras, catching gambling activity across multiple locations. The Lions were informed of infractions and fined alongside Karras but the issue was optics. The NFL was becoming the national pastime and adopting a broader corporate structure that increasingly included extreme wealth among ownership ranks. The symposium of local businessmen owning the Lions accurately mirrored Detroit's population—including roughneck elements—but could not be offered a seat at the table. Not with the broad influence held over Detroit and its players.

---

1. Karras was a key figure in Plimpton's book, who would go on to play himself in the movie—much to the team's dismay.

General Manager Andy Anderson asked Karras to "stay away from the gangsters at Lindell AC," where he worked for supplementary income.

"I need the work. I can't raise my family on a lousy twelve thousand dollars a season."

The investigation sparked national headlines. When interviewed by NBC, Karras—not yet a polished Hollywood veteran—replied to the question of "Do you ever gamble?" with "Yes, I do. With my brothers for a cigar."

"Yes I do," was the only portion aired.

A scandal was born. NFL league investigations ruled that Karras bet on NFL games, suspending him indefinitely. Gambling is an empirically proven addiction impacting dopamine receptors. The unforgivable sin is Karras, alongside a handful of teammates including legendary Joe Schmidt, bet on the hated Packers.

Suspensions and fines were levied but this wasn't enough. Not in Detroit; a place where sports gambling and organized crime were as common as assembly lines and Teamsters collecting paychecks for no-show jobs. The notorious Purple Gang rubbed elbows with Detroit elite and lingered in local lore, which convinced the NFL that any organization reflecting the city's, um, "entrepreneurial spirit," required serious scrutiny.

The NFL pushed for a single, respectable owner. What the NFL failed to consider was that a populist ownership group that may have included some underworld figures might be pretty good at running a football team.

NOVEMBER 22, 1963

An infamous date in our nation's history. William Clay Ford, grandson of Henry and heir to Ford Motor Company, became sole Detroit Lions owner. Engaged local citizens were replaced by a rich kid who people were afraid to say no to because of his last name. It beat out Kennedy's assassination as the worst thing to happen that day.

Ford had long been involved with the team and genuinely loved them, but this was his chance. The Lions were an opportunity to finally do things his way.

Being Henry Ford's descendant was no cakewalk. Henry's son, Edsel, learned the automotive world by his father's side, spending his childhood pacing assembly plants and steadfastly learning every industry detail. When it was time to follow in the family footsteps and bring forth his own innovation, Edsel was categorically stymied.

Henry took umbrage at Edsel's ideas. Developing commercial aviation, the infamous Edsel automobile, even the neighborhood he chose to raise his family in. Henry summarily quashed any attempt by his son to make his own identity, thereby reaffirming his. Attempts to stamp the name "Edsel" on the world associated it with failure.

The Ford family looks backward. Much of the family business still exalts Henry. My hometown, Dearborn, Michigan, possesses a wondrous theme park called "The Henry Ford." The museum houses Americana relics like the chair Lincoln was shot in, the car Kennedy was shot in, and the Oscar Mayer Weinermobile. The main attraction is Greenfield Village, a sprawling city re-creating the Industrial Revolution era. Structures have been relocated, and actors play key characters,[2] replicating the world when Henry was king.

This is the Dearborn way. The city's a monument to Henry Ford. There's no need for innovation, strategy, or creativity. We merely need to remind the world we already changed it.

William Clay Ford loved the Lions dearly but failed to grasp operations. The team was explicitly run for *his* benefit, not the city's. The (at the time) hard-drinking Ford partied till wee hours with players, ignoring conditioning standards and well-being. Furthermore, he was cheap. The team harshly overnegotiated contracts, even though they were owned by one of the world's wealthiest men. Detroit wanted to win, but William Clay Ford needed to win *on his terms*.

---

2. Yes, teenage Joel Walkowski did get escorted out of the park on multiple occasions for a rogue portrayal of John Wilkes Booth.

The team started losing and—thanks to Ford's meddlesome nature—continued to lose. Joe Schmidt, a Hall of Fame linebacker and bona fide leader, was brought in as coach/GM but was hamstrung by owner interference. This dynamic applied Ford's regionalized dominance to the plebe's leisure activity. It isn't enough to determine pay and working conditions. The Fords also had to control the football team. The now perennially losing football team.

This was a critical moment for Detroit. Fords intermingled with all aspects of city life, not unlike the relationship between the Wayne family and Gotham in the Batman universe. Of course, this is fiction. In reality billionaires don't care about causes outside their interests.

Things get bad. Automakers lose market share. Resulting revenue shifts rock the city to its core, negatively impacting everyone. Workers get squeezed at best and chronically unemployed at worst. The city referred to by John F. Kennedy as "the Paris of the West" fell into widespread poverty and joblessness. Yet, this was the best of our problems.

JULY 23, 1967

On a steamy Sunday morning at 3:45 AM, police raided an after-hours club where the Black community was celebrating the return of two local war heroes. Rather than turn a blind eye to the blind pig, police arrested all 82 patrons. This unfair treatment lit conflict's fuse, boiling over tensions that had simmered for generations of systemic racism and escalating into days-long riots. Shops were looted, buildings burned, and lives lost. The National Guard was called in to quell the uprising, but by the time tanks rolled in, it was too late. Detroit would never be the same.

A cycle of negativity had begun. Over the next four decades Detroit experienced:

- Suburban white flight depleting populations to such extremes that the city struggled to provide basic utilities;
- Racist real estate policies (i.e., redlining effectively imposing apartheid);

- Rampant corruption from local leaders; and
- Aside from a horrific addiction epidemic, the War on Drugs' punitive punishments jailed 25% of the city's adult male population.

The auto industry continued declining. The birthplace of the middle class faced a sudden scarcity of jobs. The most viable local income source for some was abandoned buildings, plundered like nonrenewable mining operations for copper, insurance money, and squat homes.

Causes for Detroit's decline were unavoidable. The America of the 1960s had unsolvable racial conflicts no matter what *Remember the Titans* says. Despite these issues' inevitability, actions taken by Detroit's leaders during its darkest hours fell short. The same jobs that built Detroit's golden age were outsourced to cheaper labor pools. When the city needed the automakers, the automakers went overseas.

Marketing Myopia, a seminal piece chronicling the decline of American automakers, argues that car companies tried dictating consumer wants as opposed to listening to their desires.[3] Lack of consideration welcomed foreign competitors into the market, allotting them considerable share with offerings better satiating the customer.

This is the mindset William Clay Ford brought to the Lions. His tenure saw just one playoff win, lagging the competition in not only success but organizational health.

The Lions were a side business. It showed. The NFL is a cutthroat plaything for our nation's elite. Having conquered a sector, oligarchs pivot social and economic capital behind the pursuit of a Super Bowl. Preexisting skills are applied toward sport with some of the NFL's best-run franchises operating like some of the world's best-run businesses.[4]

---

3. Please see bibliography for more details. It is the most boring part of this book.

4. The Pittsburgh Steelers, Green Bay Packers, and New England Patriots are all evidence of different managerial approaches netting positive results. These strategies are bespoke to the individual organizations, illustrating acumen.

The NFL grew in complexity and competitiveness. The Lions remained a plaything.

For most of Ford's reign, roster decisions were conducted by Russ Thomas, a former player and announcer with no front office experience. Stingy contract negotiations cost the team Hall of Famer Fred Biletnikoff and other AFL stars amid local refrains of nepotism and favoritism.

The Fords were lauded for loyalty, elevating unworthy individuals and keeping them past expiration dates if they're one of the guys. Russ Thomas was the poster child. His continued employment sparked unsubstantiated rumors concerning how he kept his job. Was he Thomas Ford's AA sponsor? Did he save him from drowning? Nefarious theories aren't the point. Conspiracy theories were the only rational explanation why such a terrible executive stayed in place for decades.

After the 1971 season, Ford announced quarterback Greg Landry was going to be traded but never communicated this to the front office, alienating his starting quarterback. The careers of the team's greatest players—Lem Barney, Charlie Sanders, and Billy Sims—were uphill battles waged against management.

The most galling thing about Ford is not failure. It's the chasm between his performance and how the team regards him.

Divisional rival Chicago's uniforms memorialize George Halas, a team founder and key to the NFL's ascent. Upon his passing the Bears stitched his initials "GSH" on their sleeves—a fitting tribute to a true pioneer.

When Ford died in 2017 the Lions honored him in the same way. He did not build the sport, win games, or honor Detroit's emotional investment. He loved this team like Lenny loved his rabbit in *Of Mice and Men.* Reading WCF's initials on the Lions' uniform sleeves is knowing they stand for: "We Certainly Failed."

One doesn't have to suffer to be negatively impacted by familial upbringing. Ford grew up with incomprehensible wealth, but one thing money can't buy is an honest appraisal.

The Ford descendants are not ingenious or special. They're direct descendants of Henry Ford. This matters more than merit. Certain wealth thresholds instill nihilism. If life will be comfortable for generations regardless of what we do, how can anything we do matter?

It's tragic. WCF was a sports-obsessed kid. Involvement with the Lions was one of the few things he chose. He gave his soul to the thing he loved and drove it into the ground.

The franchise's dark nature was cemented in 1971. Detroit was driving for a comeback when Chuck Hughes caught a pass in Bears territory. Three plays later, an undiagnosed heart condition caused him to fall on the field dead.

This is bad luck, a fluke, something that can't be held against an organization. The same cannot be said for the decision to *finish the game.* This is Lions culture.

Ford was a crappy owner but, by all accounts, a great guy. He had the desire to win. Just not the traits. WCF took over a dynasty and turned it into a perennial doormat.

That isn't to say the team was without triumphs. The era contained plenty of lovable escapades. The core issue shaping Lions' fans' perspective is that none of these involved winning.

REASONS TO LOVE THE LIONS, 1963–1988

1. Leland "Lee" Melvin retires from the Lions and becomes an astronaut and the first NFL player in space. His dogs are inexplicably featured in the publicity photos.
2. Homer Simpson is originally drawn as a Lions fan.
3. The team color of Honolulu Blue is not a specific shade. The original owner visited Hawaii, fell in love with Pacific hues, and decreed that any color the Lions wore would be called Honolulu Blue.[5]

5. They also didn't trademark the name of the shade. Benjamin Moore sells its own version of the color. The Detroit Lions: We even lose at paint.

4. George Plimpton attends training camp and writes *Paper Lion* about his experience, positioning the team as affable also-rans.
5. Marvin Gaye practices with the team and features a couple players singing background on "What's Going On."
6. Axel Foley wears a Lions jacket on the poster for *Beverly Hills Cop II*.
7. The number 20 is reserved for our high priests. The parish struggles but the sermons are mighty. Lem Barney plucking interceptions and crooning with Marvin. Billy Sims bursting through the gap, thwapping away would-be tacklers with karate kicks. This number is a clove of garlic in a franchise made of vampires.
8. The Pontiac Silverdome.

The Silverdome was the brainchild of C. Don Davidson, a Marine, architecture professor, and Pontiac, Michigan, native. Aghast at his hometown's condition, Davidson assigned his students to pick a site, launched a newspaper to support the project, and consulted with William Clay Ford, who was embroiled in a years-long familial dispute about moving the Lions to Pontiac. Davidson convinced Ford, sending the team on the same trajectory as many fans: hightailing it toward the suburbs.

The Silverdome was situated 30 miles beyond city limits and unreachable by public transportation. Stadium construction made Detroit's car-oriented engineering bolster an already stark racial divide. On the heels of white flight, why would a population want easy, affordable connections to the place they recently fled? The dome's climate-controlled interior insulated the team from weather while its geographic placement did the same with socioeconomic conditions.

Even so. The Silverdome was magical—80,000 people watching indoor football played on carpet beneath the diffused light of a fiberglass ceiling was gorgeous. Lions football had distinct aesthetics, strengthened by the *thunk* of supporters getting sucked into the stadium by revolving doors required to keep the dome inflated.

The Silverdome did not enjoy a happy existence. There are mausoleums that house more happy memories. The Silverdome hosted the Lions for 27 years but only one home playoff game. It saw more players get paralyzed than significant victories. Even a designated moment in the sun, hosting a Super Bowl, was sullied by an ice storm ensuring the host city only showcased its shitty roads and ice trucks. The Silverdome's greatest sporting moment didn't even come from football but WrestleMania III.[6]

The Lions were losers when they moved into the Silverdome and synonymous with failure by the time they left. This perfectly served a city experiencing the same tribulations. The Lions weren't Detroit's team. They were its scapegoat.

Stemming from Leviticus, the scapegoat concept exists across cultures. Humans need something to take on their sins. Jobs are lost, men are caged, streets are desolate. The Lions follow suit, telling us we are not alone, serving up shitty football. In a time of great sorrows, the team carries a city's sins.

We all need something to store our sadness.

Banjo Bob finds it twice.

He picks up a guitar as a teenager. He will never be himself without it. It electrifies him like nothing before. First strums come on a borrowed instrument. He approaches his parents, begging them for a guitar. They refuse. Now, I don't know about you, but if I committed sacred infractions against my child I would *at least* support their interests.

It is the only time in his life that it happens, but it does, at least this impactful once. Banjo Bob rebels, buying the guitar. He is home. Complete. He spends the rest of his life cradling it softly, studying chords, and executing complex solos. He will never start a band or make his own music. That would be sacrilege.

---

6. If you ask me the greatest game in Silverdome history, I'd answer "Randy Savage vs. Ricky Steamboat."

The guitar gives life meaning. How could he ask the instrument for more? Playing guitar is an act of faith. Suffering is attached to consciousness. Anything providing relief is invaluable.

Banjo Bob works and makes money. Only because those acts are necessary to purchase more guitars.

Banjo Bob discovers more of himself the first time he picks up booze. It's the secret the ancestors foretold. A shot and a beer followed by a shot and a beer. It's not a bad way to live. It's the only way to live. Alcohol provides escape. He becomes bigger and bolder until he is someone else entirely. When Bob drinks he makes people call him "Roach." *His spirit is unkillable!*

Parties are no longer attended but played. He brings the guitar everywhere, trotting out the rhythms of flamenco or Robert Johnson at a moment's notice. It doesn't matter if he's asked to play or asked to stop. He plays.

Bob's an academic, always studying, always learning. He wins second prize for Detroit-area youth writers, but the avenue is not to be pursued. He has the guitar. How could he ask for anything more? Banjo Bob lives his dream.

There's no guidance, so this dream is, uh, pretty weird? Banjo Bob gets drunk every night, plays guitar at all hours, and inexplicably dresses like some sort of cosmopolitan fish man.[7] He purchases his first suit and covers it in taxidermized carp. He plays shows and throws fish into crowds, exclaiming "watch out for the fish."

This is the man who raised me.

Prepubescent Joel asks his dad: "What do I do at parties?"

Banjo Bob sparkles with confidence. He couldn't lead the birds-and-the-bees talk, but this? This he can answer.

"You get a dead fish and throw it into a crowd of people."

"What do I do next?"

"Yell 'watch out for the fish.'"

"Will it help me meet girls?"

"Yes."

---

7. I fucking promise that these next couple paragraphs are true.

It does help Banjo Bob meet girls. He meets my mother in his hard-drinking crew of theatrical alcoholics. I know her as a chill old lady, but she'll need to be a food addict and rage addict before becoming someone I admire.[8]

Mother's one of eight. Her family's a mix of devout Catholics and witches brought together by drinking too much coffee. The family runs the gamut of artists and corporate achievers to one eccentric relative who lives in the woods. I am seven years old, riding over a bridge in the back of their pickup. They pull open the cab window and yell back, "Should we drive off the bridge so we can meet Jesus sooner?"

The moment's seriousness misses me as a boy, and even 30 years later I derive no trauma because this is the *good side of the family.*

Alcohol allows Banjo Bob to woo. He writes my mother poems and serenades. They book a VFW hall and get married. It isn't the fanciest ceremony. It can't be. Banjo Bob spends half the budget hiring an organ-grinding monkey. This is marriage.

Banjo Bob's a drunk, falling down the stairs at my sister's third birthday. Like most third-birthday parties, it's not a rager. He gets a DUI when my mother is pregnant with me. Unable to grab diapers or ferry us to doctors' appointments, he sets the stage for parenting with a fundamental inability to participate.

A friend kills himself with Banjo Bob in the room, begging him to stop. The bottle is only put down to pick up a gun.

Banjo Bob vows to quit. Bob accomplishes everything he puts his mind to. Guitar, leather, sobriety. The issue is that he never puts his mind to anything else. It's heroic to be sober, but what happened to who he became while drinking? Where did the magic go? I spent my life waiting to meet him. Alcohol gives him a chosen identity. He quits drinking but never bothers building a new one.

Both parents join 12-Step groups. Between their faithful attendance and AA meetings doled out as a childhood punishment, the groups function

---

8. My first memory of her is of her, uh, fighting a car.

as family religion. My mother loses 150 pounds with Overeaters Anonymous, becoming a pillar of the program. This isn't because she loses weight. It's because she changes her thinking.

My father eliminates behaviors but does not address underlying wounds. There's no way of demarcating where the person ends and trauma begins, so he becomes the trauma. He's a "dry drunk." No changes or growth, just abstaining. He's the rare person to have his family whisper "he shouldn't have done that" about temperance.

Dysfunction is normal if it's all you know. The world leaves Banjo Bob behind. That's normally a bad thing but not in Detroit. If you aren't building the win, the loss will find you. This town tied its identity to its football team. Someone took the identity away and they lost forever. That's how it goes.

You don't have to be shiny and new to be loved in Detroit. Being left behind to wilt makes you one of us. Evidence of this stands on the city's East Side.

Tyree Guyton's Heidelberg Project began at the height of Detroit's troubles. The block of Heidelberg, where Guyton resided, was blighted.

He began collecting discarded items from across the city. The leftover, the unwanted debris, the hoard. Guyton adorned his block with flotsam. It's fucking beautiful. Homes are covered in numbers, swathed with doll parts, a tree of shoes dangling overhead.

The forgotten can be beautiful. Reassemble discarded pieces the proper way and blight becomes bright.

The installation has gone on for decades, always evolving as Guyton continually builds. His world was tough, so he rearranged the pieces around him until they were gorgeous.

This is the process I take with the Lions and my family. I'm defined by loving these two losers. The best way to cheer isn't waiting for a winner that never arrives. We must scrape up the dregs, rearrange them in a way that makes them appealing, and view what's left like it's beautiful.

It is.

GAME 4

BARRY

• 1989–1992 •

One Playoff Win, One Division Title

1989	1990	1991	1992
7-9	6-10	12-4	5-11

The Heisman Trophy is the biggest amateur accolade in American sports. Annually doled out at a black-tie New York City affair, the Heisman is more than an award. It provides entry into the most hallowed rungs of culture: Nissan commercials. In the brand's Heisman House campaign, airing on loop during college football season, winners live on forever, commingling as frat-brother roommates.[1]

The award recognizes college football's best player but is functionally so much more. The Heisman is earned on the field but won through media campaigns; it is an athletic distinction resembling presidential elections.

---

1. If I see Baker Mayfield borrowing Charles Woodson's toothbrush or Eddie George using Tony Dorsett's coffee creamer *I will buy a car.*

Candidates compete for the honor in the court of public opinion, boosting chances with Times Square billboards or striking the iconic Heisman pose in key moments.[2]

Given how the award is won, there was no more unlikely recipient than Barry Sanders.[3] The Heisman is a lifetime pass to the limelight, but the limelight isn't for everyone. It certainly wasn't for Barry.

Barry is remembered as the greatest running back of all time. Rosters listed him as a tailback but he's closer to Halley's Comet, a whirling-dervish wizard leaving observers agog and defenders grasping at air. He transcended the sport's militaristic confines with artistry and self-expression. He wasn't Jim Brown or O. J. Simpson.[4] He was Fred Astaire, gallivanting into the collective consciousness, leaving slack-jawed awe in his wake.

The world loved Barry, but he had a pathological aversion to acclaim, avoiding positive attention like a pursuing linebacker. If he was about to set a record? He'd remove himself from the game. If he scored a touchdown? He'd eschew celebration, dutifully handing the ball to a referee. Branded as an attempt to "act like you've been there before," these actions reflected deeply held humility. These traits were present throughout his professional, college, and even high school career. They're who he was.

This was a by-product of William Sanders, a taciturn, hard-to-please father. William inundated his son with tales of Jim Brown's greatness—even when Barry surpassed him. Speaking at Barry's 2004 Hall of Fame enshrinement, William dedicated his speech to Brown's superiority. Barry spent a lifetime chasing his father's endorsement. He never caught it.

William Sanders was a diehard Oklahoma Sooners fan even as his son starred for the rival Oklahoma State Cowboys.

Sanders spent his first two seasons in Stillwater, Oklahoma, as a special teams ace and backup to Thurman Thomas, another wonderful back.

---

2. In a terrible bit of forced wordplay future, Lions quarterback and draft bust Joey Harrington will appear on a Times Square billboard declaring him "Joey Heisman."

3. Except maybe Ron Goldman's father.

4. Barry was nice to women.

Thomas ascended to the NFL, leaving the featured role to the undersized Sanders. The promotion was not without concerns. Would Barry's 5'8" frame withstand a full workload?

Worries were quickly dismissed. Barry was sublime.

During the 1988 season, Barry accumulated unmatched statistical and aesthetic feats. In 11 games, Barry contributed an unbelievable 2,628 yards and 37 touchdowns. He unleashed hell on the highest rungs of college football like Billy Madison in a grade school dodgeball game.

He was a Heisman shoo-in. Most winners strut to the stage, hoisting the trophy and crowing a victory speech. Barry, true to his nature, accepted the award via satellite phone from Tokyo.

Oklahoma State was inexplicably scheduled to play Texas Tech in the Tokyo Dome. Marching bands and cheerleaders amplifying college football's spectacle were the perfect excuse for a social anxiety–laden star. Barry appeared on television to accept the Heisman. He dedicated it to his family, his offensive line, his fullback. Everyone but himself.

Distance from the spotlight was liberating. Barry ran for 300 yards and four scores before an unfamiliar Japanese crowd. Seeing Barry sprinting and juking as your *first* exposure to football somehow normalizes him, making spectators imagine America as a country full of superheroes. Japanese fans had never seen anything like it but could not realize no one had.

The 1988 Lions, whose roster had more holes than a Shyamalan plot about a spaghetti strainer, finished 4–12. It was the club's fifth consecutive losing season but good for third overall pick in the NFL draft.

The draft combine is a road show of athletic measurables. Prospects dedicate lives to perfecting specific drills for good reason. Fractional seconds shaved off a 40-yard dash impacts draft slots and the millions of dollars attached to them.

Young, finely tuned athletes line up for drills, but no one can find Barry. He arrives late, rolling in from the airport without time to stretch or change clothes. He blows away the competition with nonchalant dominance.

The pre-draft process also evaluates a player's character. Talent evaluator Gil Brandt's scouting report captures Sanders's "unbelievable quickness" and "great leg strength."[5] More unique is the attention given to his personality. "Great person. Everyone from equipment managers to team secretaries brag about him."

Lions coach Wayne Fontes announces he's drafting Sanders. Telling opponents your draft plan is a severe disadvantage but par for the course during this era of Lions football.

Detroit selects Barry. Top selections usually march to the podium for commissioner photo ops, but Barry watches at home with family. When asked about this, Barry calls the entire process "unnecessary." He even turns down the Lions' introductory press conference, giving the excuse "people don't really care about me" before redirecting conversation to his brother's good grades. Barry only says one notable quote during his introduction: "I always wanted to play for an underdog."

Deion Sanders, picked fifth overall, tells the media, "I'd been having nightmares I might wake up in Detroit," adding that he'd "ask for so much money the Lions would've had to put him on the layaway." The Lions are so lowly that they get rejected by someone they don't even want.

From the moment Barry picks up the congratulatory phone call welcoming him to the team, he *is* the team.

The team stinks. Sanders must overcome an incompetent quarterback room in order to succeed. It stays that way for his entire career.

GM Russ Thomas announces 1989 will be Barry's last season and uses contract negotiations with him as a final chance to be a cheapskate.[6] Financial squabbling causes Barry to miss training camp. Sanders comes to terms days before the season—too late to learn an offense or assimilate.[7] He's expected to sit out.

Not if the fans could help it.

---

5. Sanders had famously muscular legs rivaling the thigh circumference of behemoth offensive linemen.

6. The *Detroit Free Press* calls Thomas "an ogre guarding Ford's fortune."

7. Barry tithes 10% of his signing bonus to his childhood church. Not interesting but I think it's cute.

WEEK 1: SEPTEMBER 10, 1989. PHOENIX CARDINALS (0-0) v DETROIT LIONS (0-0). SILVERDOME, PONTIAC, MI.

The Silverdome keeps chanting *BAR-RY*, but Coach Fontes won't put him in. It's not like the offense set the world on fire. In 40 minutes of action they amass a measly field goal.

Third Quarter, 5:43

Barry enters the game. The Silverdome roars like Hulk Hogan just body slammed Andre the Giant at WrestleMania III.

He's getting the ball. No one takes the Corvette out of the garage to park it in the driveway. Anticipation gurgles to a hilt, but the play clock expires for a penalty and a case of Honolulu Blue balls.

Two plays later Sanders totes the rock, approaching the right tackle as the defense gathers. *Whoosh!* A swivel of the hips and off he goes, jutting across the line and sprinting into daylight for a gain of 20. Deafening cheers declare Detroit's love. Barry bounces to his feet, walks to the huddle, and *literally* yawns.

The drive ends with our new normal: Defenders looking foolish as Barry enters the end zone. Collective jubilation blows the roof off the Silverdome; Sanders meekly hands the ball to a ref and jogs off. All is well and always will be.[8]

★ ★ ★

Barry's debut occurs on my third birthday. First memories are from this day; random flashes, not necessarily profound. Banjo Bob leading singalongs in the inflatable raft that doubles as our swimming pool; my mother with a *Jaws*-themed cake.

8. We blow the game and start the season 0–5.

Banjo Bob and other dads trickle toward the television. They don't want to watch the Lions; they need to see Barry. I follow the men. Watching blots of blue swirl about Astroturf's green glow makes me one of the guys. Lifelong infatuation begins. I think I've progressed but how's that possible when my entire personality is linked to initial moments of consciousness? When I say "I've been a Lions fan as long as I can remember" I do so with *extreme granularity.*

Just like Tokyo Dome attendees, I have no idea what I'm watching but know it's worth seeing.

Ritual. Each week I dutifully follow my dad to the TV. I don't know the rules, but this isn't like other shows. People are there watching, yelling, participating. You can be part of it.

"People can go?"

"Yeah, Slick. People go."

"Where?"

"Pontiac."

"Why not Detroit?"

"Good question."

"Can we go?"

"Sure."

"When?"

"Someday."

"Someday." It sounds too fucking similar to "Sunday." Each week I expect to see the Lions; each week I am disappointed. It's good practice.

Barry carries Detroit to an inspiring win streak, but life is not a sports movie. *The ragtag bunch rallies around their value-oriented superstar and . . . finishes 7–9.*

It's enough. Barry changes how we're viewed: a young team on the rise. Football's inherently optimistic. A team doesn't need to be good to be considered good. They just have to flash competency. Fandom's rose-colored glasses do the rest.

WEEK 17: DECEMBER 24, 1989. DETROIT LIONS (6-9) V ATLANTA FALCONS (3-12). FULTON COUNTY STADIUM, ATLANTA, GA.

Sanders is known for ability and humility. In the season's last game Barry combines the two to define his mythos. Legends do shit normal people don't understand, and Barry was about to do just that.

Barry barely trailed the Chiefs' Christian Okoye for the rushing title before benchmark allocation of 20 carries became 158 yards, three touchdowns, and a blowout victory.[9]

Possession reverts to Detroit in garbage time. Word circulated on the sideline. Sanders was a scant 10 yards away from the rushing title *and* the contractual bonus attached to the achievement.

Coach Fontes gave Barry the option to reenter the game and capture the title.

Barry said no.

"When everyone is out for statistics, y'know, individual fulfillment? That's when trouble starts. I'd never want to fall victim to that." If the collective achieves its objective, then individual efforts are no longer needed. Who was this balletic back? This juking jitterbug? How did he turn a rushing title into a reflection on the nature of humility?

Barry was the league's smallest player, missed training camp, and still set the league on fire. Opponents accused him of spraying silicone on his uniform to slip away. All-time leading rusher Walter Payton even concluded, "I don't think I was ever that good." How does one become the running back king by turning down the rushing title? By transcending.

The legend was a nap-loving, faith-based man who refused to practice when teammates swore and badgered his coach about why the Bible on his desk never seemed to move. Barry wasn't a legend because he was a great athlete. He was a legend because his career imposed a value system over

9. Okoye was memorably nicknamed "The Nigerian Nightmare." That would also be a good nickname for email scams from fake princes.

gridiron chaos. Character is not predicated on winning; it's the North Star for reaching any outcome.

Barry was a self-contained offensive ecosystem given a green light to take risks. The talent behind his highlight reel runs is also the reason why he owns the league record for negative yardage. Unorthodoxy contradicted traditional run game strategies. He did not play with a fullback or excel in short yardage, but it didn't matter. Surrounding Sanders with a sensible strategy would dilute his gifts. Freddie Mercury was an unmatched front man but would underwhelm in an orchestra.

The Detroit Lions were tasked with building around Barry, one of the most unique challenges ever faced by NFL decision-makers.

Detroit's planned GM vacancy dovetailed with a talented young core. William Clay Ford could finally find the right steward. Someone to intentionally craft a team, not just haggle contracts.

Ford put Chuck Schmidt, vice president of finance, in charge of football operations. Schmidt had no experience as a player, coach, or talent evaluator. When pressed for qualifications, Schmidt boasted, "I'm here because of my management skills." The Lions' unique task was assigned to yet another yes man.

The introductory press conference could've offered ideas on how to build around Sanders or find a franchise quarterback. Schmidt announced how important it was for people in his office to get along. Barry Sanders was sixteen games into his professional career, but corporate hiring practices were already closing his championship window.

Strong finish aside, Detroit was a decidedly bad team. The new brain trust was desperate to use the seventh overall pick on a quarterback. However, the draft class had few viable options, something the new regime was too inexperienced to realize.

Andre Ware's resume was loaded with equal parts accolades and red flags. The Houston Cougars signal caller won the Heisman playing against inferior competition in a gimmick offense tailor-made to his strengths. Ware was not a traditional pocket passer but excelled under wide-open windows provided by the run-and-shoot scheme. Few teams thought highly of Ware as a quarterback—at either the college or NFL level.

The Lions picked Ware. Coach Wayne Fontes proclaimed he'd lead the team to a Super Bowl. The idea of two Heisman winners sharing a backfield was easily romanticized, but the real story unfolded away from the headlines. After Ware's selection, the Lions' director of college scouting quietly resigned in protest.

He was correct. The Ware selection was a cataclysmic misfire, arguably the most damaging draft pick in league history. Top quarterback selections are a notorious crapshoot, scratch-off lottery tickets masquerading as young athletes. The Lions' quarterback desperation convinced them to take Ware as if justifications increased the likelihood of a desired outcome.

Ware arrived at training camp. The decision-makers who fought for him immediately deemed him a sunk cost. Yikes. Sorry, Barry.

The Detroit Lions entered the 1990 season as the team du jour. Barry graced *Sports Illustrated* accompanied by an actual lion and the role of NFL cover boy. Expecting Barry to save the Lions was akin to betting on Sisyphus to finally roll the boulder up the mountain. He possessed the powerful lower body needed to accomplish the task, but the boulder came tumbling down the moment he wasn't Superman.

A Week 1 home blowout to Tampa Bay boldly announces a disappointing season. The Lions' performance is like hiring a skywriter to spell out "I suck!"

Rather than dwell on the horrific team, fan interest pivots toward Sanders. Cheering on this team creates resourcefulness toward joy. Rooting for them long enough causes one to root on singular individuals like a tennis fan. The cruel irony is that a player who unilaterally eschewed personal accomplishment for the team was stuck on such a shitty one.

Detroit finishes 6–10, underwhelming on defense and in the passing game. It's the worst possible context for a running back, but the season's toxic wasteland sees Barry attain every possible individual achievement: 13 touchdowns, a rushing title, and first team All-Pro. These figures weren't garbage time accumulations. They were John Henry laying the tracks before the train.

Football gods gifted Detroit a Michelin Star chef. The Lions essentially asked him to serve as line cook to keep the lights on at a failing restaurant. The only thing limiting Barry was his employer. He means more to this franchise than anyone else but on some cosmic level? It's a tragedy that he worked for us.

The 1991 season approaches in typical fashion. We weren't going to matter. The offense was gimmicky, Barry would break down, and the team's biggest offseason acquisition was backup quarterback Erik Kramer from the Canadian Football League's Calgary Stampeders. The other notable move was drafting receiver Herman Moore, an ideal blend of size, hands, and body control who revolutionized his position despite being overshadowed by Sanders's greatness.

The season gets off to the expected bad start. A rib injury sidelines Barry for Week 1 at Washington. The Lions get obliterated, 45–0. Afterward, Wayne Fontes holds firm, promising fans a good season.

It's the rare instance in which our coach's public assurances are correct. Barry's return keys a slew of convincing victories. A win over Miami sees a Dolphins defender utilize such a wide net to capture Barry that he tackles both Sanders *and* a referee. The following week, Sanders resoundingly outplays All-World RB Eric Dickerson in Indianapolis. It's not a torch passing but a microcosm of nature's inherent mortality. There will always be someone younger, stronger, able to do what we suddenly cannot. Dickerson enters the RCA Dome as a football star and leaves it as a future broadcaster.

WEEK 6: OCTOBER 6, 1991. DETROIT LIONS (4-1) V MINNESOTA VIKINGS (2-3). SILVERDOME, PONTIAC, MI.

Hungry young Lions deem the Minnesota game their "Super Bowl." Calling something your Super Bowl is reasonable if you're my 70-year-old mother watching the Oscars but unreasonable for an NFL team with a theoretical chance at the *actual* Super Bowl.[10]

---

10. The Vikings weren't even that good at the time. They were 2–3!

Fourth Quarter, 7:00; Vikings 20, Lions 3

Time wanes. Another letdown is certain when Barry takes over. Defensive attention paid to Barry allows the passing game to thrive, cutting the lead to 3. Our defense follows suit, stepping up to do its job. Possession returns to Detroit with ample time to raise the curtains on the Barry Sanders show.

Barry takes a crossing route upfield and out of bounds. He follows it by knifing through a hole, freezing a defender with a spin move, zipping a gain of 26. Barry's a one-man hurry-up offense. No reason not to return to the well. Sanders tiptoes into the Viking line before lowering his shoulder to find the secondary. One Viking remains. The defender squares up in textbook fashion. Barry defies the laws of physics, simultaneously pausing to swivel his hips while still moving forward. The dissonance between his gyrations and a rational understanding of human kinesiology allows Sanders to ease into the end zone. *Lions win!*

The team makes good on a long-held promise to Detroit, but the city doesn't notice. The inspirational comeback takes place before a half-empty Silverdome and no local viewing audience.

The 1991 campaign is the high-water mark in a half-century-plus span. We do not enter the pantheon of the elite but approach the precipice for a single season. It won't last. The NFC's loaded with talented, forward-thinking teams. Talented young cores in San Francisco, Green Bay, and Dallas will run the conference for a decade. The best we can say is that we were better for a couple months.

WEEK 9: OCTOBER 27, 1991. DALLAS COWBOYS (5-2) V DETROIT LIONS (5-2). SILVERDOME, PONTIAC, MI.

Dallas's Silverdome visit provides the first chance for Barry Sanders to face off against Emmitt Smith outside of barstool debates.

Sanders's career exists against a backdrop of perpetual comparison to Smith, a star on the 1990s Cowboys. Emmitt enjoyed significant team success and would someday claim the all-time rushing mark Barry rejects. Great running backs can dominate by putting up four yards a carry. Emmitt was a great back.

Sometimes we're judged for our contexts. Emmitt became the face of the Cowboys success, but the team's true motor was the offensive line, the NFL's most gifted position group. These talented oafs did not appear on lunch boxes or television commercials but were among the league's most important players.

Barry didn't have this. He was expected to conjure magic as a substitute for a cohesive offense. Individual acrobatics and herky-jerky style made Barry the world's most unconventional swordsman, the one the best feared most. Emmitt got four yards a carry. One was great at his job. The other was a monument to human movement.

The Cowboys get thrashed. The key win isn't the victory itself but overcoming adversity. Starting quarterback Rodney Peete goes down with an Achilles injury.[11] Backup Erik Kramer steps on the field, confidently audibles out of his first play, and throws a touchdown. This earns him the nickname "Brass," acknowledging the balls it takes to call your number during your first NFL snap. Kramer is not a great quarterback but a stable one. It's the biggest contribution from the position since the moon landing.

11. Peete is married to a star of the sitcom *Hangin' with Mr. Cooper*, one of the team's greatest wins.

WEEK 12: NOVEMBER 17, 1991.
LOS ANGELES RAMS (3-7) v DETROIT LIONS (6-4).
SILVERDOME, PONTIAC, MI.

WEEK 13: NOVEMBER 24, 1991.
DETROIT LIONS (7-4) v MINNESOTA VIKINGS (6-6).
METRODOME, MINNEAPOLIS, MN.

Coach Fontes leverages a string of bad losses into a wake-up call. A clash with the Rams is something to rally around. Team fervor ignites wire-to-wire victory, but the game's meaning changes in the third quarter.

An unlucky collision on a routine play. Mike Utley is a titan of a man, his taped hands and large mullet-adorned frame give the impression of a hockey enforcer. Utley successfully completes a pass protection set. His target leaps to bat down a pass but lands on Utley, bringing undue impact on his head and neck.

Utley sprawls on the Silverdome turf, paralyzed from the waist down. Football's brutalist spectacle is juxtaposed against the specter of human frailty as the game grinds to a halt. The gladiators become people. Fans wonder if watching makes them complicit.

Strapped to a stretcher and loaded into an ambulance, Utley still manages heroics, raising a fist and giving a thumbs-up to the crowd. The moment is iconic, making Utley forever beloved in Detroit.

Players are rattled. Fellow lineman Eric Andolsek is visibly shaken, fighting back tears while recounting the difficulties of seeing his best friend try to walk again.

Football causes injuries, but the sport's ailments are rarely accompanied by trauma. Trauma can't be walked off. Concentrated therapy and support groups acknowledging how you've been impacted are key. The Lions are grieving, rattled by their brother's future and his fate's feasibility. A group of fearless football players become the vulnerable men they need to be, but the inconvenient truth is that games are left to be played.

Playing Minnesota six days after Utley's injury makes winning feel impossible. However, accomplishing the impossible is what Barry Sanders does best.

Lapsed protection during a first-quarter handoff lets the defense meet Barry in the backfield. The collision sends him backwards, but his lower body stays activated, propelling him into the open field. He evades four more tackles en route to the end zone.

This run is rarely featured in Barry's highlights but, when accounting for the psyche of city and team alike, this scamper is the best run of his life.

Sports do not heal wounds but can provide a moment's respite amid devastation. Steve Gleason blocking a punt in New Orleans for the post-Katrina Saints or Nyheim Hines's game-opening return touchdown after Damar Hamlin's cardiac arrest are NFL lore.

Barry's cathartic performance belongs in the pantheon of the sport's breakthrough emotional moments. His limited postseason success allowed him to be dismissed as "not a big game player" but from a human perspective, few games were bigger than this one—220 yards, four touchdowns, and a win for a city that desperately needed it. Barry avoids defenders while tending to a city's heartbreak.

Tom Wolfe in a thesaurus factory, let alone an NFL scorekeeper, could not adequately capture this dominance across athletics and aesthetics. Every fan has a favorite Barry run. Fans will spot my Lions hat and wax poetic about their favorite Barry plays. This single afternoon captures what dozens of meandering conversations cannot. Barry mattered. To us. To the sport. To anyone who ever watched.

Utley's injury turned Lions football from a self-flagellating diversion into a humanist disruption. On this day for this particular city, only Barry could make the game fun again.

DIVISIONAL ROUND: JANUARY 5, 1991. DALLAS COWBOYS (12-5) V DETROIT LIONS (12-4). SILVERDOME, PONTIAC, MI.

Detroit streaks to a division title and first-round bye. The Pontiac Silverdome hosts its first playoff game against the Cowboys. Nobody knows that Dallas is in the nascent stages of a dynasty or that this is as good as it gets during the Sanders era.

The future is unwritten, but today can be authored.

Detroit dominates in all phases. Erik Kramer sheds journeyman status, threading turkey-hole throws to become a franchise quarterback, if only for an afternoon. Sanders secures the win with a 47-yard gallop that puts Detroit into the NFC Championship Game and the throes of ecstasy.

Triumph ignites the dormant football town in Detroit's DNA. The Silverdome crowd disrupts the Cowboy offense with eardrum-shredding decibel levels that shatter indoor stadium noise records.

A storybook ending does not await.

Washington is a monolith of competence. The Lions lose 41–10, falling to one of the great teams in league history. Detroit became 1991's third-best team and bounced back from trauma to do so. That should be enough. Judging by how this team is still loved, it is.

* * *

My extended family's Catholic. Like, Latin Mass, texting with the bishop-level believers. Walkowskis were only religious when my parents found a church choir worth joining.[12] I sat through endless Sunday services thinking kickoff was the truly sacred time.

When Pope John Paul II visited Detroit, he led mass in a sold-out Silverdome. This made sense. That's where deities worked.

---

12. Banjo Bob shredded psalms for any parish that would ask. And some that wouldn't ask.

We lived in East Dearborn at the intersection of Warren and Schaefer. This zip code possesses the country's highest Muslim concentration. An influx of immigrants from Lebanon, Palestine, and other countries began in the early 1980s,[13] spurred in part by jobs Henry Ford promised long ago.

Our town blossomed alongside a thriving immigrant population. Dearborn is wonderful because new residents kept their existing cultures intact. Store signs are in Arabic, sports bars offer hookah instead of booze, and we're home to the world's best garlic sauce.

I witnessed calls to prayer, classmates fasting, and women in burkas but didn't understand it as a matter of faith. Living among two cultures with a child's perspective is to dwell on similarities. What bypasses differences to bring people together? What sparks collective joy? What turns neighborhoods into communities?

Barry Sanders.

A 2011 Oxford study found that children innately believe in God. This global study surveyed 20 nations and discovered that searching for a higher power is something humans simply do. Developing human minds inherently seek something to order the world and its complexities. The study also found that, if there's no presence of religion or faith, children generally ascribe supernatural traits to a person from their community.

I loved my parents but understood them as human. Looking back, I saw my mother wrestling with rage and food issues; my father simply struggled. My psyche longed for someone to put on a pedestal and settled on the most impactful figure in proximity: the running back.

This was not a fantastical leap but a rational one. Everyone knew him, everyone loved him, and he sparked widespread joy. Barry was divine.

Faith fosters community from collective belief. I could discuss Barry with anyone and worship him openly, knowing the rest of my region felt the same.

My adapted belief system aligned with other load-bearing cultural tentpoles. When my parents took me downtown, Barry's image stood fifteen

---

13. They probably wanted to watch me grow up.

stories high on the Cadillac building. Barry appeared in McDonald's commercials and on collectible cups alongside the Tasmanian Devil. This was significant; there was no higher feat than synonymy with McDonald's. Barry was culture.

I'd been to church but never heard about Jesus making an All-Pro team or shaking a linebacker out of their sneakers. Religion is based on miracles; that's what Barry performed all the time. Detroit was an economically depressed place in decades-long decline. Barry Sanders did the impossible. He made people happy.

I'm not saying that a running back with positive traits is an ideal choice for a Christlike figurehead. I'm saying I could've done worse. Barry became my totem and the Lions my faith.

I was a true believer about to become Job.

JUNE 23, 1992

The 1992 offseason offers a bright future.

More tragedy strikes. It's the second instance of horrific events impacting the Lions—and the offensive line specifically—in a seven-month span.

Eric Andolsek embodied everything right with the franchise. Drafted as a fifth-round offensive guard in 1988, the raw prospect developed into a solid starter. Blessed with impeccable work ethic and laden with character,[14] Andolsek was foundational.

Andolsek was working in the front yard of his Louisiana home when fate showed its cruel nature. A truck driver towels moisture from his face. It's a regular moment—a task everyone's performed—but ruins lives in this instance. The driver loses control. The truck jumps the curb, speeds across the lawn, and strikes Andolsek. He perishes.

---

14. Andolsek was suspended from grade school for (too) successfully standing up to a bully.

Hit by a truck while doing yard work in broad daylight. This demise is more unlikely than a lightning strike, requiring a confluence of unfortunate events borrowed from a *Final Destination* movie.

The young team on the rise is once again a group of confused men mourning.

Men are expected to buck up, but there's no toughing this one out. Not when the bright futures of colleagues are seemingly extinguished at random.

Collective wisdom deems the Lions an ascendent team. Collective wisdom is stupid. How can we be at our best when mourning?

Being a loser is more than coming up short. It's a deep-seated dread making our worst moments self-fulfilling prophecies.

It's *Same Old Lions.*

Every new coach is asked about *Same Old Lions.* They deny its existence, promising change.

It never changes.

"Same." Bad luck sparks a sinking feeling.

"Old." Back-breaking, improbable, *what-if* errors occur, just as they have since 1957.

"Lions." The concession that we aren't merely competing against other teams but fate itself.

The 1992 Detroit Lions are frontrunners. It's impossible to imagine them floundering until the season starts. Quarterbacks fail to develop, coaches coast on previous performance, and the team sputters within a culture simultaneously toxic and laissez-faire.

Regression is a hard truth. The Lions get off to a horrific 1–4 start, burying the season before Halloween decorations appear. Four losses by 14 points portray an unlucky team as opposed to a bad one. *How did a team with prime Barry Sanders finish 5–11?* Advanced analytics weigh efficiency and quantify bad luck indices, but all the math in the world is no match for those three little words: Same. Old. Lions.

We're a disappointment because that's what we are.

Long-term success—in the NFL or otherwise—is often predicated on how the first trappings of a win are responded to.

1991 is a feel-good story. A young star rallies a team past trauma, lifting them to new heights, and illustrating resilience. They are talented but not managerially self-aware. Success doesn't occur. It's manufactured, the net result of every habit.

The team becomes bad because they assume they'll be successful.

My father built a family. He found a wife, an income, and sired two children. He didn't acknowledge trauma or plan to overcome it. There is no plan for continued success aside from stubbornly believing it'd perpetually continue.

It won't. Shit hits the fan. The family declines. He doesn't blame himself for not acting proactively. He views this decline as inevitable. It was destined to happen to him, to us.

Anytime I tell my father about a professional success he gives the same response.

"Take the money and run."

Winning is not something you plan and incrementally achieve. It's a scam someone falls for.

My story is unlearning Banjo Bob's lessons. My inherited worldview landed me in a loathing-fueled cycle of addiction, recovery, and relapse. Being given this approach is not my fault. Not addressing it is.

Being good at something and doing well are two vastly different things. I must address my flaws. Acknowledge my shortcomings and plan accordingly. Being placed in a crappy context doesn't define me. You can still be the best while tethered to a losing organization. Stay humble and use everything in your arsenal to avoid what's determined to take you down. I learned this from my deity.

I'm given this behavioral cycle. My task is preventing it from becoming my defining characteristic. I am Barry Sanders, and the Walkowski Way is a linebacker. Hard effort and self-inventory are the only way out.

Otherwise, I will be the 1992 Detroit Lions forever.

GAME 5

SANDERS

• 1993–1996 •

One Division Title

1993	1994	1995	1996
10-6	9-7	10-6	5-11

Success stems from decisions. The "marshmallow test," conducted at Stanford in 1970, correlated lifelong success with the ability to delay gratification. A child is left with a marshmallow. If they wait 15 minutes without eating it, they'll receive two marshmallows. The study found that children who waited received more than two marshmallows—they'd get better lives. The best decision is the one serving long-term interests.[1]

Modern NFL free agency began in 1993. It was a seismic shift. Players could choose their employer. Teams could improve arsenals by agreeing to contractual terms—provided they had room under the NFL's hard salary cap.

---

1. It's worth noting the child must trust the promise. Anyhow, if you finish reading this book I'll mail you two marshmallows.

Greed destroys. There's a reason it's one of the seven deadly sins over, say, loitering or having too many houseguests. Greed skews thoughts, prompting bad decisions. Have you seen a video of someone losing everything at a casino? They fight past security, grasping at chips lingering on the table. Greed has set their fate. Those videos adeptly capture the 1993 Lions offseason.

Pat Swilling was the NFL's first free agency misfire. Hitting the open market was uncharted waters, and Swilling, a former Defensive Player of the Year averaging 16 sacks annually, was the prize catch. The Lions badly wanted Swilling, offering him the largest contract ever given to a defensive player. Swilling's previous team, New Orleans, had six days to match the offer and did so at the eleventh hour.

Swilling was happy, saying he was "grateful to put the process behind him and remain a Saint."

Unfortunately, the Lions weren't finished. It made sense for GM Chuck Schmidt to acquire the pass rushing linebacker in free agency. It made no sense for the team to double down after being rebuked, trading for Swilling. The desperate Lions offered a bevy of picks and got legend Joe Schmidt to unretire his #56 jersey for Swilling to wear. The Lions weren't just willing to mortgage the present and future for Swilling. They'd happily give up the past.

In college, at chemical exploration's peak, I *needed* a Tenori-On. If you don't know what that is: Congratulations! You probably have friends! The Tenori-On is a Japanese electronic instrument and *music visualizer.* I viewed the grid of sixteen blinking lights and sounds as my salvation—even though I'm not a musician. I didn't have money for groceries but bought it anyway, putting it on my credit card and ultimately stealing food for sustenance.

Pat Swilling was the Lions' Tenori-On.

Who hasn't pursued a dream so hard it held them back? In exchange for Swilling, Detroit sent New Orleans the eighth overall pick and an additional fourth rounder. The first rounder became Willie Roaf, a Hall of Fame offensive guard. The fourth became Lorenzo Neal, the era's best blocking fullback. These acquisitions would have greatly benefited Barry—especially after losing two top blockers under tragic circumstances.

Swilling underwhelmed, becoming Detroit's biggest sports villain through no fault of his own. He did not write the contract but was demonized like he embezzled the funds.

Detroit's feverish improvement attempts served short-term interests, inadvertently swapping the perfect supporting cast for a pariah. Instead of methodically building around their crown jewel, the Lions rushed the job, undermining the entirety of Barry's career just three years into it.

Joe Montana phones the front office. The greatest quarterback of his era wants to play in Detroit. Coach Fontes jumps with joy, but Chuck Schmidt shuts down the idea. "He's over the hill. He's done."

The real miss is opportunity cost. The 1993 team is scrappy, talented, and tough. It's especially pertinent because the Lions win their division—a distinction that will not occur again for 30 years.

★ ★ ★

Banjo Bob's a talented gift giver. This ability overcomes his limitations, letting loved ones feel seen. He grows demented and impoverished but still delights with homemade leather goods and esoteric taxidermy.

I know what I'm getting for my seventh birthday in September. "Someday" will be on the calendar. Every good grade, holiday, or visit from the tooth fairy springs private manifestation for this longed-for event. Banjo Bob pulls a crisp envelope from his breast pocket. *Someday*'s here.

We're going to see the Lions. The tickets are so official, so authoritative in my hand that sensory memory stays with me forever. Even today, in the age of digital entry, if I gift someone tickets, I remember this moment and produce facsimiles.

Someday resides in November's distant future but looms over each day. I struggle in school, unable to sit still or pay attention. Teachers meet with parents, formulating plans to get Joel to behave. I get beaten with shoes and sat on by my mother as a punishment, but the idea of taking away the game is nixed as "too cruel."

The Lions assemble a solid season, convincing me—for the first time of many—that this is the year. A journey of a thousand miles starts with a single step; the lofty goal of a Super Bowl begins with becoming a pretty good football team. The 1993 Lions are pretty good.

WEEK 10: NOVEMBER 7, 1993. TAMPA BAY BUCCANEERS (2-5) V DETROIT LIONS (6-2). SILVERDOME, PONTIAC, MI.

Everyone assumes their childhood is normal. At least as it's happening. It's impossible to know otherwise. Banjo Bob drives us in his gold Chevy Nova nicknamed "The Lung Cancer Death Mobile." The Silverdome is thronged by parking lots. Rungs of asphalt ring out, exalting urban sprawl. We drive past 'em all, parking miles away. I'm not going to a game; I'm getting a curriculum. This is *Football Watching 101*.

There's only one right way to attend a game and, fortunately for me, only Banjo Bob knows the rules:

1. Avoid traffic. Arrive early, stay late . . . More time to look at the field.
2. Never pay for parking. It's a scam.
3. Buy a program. Read about assistant coaches.
4. Good plays are accompanied by a high-pitched "oooooh."
5. There's lots of good things to do in the parking lot afterward.

And most importantly . . .

6. Never leave early. No matter what.

Being sucked through the Silverdome's revolving doors is a Pangea-slow process punctuated by a *thunk* demarcating the moment the stadium vacuums up the individual, transforming them into part of a crowd. One atom in a being of 83,000 components, each residing in the same state. We dress similarly, yearn for the same outcome, and are allowed to be rowdy.[2] I'm an ADD-addled kid, constantly in trouble. This marks the first time I don't have to alter behavior to fit in.

The offense shuffles onto the field. Even from the nosebleeds it's easy to pick out Barry. His big legs and oversized shoulder pads make him puffy, lending the appearance of a stubborn toddler.

Magic happens immediately. Barry pirouettes to the perimeter, sweeping upward for 20. The place erupts, rapturous joy wrought from a diminutive man's single action. Each first down is marked with a Lion's roar, bubbling into crescendo as we reach the end zone.

"Read the scoreboard and sing along." A band leads "Gridiron Heroes." Bellowing "Forward down the field" brings great happiness. This remains true for the rest of my life.

A confluence of timing makes it lasting. My baptism was observing a perfect game at my father's side, peak Barry feasting on the undermanned Bucs. I don't know the Lions are historically bad. I just know they're mine.

The Lions win 23–0 but we aren't allowed to go home.[3] Traffic is to be avoided, not experienced. Banjo Bob removes garbage bags from his jacket. Taking advantage of Michigan's recycling laws, we collect enough cans to purchase pepperoni pizza on the way home.

We lug our cans to the players' parking lot. Banjo Bob hands me a Sharpie, telling me to "look sad." We're the last fans left. A tricked-out truck pulls past. *Chris Spielman!* I sprint after the truck like it's a running back shooting the gap, putting up the fastest 40 time in franchise history, rewarded by the brake light's beacon. Spielman rolls down his window, signs my program, and tells me to "go home, kid."

I'm already there.

---

2. I suppose there are visitors rooting for the opposition but that's lost on me as a Lions-centric child.

3. The Lions employ a safety named "Willie Clay." I ask my dad if he's related. He says he's the owner's son but can't use the surname because "Henry Ford hated football."

WEEK 18: JANUARY 2, 1994. GREEN BAY PACKERS (9-6) v DETROIT LIONS (9-6). SILVERDOME, PONTIAC, MI.

WILD CARD: JANUARY 8, 1994. GREEN BAY PACKERS (9-7) v DETROIT LIONS (10-6). SILVERDOME, PONTIAC, MI.

It arrives. The primary feeling I'll be rationalizing for the rest of my days.

Green Bay visits the Silverdome. Winner takes the division. In 1993, matchups with the Packers are just another game, not some twice-biannual horror show.[4]

Brett Favre loses the game for Green Bay. Our secondary capitalizes on his terrible decisions like a construction crew specializing in college volleyball arenas. The Lions not only win the division but show character, overcoming significant injury to Barry.

The divisional crown is rewarded with a home game the following week, played against the Packers once again. Barry plays through a torn knee ligament, the biggest injury of his football life. He is sublime, shredding the (admittedly meager) Lions' postseason record book.

Disaster derails certain victory. The Lions are driving for a 10-point lead when Erik Kramer's end zone pass is intercepted and returned 101 yards for a score. Giving up scoring plays longer than the field is generally a bad thing.

Detroit rallies to lead 24–21. I want to throw out historical accuracy and say this is where it ends, that the last three decades were happy for my team and family, but that's not what life is. Rooting for the Lions is buying a pennant for the abyss. Other teams hang banners. We build character via ennui.

It comes down to one possession. The Packers have the ball on the Lions' 40, flirting with a field goal like Mark Chmura approaching a hot

---

4. In a rare scheduling fluke, the Lions and Packers play four times in 1994.

tub teenager. Favre spent the previous 119 minutes of football making mistake after mistake. Coaches beg him to play conservatively but gunslingers rarely follow expected value processes. Favre rolls out, finding a running lane so clear even impartial announcers beg him to take it. He doesn't.

Favre fires the cannon. It finds Sterling Sharpe alone in the Lions' end zone. Not a single defender is in frame. Lions lose. We resoundingly outplay our opponent but lose on a last gasp in maddening fashion. Even worse, the gasp awakens a juggernaut.

What hurts isn't that this occurred. It's that it transpired during what should have been Barry's finest hour.

This game kick-starts a decades-long run of Packers dominance. Their fan base descends upon the smallest town in pro sports, worshipping at Lambeau Field like it's a beer-serving cathedral. I'm no different. My biggest dream is to visit Lambeau . . . and pee on the 50-yard line.

I will be arrested, charged, brought before a judge, and asked "How do you plead?" I'll plead insanity, play back the Sterling Sharpe catch, and get off with a warning.

This is a core feeling I carry with me. Another begins in this same era. Are they significant or does whatever impacts us during certain windows simply stay with us forever?

★ ★ ★

I'm put on Adderall, ripping 40 milligrams of speed daily. There it is. Addiction. The pangs and demands of a deeply seeded creature emerge as I'm discovering consciousness. You, the reader, may scoff at this genesis. You're welcome to replicate the dosage. If you're ever gonna put a seven-year-old on 40 mg of Adderall, *try 40 mg of Adderall!*

I'm a hyperactive, happy kid put on pills to fit in and make the teachers' lives easier. If the buzz wanes I visit nuns working in the school office and re-up. Methamphetamine will supposedly help me in school. Instead, I learn the only way to accomplish a task is with pills.

I've been an addict ever since. Pills, booze, weed, hallucinogens, opioids, meth, kratom, nicotine, coffee, gambling, no drug of choice—anything that will make me feel different. I fixate on this sensation until I can get it again. It starts here, recommended by a doctor receiving pharmaceutical kickbacks. I don't mind carrying the long-term effects of short-term decision-making. I just wish it was my decision.

All this to say I love it. Speed is a perfect feeling. There's a small heaven in being seven, compulsively cracking knuckles because you're friggin' *locked in* for elementary school. I breeze through math, memorize the Lions depth chart, and swallow another pill, knowing it makes me whole.

Doing drugs allows membership in a fraternity. Uncle Joe asks me about my "hyper pills." First adult conversations are comparing the effects of my Adderall to his Vicodin. Pills are never discussed with anything but effusive praise. They make us functional, who we need to be. Us poor Michiganders scrounge for pills like they're our coveted morel mushrooms.

We're all seeking solutions. None of them work. A local saying decrees that Detroit's most popular citizen is backup quarterback for the Lions. Cycle of injuries and interceptions forges a grass is always greener mentality, prompting further attempts to address the position. Once again, it's wrong.

Miami's Scott Mitchell sits behind legendary Dan Marino, diligently holding his clipboard. An injury forces Mitchell into action, setting the stage for him to come in and . . . be kinda okay.

The Lions ravenously pursue Mitchell—who took over a 9–4 team and led them out of a playoff race. He was a passable fill-in who looked the part and possessed traits a general manager could talk themselves into. Size, pedigree, youth. He was the latest iteration of the savior and immediately hated by almost everyone. Star tackle and franchise ambassador Lomas Brown admits to deliberately letting him get sacked. When he eventually balloons and appears on the weight-loss reality program *The Biggest Loser*, a chorus of fans exclaim they already knew that.

The Sterling Sharpe catch hurts so bad. Blaming myself, I vow to buckle down and witness the team's eventual success. Much like addiction, being a die-hard fan is something best navigated when self-diagnosed. The 1994 season is my first approaching the team in a manner befitting a DSM description. Rituals include songs, superstition, and stories but the key component is how the calendar's viewed. Sunday afternoon is a week's load-bearing component. Other windows are either exposition or denouement.

WEEK 1: SEPTEMBER 4, 1994. ATLANTA FALCONS (0-0) V DETROIT LIONS (0-0). SILVERDOME, PONTIAC, MI.

I sit in church, piously anticipating the return. Visions of a 16–0 season dance through my head as sermons are resoundingly ignored. Talk of eternal damnation falls on deaf ears before a crowd of Detroit sports fans who already experience that. We bow our heads in prayer. I fold my hands, close my eyes, and channel energy toward Scott Mitchell.

Colorful Silverdome crowds use vestiges of chaos magic to repel reasonable doubts regarding Mitchell. One fan swings a noose containing effigies of opposing quarterbacks. Another holds cartoonishly large arrows, conjuring misfires from opposing kickers. There's even a bedsheet spray-painted with the manifestation "Mitchell + Moore = Score." Bedsheet graffiti actualizing aspirations tempts me to ruin Egyptian cotton with "Stay Sober & Eat More Plants."

Faith's rewarded. Mitchell's physical tools unlock Herman Moore, allowing him to key victory. *The linens were right!* Scott Mitchell is a franchise quarterback.

He holds the position for one week.

Mitchell regresses, throwing a slew of interceptions in a series of losses. We scale up Barry's carries to get us through the season even though playing "big play lottery" wears on him.

Mitchell goes down for the year, allowing Dave Krieg, an undersized but overqualified backup, to properly play quarterback. We don't need a savior. We have one. The savior needs less turnovers from his disciples.

Krieg goes 5–3 as a starter, throwing 14 touchdowns against three interceptions. Other quarterbacks faltered via mistakes. Given the caliber of weapons, the worst thing a quarterback could do is sacrifice possessions. The search for a savior failed because what we really needed was stability. The clearest path to success is not fucking up in the first place.

The season's remainder is a joyous rip roar, but a foreboding feeling takes hold. *We aren't good enough.*

I know we'll lose. This is a good thing. Instead of expecting victory, I practice optimism. There's always a path to victory, no matter how unlikely. A 17-point deficit just needs two scores, two stops, a successful on-side kick, and another score. The last wild card spot will certainly spark a Super Bowl destiny. Heck, even if we fail, next year's draft pick will right the ship.

This manner of processing impending losses are thoughts attempting to self-govern. Accepting losing as a naturally occurring process redirects neural pathways toward positivity. Training myself to see "what needs to go right" is the trait serving me best and instilled by accepting that the deck was stacked against my beloved team.

★ ★ ★

The Detroit Lions are more than a football team. At least to a nascent mind seeking structure and meaning in an otherwise chaotic world. A universal way of thinking develops from one specific circumstance. Each Sunday, I accept the valleys and train myself to always spot the way out.

I practice seeing the positive. This trait isn't something we have but something we build. The first step to solving a problem is acknowledging its existence. There will be disappointment. What's inherent in life is omnipresent in Lions football. The only way to watch is by refusing to look anywhere but the bright side. I strain to see the positives and repeat every game day until a childhood habit becomes my adult attitude toward adversity.

WILD CARD: DECEMBER 31, 1994. DETROIT LIONS (9-7) V GREEN BAY PACKERS (9-7). LAMBEAU FIELD, GREEN BAY, WI.

Barry had almost 2,000 yards. Running back production declines after 300 carries in a season—Sanders eclipses this threshold three times in four years—what can we expect?

I'm making excuses. Barry Sanders has the worst game of his career. In the playoffs. Against the Packers. At Lambeau. We fall 16–12 on "the frozen tundra." Losing is fine but not like this. Barry puts up 13 carries for *–1 rushing yard.* Linguistically unpacking the performance reaps devastation. The yardage isn't even plural. Fuck, it isn't even positive.

From Jason Hanson whiffing an early field goal to Herman Moore catching a fourth down game winner out of bounds, it clearly isn't our day.

The worst part isn't Barry's terrible day or the knife twist of close calls. Dave Krieg doesn't win a playoff game, so Lions brass let him leave in free agency. Krieg's performance is no argument against Mitchell's contract. We pay him like a starter, so he is one.

We open the 1995 season against Dave Krieg's new team, the Arizona Cardinals. He humiliates us. Even me, a feeble-minded nine-year-old, knows we deserve it. It is no surprise that Dave Krieg outplays Scott Mitchell for an afternoon. We just watched it for an entire season.

The Lions sputter to 3–6. Coach Fontes must guide the team to the playoffs to save his job. Given his record, this threat's effectively a pink slip. Detroit must play perfectly.

They do.

It starts on Thanksgiving. Barry, Moore, Brett Perriman, *and* upstart Johnnie Morton all record 100 yards and a touchdown. Broadcaster John Madden gushes over the performance while handing out genetically modified turkey legs. The bird isn't real but the team sure is.

Scott Mitchell becomes the player the front office thought they signed, putting up 32 touchdowns and 4,500 yards. These benchmarks, regularly approached by other franchises, were as absent from Detroit as ethical mayors.

It's the league's best offense. Legendary coordinator Tom Moore, who eventually helps develop Peyton Manning, creates a revolutionary passing attack. The threat of vertical passes compliments Sanders as Moore and Perriman rewrite receiving record books.[5]

We don't just beat teams, we steamroll them. Jacksonville loses 44–0, Tampa gets thrashed 37–10. We run Florida like Jimmy fucking Buffett.

The team's efforts land them on the cover of *Sports Illustrated*, an unparalleled honor in the Walkowski household. Banjo Bob gets me a subscription at age six, giving his highest compliment of calling it "good writing." Rushing home from school on Thursdays, tearing open the mailbox, and reading cover to cover makes me feel like his son. Barry gracing the front page causes serotonin spikes rivaling a snow day.

WILD CARD: DECEMBER 30, 1995. DETROIT LIONS (10-6) V PHILADELPHIA EAGLES (10-6). VETERANS STADIUM, PHILADELPHIA, PA.

A team with an opportunistic defense and unmatched skill-position players enters the postseason on a seven-game winning streak.

I am nine years old and abjectly stupid. Core beliefs are that the Lions are awesome, teachers don't exist beyond the classroom, and that "Macho Man" Randy Savage holds elected office. And yet . . . I know ball.

A playoff contender has a certain look, a particular roster balance. The Lions are the best team in football. The only thing missing from a certain Super Bowl run is a home game. Our roster construction requires a fast track, i.e., a domed stadium, to be fully unleashed. Muddy, cold-weather games are the backbone of the sport's identity but don't agree with our electric offense.

5. Herman Moore sets the record for receptions in a season with 122.

We have a chance at the division title but do not control our fate. Pittsburgh must beat Green Bay.

A single play remains. The Steelers trail 24–19 deep in Packers territory. Pittsburgh receiver Yancey Thigpen is open in the end zone. A perfect throw flutters directly into Thigpen's chest. He drops it, relegating us to an away game.

The Lions must face the Eagles and former Lions quarterback Rodney Peete before a raucous Philly crowd. Still, they aren't on our level. It's a sure thing. I have full confidence the Lions will come through in a big spot. It's what they've done all year. *This Native burial ground is the perfect place to build the family home.*

Mitchell drops back. His pass is tipped, intercepted, and sets up the first Eagles score. Early jitters. That's all.

We get the ball back, certain to answer. Brett Perriman suffers serious injury. The severity is immediately obvious, sending him from the game and compromising his career trajectory. Our Super Bowl offense gets half a quarter before suffering lasting impediment.

Sharpe's catch, Moore falling out of bounds, Perriman's injury. The annual tradition is a wild card loss accompanied by a what-if moment we'll take to our grave.

We spin out. The perfect team that cannot lose is dead. Everything that can go wrong does. Long Eagles touchdowns, Mitchell pick-sixes, even a *fuck you* Hail Mary to make the halftime score 38–7. A rollicking two-month wave of ecstasy crests into the obvious lesson: No matter the circumstances, a loss is always lurking.

It's over.

I blame Thigpen's drop, Perriman's injury, and the Ford family for not tying Fontes's job security to a playoff win.

The deficit is too deep. There's no way to win. The game ends and I immediately replicate the matchup on my electric football machine, realizing the only thing as disappointing as the loss is this crappy toy. I dwell on the loss for months. If I close my eyes Mitchell's interceptions replay. If

I open them, I see a sad-sack community kicking themselves for the sin of believing.

Sometimes a single decision is so devastating it not only ends the good times but reaches backwards in time to remove luster from happy memories.

East Dearborn's a happy place. The melting pot of thriving immigrants is the perfect base for our esoteric family. Great memories aren't something pursued but an organic by-product of a vibrant, walkable community. We thrive here because Banjo Bob thrives here. He's lead guitar in church band, heads a Boy Scout troop, and is an invested family man. Both parents attend 12-Step meetings, dragging their children to our one true church. Bill W is Jesus, the steps are commandments, and stale donuts are communion.

It's a decidedly good life. We have our problems but navigate them. We're happy. It's not eye-popping from a "Keeping Up with the Joneses" perspective but it is enough. Until it isn't.

Beware the next big move. The decision intended to push an entity over the top often sends it back to the drawing board. Had my parents paid attention to the Pat Swilling or Andre Ware acquisitions they'd have known this.

My parents visit an open house. It's a giant home on a beautifully wooded lot in an upscale neighborhood. They can't afford it but have to have it. Banjo Bob's at his peak earning powers. If good times last forever, this just might work. They throw out an offer. It gets accepted. We're moving.

Banjo Bob tells me about leaving East Dearborn at 8 AM. By 6 PM, he's pulling me aside to confide "we made a mistake" but lacks the self-worth to stop what he put in motion. This isn't my mother being domineering. This is an individual on the spectrum starting a decades-long pattern of behaviors best described as "pathologically passive."

We go from crossing train tracks for Lebanese cheese pies to living near a golf course with people who are really proud of living near a golf course.

I ride my bike across the corner of a lawn only to be told "we don't do that here"—by another ten-year-old!

The nuclear family starts eroding the moment the truck is unloaded. The new family home turns our close-knit clan into a disparate group of individuals.

Banjo Bob does not like the rich. Being around wealth sets off anger and anxiety. He loses his job, falls into depression, and is begged to attend therapy. He does. Addressing his childhood makes him announce his trauma and join a support group for Child Sexual Assault survivors. He buys a little black baby doll, swaddling it with expensive doll clothes, providing it with the great childhood he never had. From a therapeutic perspective? This makes sense. As a kid who lost out to this stupid doll? It doesn't.

He withdraws from the family. The sound of mournful guitar is his only presence in the home.

DECADES PASS

He remains the same. I wish he'd shake off decades of self-serving silence and guide me. In our final conversations I can't help but remind him of this fact, begging for wisdom.

"Is there anything you want to tell me before you die?"

I ask every hour, receiving the same answer each time.

"I like Mountain Dew."

It breaks my heart, but I keep asking, ruining Baja Blast in the process.

1996

Just like every year, it will be a good year. It's finally our year. The league's hottest team added two bruising first-round prospects. Reggie Brown in particular, a cannonball LB out of Texas A&M, promises to make us bigger and tougher, equipping Wayne Fontes's team with the brute physicality they lack.

HALLOWEEN 1996

Scott Mitchell picks up where he left off, throwing interception after interception as losses mount. The team shrugs it off for a 4–3 start but a blowout loss to the moribund Giants seals Mitchell's fate. New York puts up 35 consecutive points as Mitchell throws three picks. It's his best performance of the week.

Quarterback effectiveness is part physical skills but mostly leadership. Strong decision-making must favor collective interests over the individual. Mitchell demonstrates a fatal lack of leadership through his choices at, of all things, Herman Moore's Halloween party.

Mitchell and Fontes fight all year. Rather than handle the issue internally, Scott tosses fuel on the fire. It's his most accurate throw of the season.

Scott arrives in a fat suit and Mickey Mouse ears, chomping a cigar as part of a Wayne Fontes costume. He proceeds to give an interview with local news while in character. The message is clear: He doesn't respect his coach. Mediocre talents distract from their worthlessness by creating drama. The 1996 Lions have the same story arc as any season of *Real Housewives*.

For the second consecutive season, Fontes's job is publicly on the line. The strong close to previous seasons conditions me into magically thinking Detroit always plays well down the stretch. I am born in the equinox, erroneously thinking the world is always bright. This is wrong. We limp to the finish line, only winning one game after the costume.

We enter 1996 with Super Bowl aspirations and exit 5–11.

Wayne Fontes is fired.

William Clay Ford addresses the media: "I won't be satisfied with anything less than a Super Bowl." This message is contradicted by every action during his tenure.

Fontes makes a surprise appearance at the press conference. He isn't combative or contrite but his charismatic self. "I gave you guys hope. You never had that before I came here."

National newspapers proclaim "Lions FINALLY Fire Wayne Fontes" while Lions fans call him the best coach they've ever seen. He leaves the franchise as both the winningest and losingest coach in their history. One marshmallow might not lead to lasting success, but it's delicious going down.

Opposing players derisively dismiss Detroit as a "country club" due to laissez-faire practices, but as this era's Walkowskis can attest, it's not easy to thrive in country club conditions.

GAME 6

THE APEX, THE ENDS

• 1997-2000 •

Two Wild Card Berths, One Breakthrough Milestone, Three Crushing Exits

1997	1998	1999	2000
9-7	5-11	8-8	9-7

The house we can't afford comes with a broken-down sports car. My father's new image is being covered in grease, wearing a "Papa Roach" T-shirt,[1] and donning a sweat-soaked bandanna crowning his receding hairline. His mouth alternates outputs of cigarette smoke and curses regarding some automotive malady.

Banjo Bob writes car manuals. Glove box tomes are his livelihood. He's synthesized every bit of technical information, promising to fix up the car "you'll drive to prom." It sits there stagnating.

---

1. "Roach" is his college nickname. I get him a Papa Roach T-shirt from the nu metal band. He wears it every day for years.

He loses his job. I'm the only one he tells, sworn to secrecy as he musters enough courage to tell my mother.

"You got fired?!?" I ask.

"Laid off."

I don't know the difference. Nor do I know solid middle-class jobs have been siphoned off for decades, unlikely to return, or that our plush neighborhood is populated by those who cut said positions.

I'm Banjo Bob's safe space, his confidant. Little boys see their father as God until learning enough to know better.

News can't be contained. Stoney and Wojo host drive-time on WDFN Sports Radio 1130: The Fan. Wednesday's recurring segment, "What's Your Beef?" features listener complaints. The top grievance receives a prize.

"Joel from Dearborn, what's your beef?"

"My dad lost his job."

I don't win but my prepubescent squeaks elicit enough sympathy to receive a promotional T-shirt.

Later that day Banjo Bob comes in from a long day in the garage staring at a broken-down car.

"Hey, Slick. Did you call Stoney and Wojo?"

"No. Some other Bob must've lost his job."

We don't know what's waiting. We're steeped in the mold to be tragic goofballs. Even our darkest moments are funny, yet poignant.[2] We'll never break free of ourselves.

* * *

2. My parents send me to a cultural immersion camp off the coast of Iceland not realizing one of the scheduled activities has children assisting a traditional whaling expedition. They scrounge for me to see the world. I see Scandinavians butcher 200 pilot whales instead.

The Lions embark on the same doomed trajectory. Wayne Fontes is removed, blamed for lax practices in place since 1963. The Fords want to renovate team culture without examining their contributions.

Bobby Ross is a military man first and football coach second. Beginning his career at the Virginia Military Institute, the field general graduates into actual generaling with a tour of duty. Football's inherently militaristic. Plays resemble battle, satiating appetites for combat in a nation increasingly removed from war.

Civilian life is coaching. Ross transforms Georgia Tech into a college powerhouse, jumps to the NFL, and keys a similar turnaround in San Diego. He's well regarded with unmatched job security, but the romanticism of reviving doormats beckons.

Detroit offers the world, wooing Ross with the promise of complete control. Head coach and general manager are usually two positions. Each job requires 70 hours weekly for even average performance. The unflappable military man is given dominion over the franchise.

The coach who never lost took on a team that never won. Time for a culture war.

Ross's control over basics like rosters and game plans extends to weight room mandates and curfews. Losses to divisional foes might be inevitable, but Ross was determined not to lose to the *Same Old Lions*.

The first mandate was instilling a traditional running game. For the first time, Barry would run behind a fullback. Having a blocker clattering into run lanes, whamming linebackers, explicitly creating space makes a halfback's life easier. The Lions employed history's most talented back for *seven years* without providing this resource.

Early returns were terrible. Over the first two games Barry gets just 53 rushing yards as announcers openly pontificate the root of the issues.

There's collective panic heading into Week 3.

"Bobby Ross ruined him!"

"He can't play with a fullback!"

"His best years are behind him!"

Barry adjusts.

1997 WEEKS 3-17: 2,000 YARDS

Against Chicago, Barry doubles season rushing totals in a single half. Ross's traditional rushing attack shows intended dividends with Barry performing sorcery in the defensive backfield as opposed to behind the line of scrimmage. The offense scores 32 unanswered points, and Reggie Brown adds two sacks.

The defending champion Packers swell in popularity, cheered by legions of simpletons duped by small-town branding. The ability to coax casuals onto the Green Bay bandwagon is extremely valuable to the NFL, with NFL referees consistently residing in the team's pocket.

The Packers get away with too many men on the field during a field goal. Bobby Ross reacts with consternation. Instead of righting the wrong, officials reward 30 yards to Green Bay. Our eventual win is made even sweeter knowing the triumph's uphill nature.

Against Tampa, Sanders has *two* scoring runs longer than 80 yards,[3] possibly the most eye-popping stat in a dossier full of them. The Buccaneers are a dominant defense, but Barry beats them single-handedly. The Ross era is off to a great start. One can imagine him hunched over a microscope, altering the team's DNA a la CRISPR.

A thrilling would-be comeback in New York is squandered by Scott Mitchell opening overtime with a game-ending pick-six, but losing doesn't matter. Not anymore. Barry has a chance of reaching the rarefied summit of 2,000 yards in a season.

My relationship with the team is obsessive to the point of being at least somewhat spectrum adjacent. If you disagree, I assume you picked this up in a bookstore and read the previous sentence first. Team statistics are private totems. The 1997 season joyfully turns private quirks into collective obsessions.

---

3. Barry breaks the NFL record for 80-yard runs in a season. As the owner of multiple Philip Glass vinyls, I assure you that esoteric records are still records.

WEEK 14: NOVEMBER 27, 1997. CHICAGO BEARS (2-10) V DETROIT LIONS (6-6). PONTIAC SILVERDOME, PONTIAC, MI.

The greatest Thanksgiving performance in franchise history. John Madden and Pat Summerall are on the broadcast, and old friend Erik Kramer sparks our foe to a 20–10 lead. The Silverdome's roof cannot shelter the team from downpours of boos.

Barry breaks a routine handoff, jukes a bevy of defenders, and finds the end zone. Floodgates open. Detroit reels off 45 unanswered points en route to a 55–20 victory with Barry churning a 25-yard run that becomes a perpetual staple of NFL highlight reels. Summerall and Madden—unmatched observers of the game—are left speechless. Barry leaves to a standing ovation and munches a genetically modified turkey leg. Every individual metric that matters is within reach, provided he bothers to grab them. Barry goes down as the greatest individual performer at his position. This game formally secures that designation.

WEEK 17: DECEMBER 21, 1997. NEW YORK JETS (9-6) V DETROIT LIONS (8-7). PONTIAC SILVERDOME, PONTIAC, MI.

Stakes are at all-time highs for a home game versus the New York Jets. It's a "win and in" game for both teams, but playoff implications are just technicalities. Success isn't determined by the team but by Barry surpassing 2,000 yards. The Silverdome contains the most raucous crowd of its entire existence. Fans gather for catharsis, screaming incantations to be forever changed. The game delivers.

The metric of the day is 131 yards. Our breathless countdown to 2,000 comes down to a single afternoon. Our hero hates attention and other superstar accoutrements but we don't care. We want this for him—even if he doesn't want this for himself.

Detroit treats this like a holiday. Every individual plans to watch in a specific setting but not us. My parents attend a social engagement. I watch alone in the family room, which I suppose just makes it a room.

It's easy for a child to relate to Barry. The smallest player on the field has a mythology cast against the backdrop of a hard-to-please father figure. Parents are scary. Seeing this trait in a hero affirms this truth.

William Sanders, Jim Brown proponent and root of his son's stoic nature, evolves on this day. There's no grandstanding or appreciating other backs. He roams the sidelines draped in Honolulu Blue,[4] supporting his son like the rest of us.

The contest's nature is immediately apparent: slugfest. The Bill Parcells–led Jets are more conservative on offense than a Mississippi election cycle. The defense swallows us up, going into the half up 10–3 and holding Barry to just 20 yards.

Stymying continues. One carry for two, another for no gain, another loses a yard. A sad reality sets in midway through the third: Our hero will fall short.

Third and 3; Last Play of the Third Quarter

A three-receiver set indicates pass and fools the defense. Barry takes a delayed carry, squirting through three sequential gaps for a gain of 56. He follows it up by going off tackle, freezing the linebacker with a wiggle, to secure a Lions lead and shot at history.

The environment's so happy. "Bar-ry" chants are so exuberant that referees threaten Detroit with a penalty unless the crowd quiets down. They don't. They can't.

Chants continue, happy exclamations of a crowd that's been on ice for decades. Referees chide us once more, but there's nothing they can do. Only God can quiet us.

God quiets us.

---

4. Give the man a seat. He's in his sixties!

First and 10 on the New York 27

Jets back Adrian Murrell trudges up the middle for two. Star linebacker Reggie Brown makes the tackle, rolls onto his back, and stays down. A shocked crowd grows so quiet a single player is heard screaming, "He's not breathing!"

The medical staff isn't fast enough. In a truly heroic moment, players Johnnie Morton and Kevin Glover sprint out the stretcher to make up time. An ambulance drives onto the field as both teams kneel in prayer. Our day in the sun is eclipsed.

I wanted to watch the game with my dad. Longing to watch Barry break 2,000 together is now a need to be told Reggie Brown is okay. He's strapped to a gurney, loaded into an ambulance, and driven away across the turf as chants of "Bar-ry" segue into those of "Reg-gie!"

Even rewatching today, I am overwhelmed with the need to find out that Reggie Brown is okay. I find him on LinkedIn. The entirety of his employment history reads: "Detroit Lions Linebacker. 1 year, 1 month."

The game resumes. The crowd tries to roar but can't. Voices left in the ambulance with Reggie. New York drives down the field, poised to score. The only silver lining is that outcomes don't matter nearly as much as they did a half hour earlier.

The Jets do something stupid. Murrell takes the ball, rolls right, and foolishly throws into double coverage for a Lions interception.[5]

Barry gains 2, 15, and 8. The crowd comes alive as the broadcast informs us, "Reggie Brown is unconscious but alive." We yo-yo between agony and ecstasy.

Possession reverts to the Jets. We're up 13–10 with Barry stuck at 1,998. The Jets pick up some yardage on third and 20 and appear poised to go for it. The crowd rises, getting louder, louder, and louder still. Previous

5. At least according to the box score. Our DB did not secure the ball. The call is so bad and has such far-reaching implications that it hastens the return of instant replay.

decibel records are broken as a lineman false starts. They punt. Barry will have his moment.

Barry takes the handoff and gets the exact right amount. A Lions timeout kicks off formal celebrations that Sanders wants no part of. How to act while crossing new frontiers? Like you've been there before. He hands the ball to his father and jogs back onto the field.

A first down clinches the postseason. Barry zigs past linebackers, zagging all the way to the Jets' three. The Lions make the playoffs. Barry ends the season with 2,053 yards. These were things Lions fans wanted until events made them things we needed.

Barry's career has no shortage of miracles. This record's timing and impact make it a rare instance where the term "miracle" is properly applied to sports. This isn't just the peak of Sanders's career. This was him coming through during sad circumstances, making us hold him more dear.

Human beings sacrifice for our entertainment. Football takes empowered young bodies and spits out damaged husks. My weekly viewing supports this practice, effectively making me complicit. However, there's beauty in it. The spotlight beckons. To feel the sport's speed and aggression is to feel truly alive, a heavenly body in each play's universe.

We can't simply root for the laundry but the individuals it contains. I rooted for Reggie Brown in 1997. I'm still cheering for him.

The 1997 season will be the last good year for the Lions for the foreseeable future. It's easy to ascribe totemic importance to Sanders. He defines the team as I gain consciousness and exits as I enter adolescence. He's my yardage marker of youth.

My family's last good year is 1997. Unemployment is the catalyst for Banjo Bob's depression. His mood sinks and his physical presence follows suit. He moves to the downstairs bedroom, then the unfinished basement. He exists here, smoking on a couch, evoking Picasso's portrait of a sad guitar player.

Emotional devastation circles the family. I am immune. I am not strong, or well adjusted, but bypass impending trauma for a simpler reason: I'm already a drug addict.

Behaviors become patterns and patterns become the people. My father's issues are part of me. Barry Sanders on the Lions creates the same image as a childhood I didn't realize was hard. If I looked at the world through Adderall's intense focus, there was always something to fixate on. I never realized how fucked everything was.

The next year will suck.

WEEK 2: SEPTEMBER 13, 1998. CINCINNATI BENGALS (0-1) V DETROIT LIONS (0-1). PONTIAC SILVERDOME, PONTIAC, MI.

Ross militaristically disciplines his roster. A grueling training camp intended to condition the team makes them start the season fatigued.

The season's first possession sees Scott Mitchell fumble away a fourth and 1 snap for a return touchdown. It doesn't get better.

Sanders is heroic, going for 165 yards and three scores including a 65-yard breathtaker that *finally* gives the Lions a lead they immediately surrender. Sanders's true adversary is his employer. The game wanes. Barry ties it with an elusive run. We regain possession. Barry rushes us into field goal range. A win is within reach.

Mitchell throws a pick-six.

Mitchell is benched for Charlie Batch, a well-liked rookie out of Eastern Michigan University. Batch's offense puts up a whopping six points and is universally considered an upgrade. Barry goes his entire career without playing alongside a good quarterback.

Barry is unhappy.

It's easy to accept failures originating with us; it's harder to rationalize circumstantial shortcomings. For some, an employer is a trusted support system orienting them toward success. For others it's a pair of cement shoes on a fishing trip. Barry falls short because his team perpetually picks the wrong quarterback. My family falls apart because they picked the wrong house.

Taking a team to the Super Bowl is great. Owning a city's heart is better. Barry leveraged a rare running style into a value-oriented career allowing sheer movements to evoke human ideals. Work hard. Be yourself. Don't complain. Live life like a Barry Sanders handoff. It could be good or bad but conduct yourself the same either way.

WEEK 3: NOVEMBER 26, 1998. PITTSBURGH STEELERS (7-4) V DETROIT LIONS (4-7). PONTIAC SILVERDOME, PONTIAC, MI.

Enthusiasm pivots to Barry's pursuit of the all-time rushing mark. Barry will certainly break the record, likely sometime in 1999. However, for Sanders, the only authentic exit is avoiding the spotlight one final time.

My mother's parents separate after 50 years.[6] Long-standing Thanksgiving traditions are scuttled but that's irrelevant. We're free on Thanksgiving.

It's not a food holiday in our home. My mother is a recovering food addict, and my father's trauma stunted his palate alongside the rest of him. I only ever see him eat four foods: hot dogs, pizza, potato chips, and peanuts. Family dysfunction is passed around our dinner table. So we eat alone. I eat ramen and Pop-Tarts in solitary confinement, understanding it as a form of heaven.

Left to forge our own traditions, we squander a perfect autumn day in the Silverdome's ziplock-bag aesthetic. Pittsburgh's superstar Jerome Bettis is a Detroit native, creating a wholesome narrative where the city wins with any outcome. The afternoon feels like a collaboration between Norman Rockwell and Budweiser.

Detroit gets jobbed on several early plays, but referees make it up to us.

---

6. As opposed to the alternative of, um, waiting a few months.

We go into overtime, still sudden death at this point. The referee tosses a coin to determine possession. Bettis plainly calls "tails." The referee mishears him, insisting he called heads. It's tails.

Steelers escalate the argument but referees never back down, especially when they're wrong. The Silverdome pops figurative bottles of champagne, reveling in the impending win. Dumb luck works like this. When an inane, illogical event transpires, whatever outcome compounds it most is a lock.

Moore catches a pass. Barry breaks a run. Hanson boots the winner. Details are lost to time. The coin toss overshadows all. It's the only thing to happen that day.

Banjo Bob and I collect cans for a pepperoni pizza and ride home in the Lung Cancer Death Mobile. We could have unpacked feelings or savored the moment but don't. We discuss the coin toss.

It's the last win of Barry Sanders's career.

The team gets listless. A loss at Baltimore mercifully ends the season. On the plane ride home, Barry gathers teammates, telling them he's done.

News creeps through the organization. Bobby Ross resorts to sending Barry handwritten letters, begging him to return.

Barry remains silent.

He faxes his hometown paper, *The Wichita Eagle.* "My desire to exit the game is greater than my desire to remain in it."

How could the rushing record mean so little to him when it means the world to me? I feel deeply childish—even though I'm 12.

I've come to understand Barry's disdain for records as beautiful. It was his way of letting the world know his priorities without having to explain them. He conquered a brutal game, walking away on his own terms.

Teammates discuss Barry like an endearing sloth. All he did was take naps and express a desire to retire. I've stayed at several jobs because it was so enjoyable to imagine quitting. *I get it, Barry.*

Without their leading man the 1999 Lions aren't written off or dismissed. They aren't even considered.

WEEK 9: NOVEMBER 7, 1999. ST. LOUIS RAMS (6-1) V DETROIT LIONS (5-2). PONTIAC SILVERDOME, PONTIAC, MI.

In a surprise to all, the Lions cobble together a .500 record. The roster contains more question marks than The Riddler's laundry, but Barry's departure galvanized them into above-average performance.

The St. Louis Rams are the feel-good story of the year. The Greatest Show on Turf streaks into the Silverdome with Kurt Warner going from grocery store clerk to lynchpin of a historically good offense.

The Rams are one of history's great teams, but on this day, we are better. It's the high point of the next decade. Barry's abrupt departure wounded the franchise's self-image so deeply that besting the eventual Super Bowl champions was worth raising a banner for—*1999 Detroit Lions: Beat a Bag Boy.*

The season has peaked. Emergency triage mode can only last so long. Starting 8–4 and winning on Thanksgiving empties the tank. We lose every remaining game. It's an inspiring success.

We rally for mediocrity. What seem so-so are the salad days.

★ ★ ★

Something needs to be done about Joel. Being hopped up on speed *actually* isn't that good for sitting still. I am kicked out of Catholic school for constant disruption. This is not hyperbole: A week before expulsion I'm cast as Jesus in Stations of the Cross and crucified before the student body.

A decision is made to save me. My family will have another child. Specifically, an enthusiastic Thai exchange student named Boon. He's handsome, charismatic, and spends his first day as a Walkowski kickboxing neighborhood kids off our secondhand trampoline. We call each other "brother" by sunset.

He's immediately the most popular kid in high school. He shares his status, bringing me to raves and gifting me old pornos. All I have to give in return is Lions fandom. Boon is initially skeptical but warms to American football upon learning Johnnie Morton is of Asian descent. Understanding the vital role football plays in male bonding, I introduce him to the game and painstakingly imbue various reasons why the Lions will be good. He believes me.

Bobby Ross builds a great defense. Dominant linemen Robert Porcher and Luther Elliss disrupt opposing offenses, allowing the rest of the unit to fly around fulfilling functions. The team has no real stars, but Ross has imprinted his personality on the team. They are disciplined, tough, and watch *Full Metal Jacket* to unwind.

WEEK 10: NOVEMBER 5, 2000. MIAMI DOLPHINS (6-2) V DETROIT LIONS (5-3). PONTIAC SILVERDOME, PONTIAC, MI.

A strong Dolphins team embarrasses us. Miami returns the opening kickoff to midfield, immediately scores a long touchdown, and successfully converts a surprise onside kick to cue another score. The meager Lions are pressed to answer but fumble into their own end zone.

The Lions lose 23–8. It's disheartening but hardly registers on the Richter scale of Lions' letdowns.

What's normal to Detroit breaks Bobby Ross. Postgame, he tells the press, "If there's one thing I want to leave the city of Detroit it'd be that I do fight and I do compete."

He quits the next day.

Ross arrived in Detroit determined to change culture and expel *Same Old Lions* but we break his spirit.

This is what happens in a toxic culture. Talented individuals arrive, bursting with character, only to get bested by the task at hand. Ross thought he was the man for the job but was not the man he thought he was.

Same Old Lions.

The drill sergeant's sheepish exit leaves the team so high and dry that interim coach Gary Moeller, former heir to the powerhouse Michigan

Wolverines football program, is given a three-year contract. He'll coach seven games.

The situation's dire, but Moeller beats Atlanta. The team then travels to the Meadowlands, storming to a 28–0 lead with no resistance from the Giants aside from a strong performance from blocking tight end Dan Campbell. Two straight wins is enough to let delirium run wild, reaching fever pitch to celebrate Gary Moeller.

It's an endearing redemption arc. Moeller was the handpicked successor to legendary Michigan coach Bo Schembechler. He took the job and performed well, leading the team to multiple Rose Bowls. Unfortunately, his relationship with alcohol contributed to an ugly incident in which a drunken sports bar tirade ends with Moeller putting hands on a police officer. He resigns from his dream job in disgrace.

Ross's lack of character lets Moeller show his. The embarrassing team becomes an optimism-inducing curiosity.

Banjo Bob takes me and Boon to the Thanksgiving game. The Lions lead Bill Belichick's doormat Patriots 34–9, but "real fans stay to the end" applies on holidays. The Patriots bring in the backup. Former Michigan quarterback Tom Brady comes out to a smattering of applause for his first NFL snaps and drills a halfback in the head. Brady obviously won't amount to much but it's good to cheer on a Wolverine.

WEEK 17: DECEMBER 24, 2000. CHICAGO BEARS (4-11) V DETROIT LIONS (9-6). PONTIAC SILVERDOME, PONTIAC, MI.

If Moeller's story ended on Thanksgiving, he'd exit a hero. It doesn't. Persevering is not always enough. The inspiring cat clinging to a tightrope on the "hang in there" poster eventually slips. The team that lost everything drastically outperforms expectations. It won't be enough.

We host the uninspiring Bears on Christmas Eve. A win sends us to the playoffs and secures Moeller's job. A loss sends us back to the drawing board. It's a decidedly big game no one cares about.

NFL policy favors in-person attendance. Any game not sold out 72 hours prior to kickoff is not aired on local television, punishing economically devastated towns for any lapse in loyalty.

Capacity is not reached. The often burnt fan base is not willing to bet holiday cheer on Honolulu Blue.

Television sets go dark. Moods follow suit. My angsty teen brain wonders, "What did I do to anger Paul Tagliabue?" A make-or-break game isn't second to the holiday. It *is* the holiday.

Boon and I ride in the Lung Cancer Death Mobile to a family party, cursing loved ones for audaciously attempting to connect on game day. We get stuck in traffic. Banjo Bob dusts off a wry smile, pulling three crisp tickets from his breast pocket. "Should we go?"

A lifetime of disappointments has no chance against this singular, perfect moment. I have no choice but to love him forever. It's my happiest Christmas memory. It's also Boon's since it's his only Christmas memory.

10–0 Lions

A double-digit lead sees Chicago pull quarterback Cade McNown, but an injury thrusts him back under center, spurring sarcastic ovations. Nonplussed, he puts the Bears on top.

Charlie Batch leaves with injury. Batch is often injured, disappearing into tunnels more often than an NYC subway car. Terrible backup Stoney Case enters the game, the canary in the coal mine for the team's impending decades-long downturn. He puts us on top with a cool-headed scramble, then gives the lead right back with a pick-six.

20–17 Bears

Luther Elliss produces a Christmas miracle. With the Bears pinned deep he finds the ball carrier, forces a fumble, and gains possession. The Lions are 10 yards from the postseason but don't gain a single one. Hanson makes a field goal.

20–20 Tie

Elliss keys another stop. The Lions are driving for the winner, a single positive play away from Hanson's range. Case drops back, takes too much time, and gets hit. *FUMBLE!*

Bears recover.

An exhausted Lions defense surrenders a fourth and 1 conversion. Chicago's in range. It's the longest attempt of kicker Paul Edinger's life amid a pressure situation but range, nonetheless.

I cling to my father as Edinger steps onto the field. Every individual in the Silverdome knows what's coming. The point of existence is to transcend suffering. The point of this team is to provide suffering.

I bury my head in my father's sleeve as Edinger lines up. I turn to watch the snap. It's perfect. A coiled leg sends a ball hurtling through the uprights. The Bears win but it's more complex than that.

The Silverdome's vacuous mechanisms suck me into the shocking cold of a Michigan December a changed man.

What belonged to us is gone forever.

We aren't special. We're losers needing a blueprint. William Clay Ford vows changes. He's the happy young family who upgrades, not knowing how good they already have it.

A miss would have validated resilience. We would have seen the fight pay off, learning that no single thing can keep us down, but that's not the lesson.

The lesson is that we're losers. This fact can't be escaped. Nothing will change until it is accepted. Barry was right to leave us. Bobby was right to quit.

I move forward but part of me, arguably the best part, remains in the Silverdome, willing Edinger to miss.

The Lions were my connection with Banjo Bob, a substitute for paternal relationship. I know he loved me more than anything, even if the only demonstrable gesture was taking three crisp tickets from his breast pocket.

We are defined this Christmas Eve. A made field goal is Scrooge's ghosts, representing all we've been and will ever be. I still see the kick and feel its pain. It cannot compare to the joy of going.

The best memories of my father are being separated by the Silverdome's revolving doors, instinctively reaching out for each other upon entering the concourse. Family framework doesn't exist outside this team. My parents find the pornos and send Boon back to Thailand. I haven't seen him since but will call him "brother" when I do.

The Lions have to be enough. There's nothing else.

I can get past resentments but can't forgive Paul Edinger for the sin of being good at his job.

The kick summarizes us. It's a painful core memory inducing the same feeling as performing self-inventory and seeing how I've failed. Painful memories can still be great ones. This day begins a decade of unmatched losing, but the fact remains:

I wouldn't change a thing.

GAME 7

A MILLEN REASONS WHY

• 2001-2002 •

Everything Sucks

2001	2002
2-14	3-13

Fast-forward to my adult life, and my simple existence mirrors that of longtime Lions owner William Clay Ford. Both our lives revolve around competition, specifically within our social circles. I don't own an NFL team, but each September I throw a charity basketball tournament. It's hard work but the thing that makes me happiest. This isn't a coincidence.

A schoolyard style pick 'em fills 16 rosters, and a single elimination tournament is conducted. My personal paradise celebrates the community of comedians I've cultivated, with efforts channeled toward a good cause. The cocktail of jokes, basketball, and competition raises a significant amount of money for organ donation in honor of our departed friend Kenny and his status as an organ donor. The tournament grows every year with ideas from the community universally "yes and"-ed and incorporated.

"The Big Walkowski" tournament has evolved into a great cause and is the highlight of the NYC comedian social calendar.

My community gives time, energy, and money toward a cause noble enough to offset the narcissism of throwing an event named after myself.[1] Each year I look around the festivities, see peers having the time of their lives, and remember how good I have it.

But if I'm honest? The most important thing about the tournament is winning. I live to compete against my peers. WCF and I have this in common. Competing within our social circle is what we care about most. The difference? All he did was lose, and I win—at least some of the time.

I'm a winner. My community knows it. Peers attend, telling me they're impressed with the operation before I pulverize them into blacktop. Beating peers is heaven, losing to them is hell.

William Clay Ford experiences hell. He's owned the Lions for 37 years. Like me, his life revolves around competing with peers, but we're nothing alike. He's a billionaire who exclusively loses; I'm a pauper who sometimes wins. At life's end, I'll close my eyes and delight in silly conquests.

WCF possesses every luxury but this one. The one that matters. Yes-men and account balances say otherwise, but deep down he knows. Not a single track record calls him a winner. The team became his Edsel.

Edinger's kick ends delusions. Laid bare before the NFL universe is indisputable fact: WCF can't win. This must change. No one wants the thought of *why couldn't I get over the hump* circling their consciousness forever.

The 2001 offseason brings new urgency. WCF is ravenous to build the team in his image. *It's winning time!*

---

1. Author's Note: I struggled with this chapter. This is partially due to transitions from childhood to personhood but mostly because I wrote the first draft by hand and left this one on top of my car when driving to the dentist. It flew off, got hit by a truck, and I fished pages from the sewer.

We're about to lose. More than anyone in the sport's history—all because of one man.

Matt Millen is a football guy. A circuitous gridiron career saw Millen win at every stop, achieving an unmatched reputation. The thumping linebacker's storied career at powerhouse Penn State spurred starring roles on Super Bowl teams for an astounding three different franchises. Joe Paterno, Bill Walsh, Al Davis, Joe Gibbs—every great 1980s football mind employed Millen as protégé. He received an unparalleled education, and his playing career proved he absorbed every lesson.

Millen retired and excelled as a color commentator, wowing viewers—including NFL owners—with his knowledge. Millen didn't just know how to win; he broke down the process into incremental, actionable steps.

WCF had been long enamored with Millen, offering him a job in 1999. Millen tells his prospective employer he isn't qualified. It's the only time he'll properly evaluate talent.

Millen interviews again, telling Ford what he wants to hear. The team is good; there are few differences between Detroit and the NFL's elite. WCF's circle prefers he fail forever than be momentarily uncomfortable.

The interview process co-opts WCF's biases to project meritorious traits onto Millen. The Lions have structural, procedural, and personnel problems, but Millen is the salve!

Millen takes over the Detroit Lions.

It's historic. Millen's the first lead executive with no experience in coaching, scouting, or player personnel. He'd never even worked in an office. Millen tells *Sports Illustrated* the only thing he ever managed was a home renovation project before rambling about difficulties with a cistern.

Widespread belief is that Millen will turn around the franchise. He's believed to possess unmatched wisdom even though his resume looks like this:

- College linebacker
- Professional linebacker
- Person on television talking about linebackers

Millen rides a motorcycle, decorates his office with "Three Stooges" memorabilia, and insists on hugging coworkers. These traits are presented as colorful evidence of an independent thinker when they're just red flags. His first official act ties employee bonuses to division championships and playoff wins. It's one of the greatest cost-savings measures in fiscal history.

I couldn't be more optimistic. I don't know I'm an addict, or that my family's screwed up, or that hearing "Matt Millen" will someday trigger Lions fans like "Voldemort" does in *Harry Potter*. All I know is that the Lions are about to win.

Enthusiasm is compounded by adolescent agency. I *need* to be a part of this. That means season tickets. My family lacks money for frivolous expenses. This desire, not family need, inspires a decision to enter the workforce.

"Dad, how do I get a job?"

Banjo Bob asks himself this so often it's a defining trait. He looks in the mirror for answers. When none arrive he retreats to the basement, avoiding the family he can't provide for.

I look for guidance. Chuckling to himself, he says, "I don't know, Slick," and pulls out a cigarette.

I ride my bike along nearby Michigan Avenue, asking businesses if they're hiring. My mother notes this, pulling Bob aside for a hushed but stern conversation. The next day he's doing the same thing.

We both get minimum-wage jobs on Michigan Avenue.

I'm a busboy at a German restaurant, reprimanded for eating leftovers and my shirt untucking from lederhosen. The $2.85/hour *plus tips* goes toward two seats at the Silverdome.

Banjo Bob works at AutoZone. He's a great worker, voluntarily fixing customers' vehicles while a run-down sports car sits in his garage. Hard times are a white-collar employee biking to work at an auto parts store. Worse times are abandoning a long-term project. Not because you can't do it, but because you can't imagine the future.

All I do is imagine the future. Zooted on Adderall, every waking moment manifests what the Lions will be. They're my developmental proxy. We'll come of age together with Millen's expertise leading the way.

I'm wrong. Losing becomes so frequent there's no apt comparison. Imagine the Washington Generals going into every matchup against the Harlem Globetrotters expecting to win. Many fans walk away but I can't. Losing draws me further in.

I want to build a time machine, go back to 2001, and warn my teenage self, but he's too enamored to listen. In hindsight, perhaps the deepest indictment of Millen is how deeply he resonates with a 14-year-old.

Lies and exaggerations proliferated during the regime's dawn. Millen starts his introductory press conference boasting about contacting Barry to return, which is equivalent to an actor bragging about an audition they did not book.

One of the first questions is about Gary Moeller. Millen calls him the team's coach. Moeller is unceremoniously fired, not even granted an interview.

The coaching search comes down to two men, Niners offensive coordinator Marty Mornhinweg and Bengals defensive coordinator Marvin Lewis. One candidate assembles a long, successful coaching career. We pick the other guy.

New coach Mornhinweg imitates Millen—growing a goatee and riding into town on a Harley. Millen praises him for "being his own man."

Both men fail. They're inexperienced and face steep learning curves. Rather than support them with experienced veterans, Ford offers unchecked, autocratic power.

A contract extension provided by Bobby Ross makes Charlie Batch the regime's redheaded stepchild. First, Millen tries trading him. When that doesn't work he trashes him in the media, outwardly pining for his replacement.

Batch knows he'll lose his job at the first failure. Sloppy play in a season-opening blowout reflects this anxiety. Throughout the broadcast, the television crew cuts to the angry, vein-bulging face of the franchise: Matt Millen.

Millen trades for another quarterback that evening. Moving on from Batch is such an emergency it cannot be tabled until the next business day.

Ty Detmer starts the next game, throwing seven interceptions in a 32-minute span. The mother who bought her son a Chucky doll in *Child's Play* got a better return on investment.

WEEK 4: OCTOBER 8, 2001. ST. LOUIS RAMS (3-0) V DETROIT LIONS (0-2). PONTIAC SILVERDOME, PONTIAC, MI.

A Monday-night showdown versus the electrifying Rams is my first season ticket–holder experience. The 9:07 PM kickoff throttles my school week, but I must tithe allegiance toward our ascendent regime. I'm confident that a new era of Lions football starts . . . *now!*

We get dusted, obliterated beyond recognition like atoms caught in the Big Bang's crosshairs.

Rams 35, Lions 0

Charlie Batch is inserted to ward off a shutout, throwing such an egregious interception the only explanation is passive aggression.

Fans file for the exits. Banjo Bob insists we remain. "Where else would we want to be?" We sneak into front-row seats behind the Lions bench, learning the best seats in the house are someone else's.

The 2001 season is a string of horribly one-sided losses. Losing is organic. Illogical, repeated defeats are part of the natural order like the tides and sun and stars. We exist to fall, but joy can be found from mere existence.

They're gorgeous losses. A Titans DT named Henry Ford blocks a field goal, a Chekhovian scenario wherein any Ford existing near this team guarantees a loss . . . Bengals running back Corey Dillon takes the game's first play 96 yards to paydirt causing a good fraction of the stadium to exit the moment they enter . . . Tampa Bay wins on a last-second field goal and gets chided for celebrating . . . Jay Leno frequently targets the Lions in his opening monologue, comparing them to the Taliban.[2]

Attendance plummets. I watch the entire season from the front row, absorbing my own personal football team. These aren't just losses. These are cruel, character-building defeats. Others are ashamed, wearing paper bags over their faces to conceal identities, but I look for something worth rooting for. I fixate on promising, young DT Shaun Rogers like my life depends on it. It might.

Each week, when defeat's secured, the broadcast cuts to Matt Millen. The season's nearly over. They've yet to catch a smile.

The team that hired Millen to answer the question "How can we contend?" now asks, "How can we win a game?"

It takes until Week 14, but it happens. We win! The broadcast cuts to Millen, capturing the season's first smile on December 16. Johnnie Morton proclaims, "Jay Leno can kiss my ass."

Jay fires back that the cocky Lions "are considering winning a game next year." Leno good-naturedly accepts his portion of crow, inviting Morton on the program. The resulting milquetoast segment is the highlight of my year.

WEEK 17: JANUARY 6, 2002. DALLAS COWBOYS (5-10) V DETROIT LIONS (1-14). PONTIAC SILVERDOME, PONTIAC, MI.

Remaining games have fewer stakes than a vegan barbecue. The only significance is the Silverdome's closing. Losses don't end when the games do. With no long-term plans for the building, the Silverdome gets abandoned and ultimately imploded.[3]

---

2. "What's the difference between the Detroit Lions and the Taliban? The Taliban have a running game!"

3. It also served as a roller rink!

We play a crappy Dallas team. I place my first-ever bet, putting $20 on the Lions to win. Wagering is the way of the ancestors, a cavalcade of drunken Polacks. Johnnie Morton catches the winner. The Silverdome's final bow is Morton doing the worm in the end zone as a 14-year-old gets a gambling problem.

I play checkers with my non-pedo grandmother as the Rose Bowl flickers in the background. I discuss the Lions' plans for the third overall pick in the upcoming draft, rudely fixating on a future my conversational partner won't be around for.

Oregon romps thanks to Joey Harrington. Joey's a good Catholic boy and college football's poster child. Grandma loves him and vows, "This guy's gonna be great." This conversation serves as her Sermon on the Mount to my young ears.

The Lions select Harrington. I'm certain he's a superstar. Not because of Joey's gleaming resume or perfect pedigree, but because Grandma said so.

Hope's restored. This is the impact of a fresh, new quarterback and a sparkling new stadium downtown.

Ford Field returns the prodigal Lions to city limits, generating excitement and incorrect choruses of "they'll be good in time for the new stadium." This reaction is necessitated by cash-strapped Wayne County providing over half of the $500 million construction budget. Other cities have taken worse stadium finance deals, but none of these places ever declare bankruptcy.

Ford Field is beautiful, highlighted by a glass mezzanine built from an obsolescent warehouse for Hudson's—a defunct Detroit department store. It's a fitting nod to history even if paying homage to a belly-up business sets a bad precedent.

The only downside is the fervor pricing the Walkowskis out of season tickets. Like non-pedo grandma, we won't be a part of this bright future.

An endless summer of waiting. When the season kicks off, Detroit will receive its crown jewel and heir apparent to Bobby Layne.

We suck. Back-to-back blowouts. Believing something good might happen is foolish.

WEEK 3: SEPTEMBER 22, 2002.
GREEN BAY PACKERS (1-1) V DETROIT LIONS (0-2).
FORD FIELD, DETROIT, MI.

For the first time Ford Field hosts a football game, and Joey appears before the city destined to be his. The Lions score on their first touch via punt return, a promising beginning.

Harrington immediately throws a pick-six, but growing pains are part of the job. He throws another but the pass was tipped. Rooting on a quarterback prospect that doesn't pan out forces fans to ingest more toxic Kool-Aid than Jonestown residents. Harrington isn't good but I spend the next four years making excuses.

Fourth Quarter, 0:35

Joey gets the ball with a chance to win. Local immortality's there for the taking. Another interception.

Losing's supposed to be hated. Not anymore. Not with a fancy new quarterback in a fancy new building. The loss is celebrated as being "not that bad." Mistakes stop us from experiencing something wonderful, but reframing the day lets it stay sublime.

Joey bounces back, winning his next start as Detroit anoints its supposed star.

The Lions practice facility relocates to Allen Park, mere miles from the family home. I keep my eyes perpetually peeled for Joey. Although I'm unsuccessful, a classmate's lucky enough to bag his groceries at Kroger.

Joey signs up for a Kroger Plus discount card. The grocery chain's rewards program offers product discounts, coupons, and more! It's a great decision. The bad decision is using his real phone number. It's the worst decision in an NFL career recording 85 picks.

Joey's number travels like wildfire through the sophomore class. Dearborn High's most coveted digits aren't attached to a popular girl for dates but the quarterback for prank calls. *Hey Joey! Is your refrigerator running? Because your offense can't!*

The handsome quarterback has star quality but not ability. He's the best Lions quarterback in decades but the best we've ever had isn't good enough.

NFL public relations is determined to make Harrington a star, featuring him on *Sports Illustrated*'s cover. My beloved magazine greets me at the mailbox, headlining an article featuring Tom Brady alongside the damning quote, "I know I can play in this league."

The article presents optimism as a key cog in Detroit's turnaround. Joey's even compared to Eminem—an impossibly high bar. No ink's spared detailing the lack of infrastructure that will ruin Joey. He's not allowed to audible or pass downfield without permission. Lions decision-makers bar Joey from playing like the player they drafted.

WEEK 12: NOVEMBER 24, 2002. DETROIT LIONS (3-7) V CHICAGO BEARS (2-8). SOLDIER FIELD, CHICAGO, IL.

Close losses are worse than blowouts. A string of embarrassments is followed by a hard-fought defeat that's infinitely worse. Losing by a hundred and having our state stripped of Electoral College rights *still* wouldn't hurt like this Bears game.

Detroit blows a double-digit fourth-quarter lead. On a game-deciding fourth and 20, Chicago's quarterback has enough time to fall down, get up, and still complete the throw. This would be most regimes' defining moment of malfeasance but is a blip of frustration for the afternoon.

The Lions win the overtime coin toss. Rather than take the ball, Marty Mornhinweg makes the worst decision in the history of human consciousness.

Marty elects to kick off. In sudden-death overtime.

The Bears are stopped on third down just outside of field goal range when a late flag flies. *Holding on Chicago.* Mornhinweg, in the throes of psychosis, accepts the penalty. The Bears convert third down, and Paul-fucking-Edinger kicks the winner.

Mornhinweg defends the decision, citing the wind. The wind! An entire team of professional players and coaches, discredited in favor of "*the wind!*"

Marty Mornhinweg never wins another game, fired after a 3–13 season. No word on whether he left team facilities on a Harley.

The Lions are the league's worst team. Joey matters an irrational amount because he offers the only way out. Even then, he throws interceptions, takes checkdowns, and has a soft reputation. He's a great guy in one of the few professions where that's actively held against you. Joey's an accomplished concert pianist maligned for "hanging out at the wine-and-cheese part of the bar."

The realization that Harrington sucks creeps into collective consciousness—at least the dozens of brain cells dictating what's funny at my high school.

★ ★ ★

We drive around on Christmas Eve stealing Baby Jesuses from front-yard nativity sets. Don't worry. We return them on Easter alongside notes reading, "He's risen. Never stop believing." It's a gentle crime affirming faith while spiking my adrenaline.

We come down from our haul, skulking through a Walmart at 3 AM, tossing a football while discussing our forlorn signal caller.

"Joey needs to stop dicking around and improve."

And then—*Eureka!*

I hold the football before my crotch and declare, in mocking tones, "I'm Joey Harrington."

It gets a laugh and spreads like venereal, becoming as en vogue in our hallways as Abercrombie & Fitch. The next year's spent holding objects like they were my dick and declaring, "I'm Joey Harrington."

The thing is: I am Joey Harrington. My situation sucks. I'm overmatched. No one will help me improve. The only way forward is becoming a star.

Rookies of Harrington's caliber usually receive specialized scheme and player development tracts. Joey is forced into Marty Mornhinweg's variant of the trendy West Coast offense. The scheme's quick, timing-based routes refute Harrington's strengths. Millen takes his quarterback and that's that. Millen's too overmatched to know team architects must also provide contexts conducive to success.

Amphetamines and adolescent hormones make me look inward, feverishly analyzing my family. Get to a certain age and *beep beep!* There goes the bullshit detector.

It's not about Joey or the team. It's about how they're applied. Seeing the quarterback struggle makes a Lions-obsessed kid realize he needs to do the same thing: improve enough to bypass the circumstances and disorganization holding him back. There's no plan for my success. Just like Joey, I must forge my own.

A new feeling arrives; a sensation that becomes my home. I don't have the grades for college but need a way out. Accomplishing some self-imposed goal becomes the backbone of my personality, fuel for addictions, and impetus for development and detriment alike. It's who I am. It starts here, sparked by the realization that, like my quarterback, I'm not enough.

"I'm Joey Harrington."

GAME 8

SAY NO TO MICHIGAN

• 2003–2005 •

Everything Is Still Terrible

2003	2004	2005
5-11	6-10	5-11

It's time to lock in. Locking in can be a good thing. Just not when it's the only thing. Realizations occur. The home's broken. The people are too. I live vicariously through my quarterback but not because he's good. Some lessons are best learned from an effigy.

The feeling starts. The pressure that's my home. Addictions feast on it. Others grow fat and happy from serving as ballasts.

Familial preconditions and pharmaceuticals lay the groundwork, but the ignition gets switched. Addiction starts here and thrives here, but the context began long before.

Russ Gibb is a legendary Detroiter. He manages the seminal band MC5, owns the iconic venue Grande Ballroom, and consistently stewards world-altering entities.[1] He's a small but vital part of rock music history with a legacy just three words long:

"Paul is dead!"

It's October 12, 1969. A listener phones Russ's weekly radio show claiming that Paul McCartney has been dead for three years, discreetly replaced by the Beatles. Playing the band's "Revolution 9" backwards reveals subterfuge with a message declaring, "Turn me on, dead man."

Paul McCartney isn't dead. That doesn't matter. Speculation circles the globe, becoming part of Beatles lore. This is how Russ Gibb is remembered. The pioneer becomes a historical footnote. It's more than most get but less than Russ deserved.

Throughout his music career Russ worked as a Dearborn High School teacher, once famously arriving at school in a helicopter.

Russ understood what was coming next, like Biff in *Back to the Future*, and purchased municipal rights to cable television. When these rights were sold, proceeds were put into a high-yield investment that funded his greatest achievement: WDHS Student Video.

Mr. Gibb made WDHS the nation's preeminent media arts program. Our shabby public school hosted a state-of-the-art production program with broadcast studios, editing rigs, and a recurring time slot on local television.

Despite these resources, the most important thing students received was free rein. Students enjoyed complete autonomy. "Don't dream it, be it," an adage borrowed from *The Rocky Horror Picture Show* was the program's constitution.

A pipeline from Dearborn to the entertainment industry was created. Hundreds of kids, myself included, built lives for themselves thanks to Mr. Gibb.

The beloved teacher was far from the cuddly individual one might imagine. Mr. Gibb's program was the district's crown jewel. He had "made

1. Introduced *Tommy* to a US Audience, first road booking agent for Jimi Hendrix/Janis Joplin/Cream, and produced Day-Glo posters hawked at flea markets to this day.

man" status and acted like it. He parked on the lawn, hit kids with yardsticks, and eschewed curriculum to ramble about Republican politics.

Favorite students were asked to shave heads and dress like British skinheads. We saw compromising pictures of teenage peers wearing little more than suspenders and Doc Martens, but no one cared. Becoming a "Gibblet," as favored students were called, brought scholarships, opportunity, a life beyond Dearborn.

I'm desperate for acceptance but resoundingly rejected. Russ points out my loud clothes and slovenly nature, shaping my future with three words: "You're a flake."

It's the best thing that could happen. Everyone in my vicinity is miserable. The same awaits me unless I change. I don't want him to like me; I need to become undeniable. Making my mark on a high school video program—even the best one—is a silly goal but the only way out. I'm all in.

Michigan faces dour economics. My father has fallen from provider to destitute as recession swallows up our state.

Still, we love our home.

Michigan is killing it culturally. During this span, Detroit's music scene produces genre-defining acts like Eminem, the White Stripes, Aaliyah, and the Grammy Award–winning Insane Clown Posse.[2]

Michigan loves Michigan. The best approach to a coaching vacancy and second overall draft pick is to stay local.

Steve Mariucci, recently unemployed coach of the Niners, built an offensive juggernaut without high draft picks or a franchise quarterback, but that's secondary.

He's one of us. Mariucci hails from Iron Mountain, Michigan. Coaches of his caliber rarely hit the open market, let alone come home.

Millen hires Mariucci. There's one problem. The hiring violates the Rooney Rule. Implemented to affirm fair employment practices, the

---

2. ICP warrants inclusion by virtue of creating the world's largest independent record label and inventive usage of Faygo Pop soft drinks.

Rooney Rule stipulates that minority candidates must be interviewed for key positions prior to hires becoming official.

Millen ignores the well-intentioned rule, drawing the ire of Johnnie Cochran, lead counsel of the O. J. Simpson trial, who states that Lions job postings should be caveated, "minorities need not apply." This decision strips the franchise of draft picks and puts veteran leaders in the awkward situation of having to defend institutional racism.

Charles Rogers hails from hardscrabble Saginaw, affectionately referred to as "Saginasty." Saginaw's a breeding ground of athletic excellence, producing luminaries like Draymond Green, but Charles Rogers is the city's greatest athlete. There's no debate. It's a fact.

The legendary prep athlete attends nearby Michigan State University, thriving before an invested local community. Rogers is as good a college football receiver that ever existed.

The Lions select Rogers second overall. A locally sourced rebuild is upon us. The idea of native sons winning games in city limits is easily swooned over. Mariucci and Rogers will create wins, a ban on foreign cars, and gift Stevie Wonder sight.[3]

2003 REGULAR SEASON

Hype's justified. Rogers glides open for two touchdowns in his debut. The Harrington-to-Rogers connection appears to be a viable meal ticket for the coming decade.

This optimistic beginning was just a red Harring-ton. The 2003 Lions are abysmal. There's no physicality, a sputtering offense, and a defense that surrenders. Rogers is the bright spot in the abyss. He's a beautiful athlete, blessed with not just athleticism but the grace and coordination to maximize his gifts.

---

3. JK he can see.

Tragedy strikes at practice. It appears as bad luck, but years tick by, and events unfold, revealing devastating ramifications. Charles Rogers breaks his collarbone. He's lost for the season and, ultimately, so much more.

★ ★ ★

It's my birthday. My girlfriend comes over for dinner.[4] The table's set for a normal meal, but those don't exist in our household. My parents let *both of us* know they're divorcing. Personally, I would've waited until dessert.

My folks obviously had a bad relationship, but confirmation is still painful. I don't know how to process these emotions, so I deflect them with ambition.

I multiply my Adderall dosage and make an arrangement with Mr. Gibb. I get keys, security codes, and 24/7 access to the video studio. Most kids can't wait to leave high school. I start living there.

I make a cutout animation telling my life story influenced by '70s avant-garde and, true to form, completed in a 48-hour amphetamine binge. I take a break from editing, crunch on a packet of uncooked ramen, and consider how making a work about my fucked-up family allows me to accept them.

At 7 AM bleary-eyed teachers and students roll into school, where I expectantly wait to show my work. *It's a hit! I'm good at something!* The project wins dozens of awards, providing a burst of self-worth that tells me who I am. Adderall makes me an auteur.

I must keep going. There's nothing else. Mr. Gibb endorses me, and the city funds my feature film. All things are possible. You just have to take drugs. I do.

My film premieres at a local theater. Eight hundred people attend, validating habits every time a punch line hits. The local paper writes an

4. Diana is an all-American Muslim. With so much propaganda espousing Dearborn's supposed Sharia law, it's worth noting that cultures intermingle beautifully enough for us to meet discussing pro wrestling during sociology class.

article about my filmmaking.[5] I'm outwardly an overachieving art kid, but every accomplishment is an addict covering his tracks. The video program provides life skills and technical knowledge, but my takeaway is that I'm only worthwhile while bingeing speed. Love is Russ Gibb's approval. It depends on creative excellence and quadrupling prescribed dosages but is love nonetheless.

★ ★ ★

Charles Rogers receives no team support or personal development plan. The football player stripped of identity finds a new one in a pill bottle. Dearborn, Michigan, circa 2003 is a great place to start a downward spiral. I spend sleepless, tweaking nights driving around the neighborhood, passing a Mercedes SUV rumored to belong to Rogers. I try peeking past tinted windows for a glance at our sidelined star but can't see into that much darkness.

Charles had all the talent in the world. All he needed was a couple lucky breaks. He got a broken collarbone instead.

Rogers will eventually pass away at age 38 from liver cancer, the by-product of injury treatments applied to life's pain. Matt Millen doesn't have the ability to nurture employees as people, especially the sidelined local kid bearing the weight of the world on injured shoulders.

The season wears on without Charles, leadership, or hope. All Detroit can do is meekly bench Harrington, a measure as effective as changing the Hindenburg's taillight. The key question shifts from "Will Joey become a star?" to "Will Joey keep his job?"

---

5. "My dream is to be a hermit and emerge every few years with a great work like Stanley Kubrick," I tell the reporter while wearing a bedazzled button-down shirt.

WEEK 13: NOVEMBER 27, 2003. GREEN BAY PACKERS [6-5] v DETROIT LIONS [3-8]. FORD FIELD, DETROIT, MI.

Banjo Bob scrounges up enough cash for the Thanksgiving game, our first visit to Ford Field.

Walking on eggshells en route to the stadium, Banjo Bob and I pass vagrants emerging from the woodwork of abandoned homes, collecting cans the moment they're discarded. *No pepperoni pizza for us.*

"I've been going to a group."

"What kind of group?"

"A group for men who had something bad happen to them."

"How's this different from AA?"

"Good question."

It's hard for men to say what happened to them—even if it burdens them forever. It's brave of Bob to tell me this, even half-assed with no details. His goal is to *tell his son* not *thoroughly unpack trauma to his son*. It's the last time we employ a father-son dynamic. He tells me what happened to him as a child and spends the rest of our relationship reverting into that little boy. Learning this secret changes him from my father into someone I must fix.

The Lions play terribly but beat Green Bay thanks to four Packer turnovers. Winning by surviving crappy circumstances is fitting.

This is one of two direct conversations we have about molestation. Big themes enter my world, but no one addresses them. My only outlet is acting out.

I drive a hand-me-down minivan, borrow Bob's trench coat, pencil on a mustache, and park outside elementary schools waiting for cops to get called and reveal that I, too, am a child.

Police arrive. I'm cuffed and thrown on the sidewalk. A friend's mother drives by. "Joel's harmless. He's a kid with a terrible sense of humor."

I cringe at the memory of a creative-obsessed amphetamine addict satirizing family secrets but still contend it was a good bit.

The season limps to a close with a 45–17 blowout at Arrowhead Stadium, far more embarrassing than the score. Johnnie Morton, cut by Millen for being well liked and good at football, finds a role with the Chiefs.

Millen tries stopping Morton for a postgame hello. No one wants to exchange pleasantries with someone who fired them. Morton understandably ignores Millen, causing him to take the high road, repeatedly calling Morton a f****t before dozens of cameras.

Millen flaccidly apologizes. "I'm sorry *if* I offended anyone." The season that starts with institutional racism is bookended with homophobia. William Clay Ford rewards Millen with a contract extension.

Detroit possesses an early pick in a quarterback-laden draft. Sunk-cost fallacy makes moving on from Harrington impossible. Millen, too dumb to realize doubling down on a bad investment makes it worse, passes on quarterback Ben Roethlisberger for statuesque wide receiver Roy Williams.[6] Consistently using high draft picks on weapons concedes that Harrington can't produce a great offense, only be a by-product of one.

2004 REGULAR SEASON

No one can move forward. My parents can't split until their unaffordable house sells in a recessed market. Mr. Gibb gets me a job at Ford while I attend community college. I'm in teenaged stasis in a decaying home, but excitement strikes the neighborhood.

Roy Williams moves in down the street. I pester Roy with welcome gifts and hellos but he's too friendly to act hassled. I will not say whether I ever rifled through his trash but can confirm he doesn't eat pizza crusts.

Roy will pair with beloved Charles, recovered from injury and grief from losing a grandmother described as "the only person who ever cared for me." The state roots for Charles so ardently it's impossible to imagine him faltering.

6. Bad news for the Lions but great news for the women of Detroit.

Rogers suffers a season-ending injury on the year's first series. He doesn't catch a pass or receive a target but confirms the idea that his career exists to sow suffering.

His absence is exacerbated by Williams showing immediate stardom, opening his career with a juggling one-hand grab in traffic.[7] A victory over Chicago snaps a three-season-long road losing streak and powers momentum.

A convincing win over Houston is followed by a shellacking from the Eagles, but we bounce back to best undefeated Atlanta on the road.

Prolonged road woes now become a winning streak. Mariucci's building a winner and nudging Harrington back toward star trajectories. Powered by complementary football, the Lions seemingly possess a winning recipe. Flashes of greatness will surely become sustained excellence.

Just like that it vanishes.

A string of torturous losses resumes. The team goes from "must watch" to "I should have gone to Kohl's with my mom" in a matter of weeks.

WEEK 12: NOVEMBER 25, 2004. INDIANAPOLIS COLTS (7-3) V DETROIT LIONS (4-6). FORD FIELD, DETROIT, MI.

Banjo Bob moves in with his CSA support group and insists on hosting Thanksgiving. I visit his putrid house and watch the game on a 13" black-and-white television. We go around the table saying what we're thankful for. One guy says, "I'm glad my rapist is dead."

Being as miserable as possible is Bob's modus operandi. He didn't need to invite me or purchase the saddest possible television but having his son ask, "Are you sure you're all right?" is his love language.

I try compartmentalizing, but Peyton Manning's Colts deliver the worst blowout in Thanksgiving history.[8] I'm glad Bob has a support system,

---

7. And *light* stalking.

8. Aside from the Pilgrims.

even if they're terrible cooks, but the day fills me with tension. I don't want to compliment my father on his rented bedroom. I want a family.

Uncomfortable feelings escalate. I'm filled with urgency, holding a deep breath that refuses to exhale.

I've never drank before. It's a point of pride. My dad's an addict, but there's been no conversations about the issue I'm as certain to inherit as 17 fucking banjos.

No one IDs in city limits. I buy a bottle of André champagne and drink it alone in my mother's backyard. Deep breath exhaled. My first drink is consumed alone, done to dull the pain, with evidence immediately disposed of. This act has more red flags than the Republican National Convention. I'm an alcoholic from my first sip.

I feel warm and wavy. My overarching thought is *Why don't people do this all the time?* not realizing that many do, and I will too.

This loss starts the habit that tries to kill me. It's not the worst loss of the year.

WEEK 15: DECEMBER 19, 2004. MINNESOTA VIKINGS [7-6] V DETROIT LIONS [5-8]. FORD FIELD, DETROIT, MI.

Writing this book began as a SMART Recovery exercise.[9] Describing the Lions' importance on my hierarchy of values hypothesizes that a lifetime of disappointing Sundays made hard days slightly easier.

Week 15 contradicts that premise.

Detroit goes toe-to-toe with the heavily favored Vikings. Joey plays the best game of his career, standing in the pocket threading needles before the blitz evaporates him.

---

9. Self-Management and Recovery Training.

Fourth Quarter, 1:43; Vikings 28, Lions 21

Minnesota goes up but, undeterred, the Lions march down the field.

Fourth Quarter, 0:08; Vikings 28, Lions 27

Harrington finds Roy. *TOUCHDOWN!* All that remains is an extra point, the sport's easiest play.

Placeholder John Jett muffs the snap. Detroit finds a new way to lose yet again. I am sick over this game for weeks, still exhibiting symptoms as I type this. A new relationship forms. The Lions aren't my team. They're my cautionary tale. They'll tell me what not to do, where not to go.

I smile at my wisdom and reach for a drink.

2005 SEASON

Most successful football rosters are built from the inside out but Millen insists on wide receivers. They're the fourth step on football's assembly line, their success dependent on everyone else doing their job.

Millen uses the tenth overall pick on Mike Williams,[10] an oversized receiver nobody wants. The real desire is replacing Harrington with Aaron Rodgers, but William Clay Ford allegedly blocks the selection.

Rodgers tumbles in the draft, falling into Green Bay's lap as heir apparent to Brett Favre. This creates the darkest possible timeline. Rodgers terrorizes the Lions for over a decade, knifing the franchise with genius-level abilities and well-timed referee assistance.

Matt Millen nearly makes a career-saving decision but gets vetoed. He goes down as a pariah, leaking this nugget to redeem his legacy, not realizing he comes off as a coward with no faith in his gut.

---

10. Mike Williams unsuccessfully petitions the NFL for early draft entry. He loses college eligibility and makes a website declaring himself a "Future Hall of Famer." He scores five career touchdowns.

The team approaches the season like parents killing time before divorce finalizes. A few small tweaks but no meaningful attempts to change outcomes. Mariucci imports old flame Jeff Garcia to challenge Joey and the team starts wearing crappy black uniforms. Charles Rogers is suspended for violating the league's substance abuse policy, ending his once-promising career.

WEEK 4: OCTOBER 2, 2005.
DETROIT LIONS (1-1) v TAMPA BAY BUCCANEERS (3-0).
RAYMOND JAMES STADIUM, TAMPA, FL.

The Super Bowl will be in Detroit. The city's feverish with enthusiasm, but I despair at Ford Field's first big game being a neutral field. I know we're as good as other fan bases, just too beaten down to have an opportunity to show it. The Super Bowl will bring an economic boom, but after subsidizing two stadiums in 50 years, an economically depressed region deserves to flex home-field advantage.

Fellow players blame Harrington for Mariucci's job insecurity, creating a toxic locker-room atmosphere.

Joey plays terribly against Tampa. Until he doesn't.

Fourth Quarter, 5:14; Buccaneers 17, Lions 13

Backed up at his own 7, Harrington shrugs off negativity and starts dealing, using his last gasp to correct the narrative.

A beautiful ball finds tight end Marcus Pollard for the win. Pollard secures the rock before tumbling out of bounds. It's a striking catch, a thing of beauty. The team celebrates Joey, euphorically bound by a single man's catharsis.

The call's overturned. Zapruderesque analysis reveals Pollard controlling the ball inbounds but refs ignore this, setting a precedent where creative interpretations of the rule book are allowable provided they make the Lions lose. This type of refereeing continually targets the franchise, making me insufferable to talk to at parties.

★ ★ ★

A parental divorce, like all things, is not without silver linings. Great joy comes from watching parents try on different identities, stepping outside the framework of "mom" and "dad" to show who they are.

Banjo Bob enthusiastically supports my creative endeavors,[11] becoming the audience I create for. I'm pathologically wired to be a little creative whiz but rebelliously inclined to be a cheeky little asshole. Life revolves around jokes—even if I'm the only one laughing. I pitch the worst idea I can think of, but Dearborn Heights Civic Theatre has the last laugh by greenlighting my original musical, *I Guess I Can't Play Piano Anymore.*

The play's about a man who eats his own fingers. Stranded on a desert island, each finger is soliloquized before the protagonist chomps down. Lights fade for a scene from that digit's existence—childhood thumb-sucking, a reporting career, etc.—before 10 sexily dressed finger Rockettes sing a musical number interrupted by a terrifying mouth dragging a phalange away.

It starts with a plane crash.

Bob serves as the musical director because he's a guitar player and tech director because he's my dad.

We play football in the theater before dress rehearsal. An errant throw knocks down the rigging for the show-opening plane crash. Bob climbs a 20-foot ladder to fix it. He falls, landing with a *thud.*

I think he's dead but it's worse. Body weight and ladder crush his wrist, ruining it for guitar. Bob's suffered a severe concussion and is in terrible pain, but the only thing he asks paramedics is, "Will you see the show?"

The play is staged. My dad recovers. His shattered wrist will never hold a guitar again but can strum a banjo.

New instrument, new man.

---

11. I sigh and admit that this, too, is for his enjoyment, staring out the window and lapsing into grief-fueled fugue states.

Life is now dedicated to the banjo. Several months into his journey he tells me, "Hey, Slick. You need to meet someone." Unbeknownst to me, Banjo Bob has corrected his shitty upbringing by building a replacement family of jazz musicians.

I meet him at Bert's near Eastern Market. He introduces me to Dr. Jazz, an elderly black crack addict who exclusively wears wedding dresses and insists she's Billie Holiday.

"This is your new grandmother." He drops his voice an octave, becoming as serious as I've heard him. "You need to call her 'grandma.' Her child was murdered."

Dr. Jazz lives in a squat house. Her only possession is the most beautiful singing voice in existence. What seems like another instance of my family's burdensome eccentricity is actually life-giving. We're taken with each other. Dr. Jazz truly sees me, writing scripts for my next films.[12]

She becomes the best part of the family. One day she is found frozen to death in her squat house. The Detroit coroner rules it natural causes.

I live with my mother in the boarding house she creates in her new home. The "normal" side of my family shares a roof with a seven-foot Nigerian, flamboyant Italian engineer, and an albino IT technician sleeping in the basement next to the water heater. I call him "the baby man."

I get good grades at community college and search for an exit. The season must be played.

★ ★ ★

The Lions are one stop away from a win against mid-career meltdown Jake Delhomme and the Panthers. Delhomme dives for a first down only to get

12. One called *The Basketball Man* reimagines the grim reaper with a basketball instead of a scythe. As one lays dying the sound of dribbling gets louder and louder.

reamed by a safety. His backup has not played in three years but puts Carolina on top with ease.

A great return brings us to the cusp of field goal range. All Joey needs to do is complete one pass. He doesn't. Four straight incompletions secure the loss and end the Harrington era.

Jeff Garcia isn't a game-changing player but is an adult in the room. The Lions win his first start due to defense, but life is unfair so credit goes to the quarterback.

Desperate to move on, we arrange delusions accordingly. Discussion of losses focuses on Garcia's positives, even when ill-advised scrambles cause injury. Harrington returns, making up for lost time with two turnovers. There are 53 players on the roster, but only two are relevant as the season boils down to substandard signal callers' toothless dueling. Rooting for the 2005 Lions is like being asked, "Which ocean would you like to drown in?"

WEEK 15: DECEMBER 18, 2005. CINCINNATI BENGALS (10-3) V DETROIT LIONS (4-9). FORD FIELD, DETROIT, MI.

More losses. The Lions unceremoniously fire Mariucci. Matt Millen, the man buying ingredients, deflects blame and throws his chef under the bus. Millen stands before the media, declaring the roster "playoff worthy." Well, operations certainly aren't.

Millen waits until days before the next game to dismiss his coach and promotes Dick Jauron, a friend of Mariucci expressing guilt over the job. It's stupidity to the point of callousness. Millen sucks so bad he can't even fire someone correctly.

Ford Field's sad atmosphere shifts to wrath as Detroiters stage "The Millen Man March," an effort to oust their leader. Thousands picket, chanting for Millen's removal. The cowardly Lions don't acknowledge the movement, brushing it off as "not a part of game-day activities." Frustrations with leisure activities reach a fevered pitch normally reserved for politics or the labor movement. Management doesn't care.

Millen's a totemic figure for a city ruined by administrators. The path to Detroit's decline was greased by poor decision-making. It's easy to reallocate broader frustrations toward the man continually sullying Sundays.

"Fire Millen" chants spread throughout our stadium, city, and reach as far as North Carolina college sports. The world screaming about our organizational failure falls on ownership's deaf ears. We lose 41–17. It's the most fun game in years.

We've lost our coach, our favorite son, and ruined a quarterback prospect. Detroit ignores the Lions, vibrating with excitement over the Super Bowl.

Being "cucked" is not yet a popular word but perfectly describes rooting for native son Jerome Bettis's Steelers to win a Super Bowl in our building. Fans adopt Six Degrees of Kevin Bacon just to feel like winners.

There's a lesson in Bettis's victory. You can win. You just have to get out of this town.

★ ★ ★

I apply to USC,[13] and then I fly to Europe to spend four months hitchhiking. I have no money so my primary activities are walking around and reading found paperbacks. It's happiness.

My appendix bursts. I pass out beside the Autobahn and wake in a German hospital. I can't go back. Not when I've already left. I convalesce reading *Don Quixote* on the beach, immersing myself with a delusional man and his windmills.

I go weeks without checking email. Drunk at 3 AM in Prague, I log on and find an acceptance email from USC. *Suck on that, Lori Loughlin.*

I prep my exit from Detroit. My mother kicks me out of the house for throwing a drunken spelling bee party. My only housing option is converting to Islam and moving in with my Muslim girlfriend's family. I have a

13. University of Southern California or University of Spoiled Children. Depends on who you ask.

great summer as a Muslim son but never redact the faith, covering my bases for the afterlife. We break up, become good friends, and laugh at our youth.

★ ★ ★

Millen rebuilds for his sixth consecutive offseason, acknowledging the team as "too soft" and promising never to quit. These are the words of someone who knows they're in over their head.

Matt hires his third head coach, defensive line expert Rod Marinelli. He's never served as head coach at any level. When pushed for qualifications, Marinelli yaps about serving in Vietnam. Bristling at reasonable queries, insisting work history is secondary to life experience, are telltale signs of bad leadership. Marinelli bills himself as a hard-boiled leader of men when he's Bobby Ross without the resume.

I drive toward USC. I've never set foot on campus or in California but need to escape. My beaten-down old car breaks down outside Joshua Tree beside renewable energy fields. Life imitates art. The new me begins in a field filled with windmills.

I call a cab, fill it with my shit, and ride to my new life. There are many problems but I can't help but smile. I got out. I've already won.

GAME 9

ROCK BOTTOM

• 2006-2008 •

Somehow Even Worse

2006	2007	2008
3-13	7-9	0-16

As Midwestern males, everything is always "fine" even when it isn't. The years covered in this chapter were abundant with joy and crucial to my development. They were also "fine."

It's my first day at the prestigious USC film school. New classmates are children of the elite with glistening new BMWs and surnames likely to get emblazoned on campus limestone. No one else took a cab from the desert to get here.

I worry about making friends but meet one on my first trip to a urinal.

"You from Michigan?"

"Yeah. You?"

"No. Just a fan of the peninsula."

Pablo is the college's most popular person. It's easy to see why. His disarming charisma puts strangers at ease—even with their dick out. The prematurely balding alpha male with a Burt Reynolds aesthetic hails from working-class Chino, California, but is equipped with a laissez-faire attitude reserved for the uber rich. He doesn't just know who he is. He's comfortable with it.

I become friends with him immediately because everyone does.

Pablo's a devout Christian and a devout drinker, setting the standard for debauchery for USC fraternities. He's everything to everyone.

He takes me under his wing, sharing his blissful existence of horchata shacks and frat parties. He's my teacher; I'm a quick learner.

I keep pace with his drinking by swallowing additional Adderalls. Amphetamine salt's supercharge lets me drink without impediment, eliminating hangovers without so much as a drop of water.

Every day in California feels like Saturday. Days start with pills, box wine, and mandates to maximize each moment. Reckless attitudes and usage attached to ambition now accompanies fun.

I tattoo Michigan on the palm of my hand, win a gold cup as the school's competitive eating champion, find a full keg of beer in an alley, and rescue a "pet" chicken from a slaughterhouse. A man-child with horrible tattoos rolls a keg of stale beer around Los Angeles, sipping from a golden chalice, trailed by loyal fowl. What can I say? I'm blossoming.

The Lions transform too. Joey's jettisoned to Miami, replaced by Jon Kitna, but the offseason's forgettable save for the signing of Dan Campbell, blocking tight end.

Campbell will ultimately change the culture but is merely a depth piece during this era, torturing competitive spirit by being tethered to the worst team in NFL history. To win in the future, one must lose in the present.

2006 REGULAR SEASON

I drag myself out of bed for 10 AM West Coast kickoff, scuttling to snag a seat at a sports bar under the illusion Californians care enough to crowd a sports bar on Sunday morning. I never take pills on Sundays. I don't need help focusing.

The defense dominates the NFC champion Seahawks as Shaun Rogers blocks two field goals. Seattle steals a last-second win, but a ragtag unit holds their own against the conference's best. A loss has never felt so much like a win.

Burgeoning optimism is betrayed by disheartening defeats. A loss to Minnesota secures a 0–5 start. Blocking tight end Dan Campbell provides an early lead, but Detroit craters at pressure's first sign, fumbling into the end zone for a Viking recovery.

Genius coordinator Mike Martz pledges offensive fireworks but appears determined to end Kitna's life via blunt-force trauma. Despite heavy investment, the receiving corps is so paltry the number two target is converted defensive back Mike Furrey.[1]

Walking into the bar, I chug a Gatorade bottle filled with Franzia but buoyancy fades. I'm hungover by kickoff. I don't consider choices or entertain that there are better things to do, other ways to live. There's no reason to question habits when I've overachieved by simply getting away. *I must be doing something right. Have you seen my zip code?!?*

I swallow pangs of regret tasting of regurgitated wine, look for something to say in barstool conversation, settling on: "That receiver used to play defense."

If there were a time to ditch this team, this is it. I spend 165 hours a week as a carefree Californian but three hours each Sunday as a disappointed Detroiter. This window's more important—it's who I am.

Losses sting but I know how to deal with emotions: hitchhiking to Malibu and getting drunk on the beach. I swill terrible wine on the sand, wishing the rest of the fan base could be so well adjusted.

---

1. Furrey's second NFL act is a wonderful story wasted on a crappy team. The Lions convert the DB to WR, and he catches 98 passes for 1,000 yards during 2006. What I'm saying is: He deserves a Disney movie.

WEEK 12: NOVEMBER 23, 2006. MIAMI DOLPHINS (4-6) V DETROIT LIONS (2-8). FORD FIELD, DETROIT, MI.

Thanksgiving. Joey Harrington starts for Miami, lending the game the feeling of running into a former partner. We built a future around the idea of us working out; they had the audacity to keep living when it didn't.

It's personal. Ford Field's jumbotron shows a montage of Joey's worst moments,[2] but the attempt to rattle Joey inspires him. Harrington thrashes the defense with three touchdowns, ending the day munching a genetically modified turkey leg.

Joey becomes the quarterback we hoped for. He's just wearing the wrong uniform when that happens. One of the sport's endearing rituals is showering the winning coach with Gatorade. Joey's postgame fruit punch shower is a rare instance in which a player receives the honor.

★ ★ ★

Harrington's not the only reinvention. Banjo Bob falls in love with a saxophone player and subsidizes her dream of owning a farm in rural Indiana. The property's in the red, but Bob's worldview dictates that people ask for money when they really need it. Lack of agency turns a passing suggestion into sage financial advice. He forks over everything. Being taken advantage of makes him a good person.

Williams, Indiana, is 20 minutes outside of Bedford, Indiana, which is 30 minutes outside of Bloomington, Indiana, a place only interesting because the rest of the state is such a shithole. The 20-acre farm has tractors, barns, chickens, goats, even a llama named George. Everything a farm needs except a way to make money.

"Why do you live there?"

"I like it."

2. Harrington receiving prank calls is unfortunately not featured.

"What do you like about it?"

"It's quiet. The excitement is someone stealing the buffalo skull from the general store."

He doesn't want me to approve of rural, impoverished cosplay. He needs me to think it's great. He enthusiastically describes another midlife crisis but lacks the self-awareness to realize what he likes is being as poor as everybody else.

He phones each week, lengthily expounding about Dinky's, a local livestock auction cheerfully described as "Amish Woodstock." I want him to check on me, maybe give advice, but I must pretend that eating a hamburger and watching a pig get purchased is profound.

My only interactions are letting Bob talk about his interests. He tells me what makes a good banjo, who makes a good banjo, and details the act of acquiring said good banjos. I learn these things, but he ends the call when it's his turn to listen.

I'm a full-blown addict—relying on booze to be fun and speed to be smart. All life's problems have solutions. It's about knowing what substance to reach for.

Some things will never change. I'll always get plastered. I'll always gobble pills. The Lions will always lose at Lambeau.

* * *

The Lambeau losing streak looms over the franchise's psyche. Blowing a late-game chance causes no disappointment, just the sweet relief of things being as they should.

Christmas Eve. If there were any karmic justice we'd upset Chicago and reward fans willing to spend their holidays at Ford Field.

A Christmas miracle is on the table. Trailing by five, Detroit advances the ball to the Chicago 22 with seven seconds remaining. Kitna evades pressure, finding Mike Williams alone in the back of the end zone. The self-described "future hall of famer" picked over Aaron Rodgers reaches for the ball.

He drops it.

Merry Christmas to all and to all a good night.

The season closes by unexpectedly blowing out Dallas. It's equivalent to leaving a five-star review for a restaurant that served you a turd because the after-dinner mint was good.

Detroit possesses the second overall draft pick after the Oakland Raiders. Owner Al Davis fosters a close-knit fraternity among Raiders alumni that includes Matt Millen. He might run the Lions but is still a Raider for life.

The conflict of interest rears its head during evaluations of quarterback JaMarcus Russell. JaMarcus is one of history's biggest draft busts, but no one yet knows his unmatched physical abilities will be undone by horrific attitude.

Russell pays no attention during a Detroit pre-draft interview, zoning out and checking his watch until getting thrown out of the facility.

Millen phones his old boss Al Davis, warning him not to take JaMarcus. It's a severe lapse in loyalty directly contradicting Detroit's interests. We're saved by Millen's reputation. His indictments convince Davis to take Russell first overall.

Millen has spent four high draft picks trying to find a franchise-changing receiver. He finally gets it right with Calvin Johnson out of Georgia Tech.

Johnson is unreal; a blend of size, coordination, and explosivity unmatched in human history outside of LeBron James. Even other NFL players are blown away. Roy Williams tries to describe what it's like watching Calvin practice, but the closest comparison comes from the *Transformers* movie series: "He's Megatron."

WEEK 1: SEPTEMBER 9, 2007. DETROIT LIONS (0-0) V OAKLAND RAIDERS (0-0). OAKLAND COLISEUM, OAKLAND, CA.

Overlap between interior life, addiction, and team is self-imposed but spurred on by coincidence. The Lions open the season within driving distance on my 21st birthday. This convergence is proof of intelligent design, at least on the part of schedule makers.

I attend with high school friends, now USC classmates, the country's best film school. We buy a Lions balloon at Ralphs and drive overnight, batting the inflatable out of the rearview.

The Coliseum parking lot crowd, affectionately known as "the Black Hole," turns en masse to boo our first step into the stadium. The atmosphere's menacing, suggesting physical danger but spurred on by me wearing a Lions Santa hat with a balloon tied to my wrist. One festively costumed fan is nice enough to take a photo in which he pretends to slit my throat.

An opening Kitna interception is celebrated by an overweight fan next to me gesticulating her FUPA against my person, intoning, "Raaaaaaiii-iderrrs." Roy Williams breaks the scoreless tie, and I learn gyrating FUPAs aren't reserved for celebratory reasons. It knocks off my hat.

Calvin Johnson scores his first career touchdown. I break out a spirited rendition of "Gridiron Heroes." One fan likes the song so much he contributes a percussion section by whipping a bottle at my head.

Oakland takes a lead, boiling the crowd dressed like Hot Topic employees to a hilt. The FUPA will shake forever. Broken coverage gives Detroit a field goal, and turnovers result in multiple Detroit scores. The Black Hole goes ashen; the FUPA goes still.

A clinching score prompts another chorus and another beer bottle whipped at my head. It hits a kid. The child's father and the bottle tosser fist fight. I let go of my balloon, watch it ascend into the cloudless sky, and exit.

I pull over at a truck stop and legally purchase a bottle of Hpnotiq for its Honolulu Blue color, figuratively sipping the Kool-Aid.

WEEK 7: OCTOBER 21, 2007.
TAMPA BAY BUCCANEERS (4-2) V DETROIT LIONS (3-2).
FORD FIELD, DETROIT, MI.

Mired at midfield, Detroit makes a prudent decision, one that guides them for the next decade.

Calvin gets the ball. After catching a diving slant for 18, the defense reshuffles to mitigate his size and speed. Trickery's ratcheted up. Calvin gets the ball in space. He's a different species, standing out on a field of world-class athletes; an actual lion on a gazelle-crowded savanna. Calvin shrugs off three tackles, gallivanting for a score.

Barry made impossible plays; Calvin's the opposite. Every achievement makes perfect sense. The only question his jaw-dropping contributions prompt is "Why does anyone else get the ball?"

This is the high-water mark, the eye of a hurricane in a depressing decade. A win over Chicago pushes positive vibes into downright goofiness. Roy Williams gets criticized for offhandedly mentioning not tipping Pizza Hut delivery drivers. Admitting this to a low-per-capita fan base is a bad look for a millionaire. Roy dons the Pizza Hut uniform, delivering pies across the neighborhood. It's the only time I regret moving.

WEEK 9: NOVEMBER 4, 2007.
DENVER BRONCOS (3-4) V DETROIT LIONS (5-2).
FORD FIELD, DETROIT, MI.

Ford Field finally hosts a winning Lions team in a high-stakes game. Shaun Rogers dominates, bowling his way into the Denver backfield, decimating their quarterback. It's far from his most memorable play of the day.

Detroit's on the right side of a garbage-time blowout when Denver hucks a pass into Rogers's oversized gut. The ball wedges into a fold of fat and Rogers runs—well, not exactly runs—but advances the ball 65 yards for a score. The victory cigar of a fat guy chugging along, collapsing in the end zone, and huffing sideline oxygen is everything I've ever wanted. The Lions win 44–7, advancing to 6–2. The heart has never been this full.

Downfall's first steps can be goofy; deepest failures are regrettable and repetitive. Once again, a Halloween party derails a promising season. Over the offseason, Assistant Coach Joe Cullen is arrested for going through a Wendy's drive-thru drunk and nude.[3]

---

3. This is also my uncle's name. This became a fun running joke as this is something he'd probably do.

It's a personal rock bottom sending Cullen into sobriety programs. Imagine painstakingly working a program only to have the golden boy at work lampooning your lowest moment via Halloween costume.

Quarterback Jon Kitna attends the party in a nude suit with his wife cosplaying Wendy in a red wig. They do not warn Cullen about the costume because "they wanted it to be a surprise."

There are more surprises. Everything this team counts on—physicality and passing—falls apart. The Detroit Lions we come to believe in will lose 24 of their next 25 games.

A little success makes it easy to deny a problem. Just as a 6–2 start gives a useless regime benefit of the doubt, enrollment at a good university shields concerns of alcoholism.

I drink most days, chasing consequences with pills.

WEEK 15: DECEMBER 16, 2007. DETROIT LIONS (6-7) V SAN DIEGO CHARGERS (8-5). QUALCOMM STADIUM, SAN DIEGO, CA.

Our fall from grace is a difficult pill to swallow,[4] laying waste to reframing tactics. A record that would have thrilled before the season now induces misery.

Friends take me to Joshua Tree. Reddened boulders and cactus formations feel otherworldly—even more so when I try LSD. It's the initial link in a lengthy chain of chemically induced "best days of my life." The feeling of watching Shaun Rogers jiggle for a score can be conjured at will. All you need is good friends, unmatched natural beauty, and the right chemical. I give full credit to the substance. My drug of choice is now any and every.

The entirety of being is disrupted by a tongued tab of paper, but I scrape myself off the mattress and make it to San Diego. We're technically alive for the postseason in the same manner I am technically eligible for the NFL draft.

---

4. The only one I have difficulty with, tbh.

A drunk old man falls over a row of spectators, accidentally crowd-surfing an entire section while keeping his beer intact. Prioritizing a beer over well-being is more majestic than my Joshua Tree vision quest and a perfect proxy for how I'm living. We lose 51–14.

A 6–2 start is squandered. Bigger losses await.

I've wasted USC. Private pursuit of creative excellence is useless in a USC caste system of networking celebrities. I'm so amphetamine zoomed, I don't realize that's the point of university.

The decision is made. I'm a writer. I'm not choosing a career but a lifestyle: mixing Adderall, whiskey, and chewing tobacco until flow state is reached.

Something happens. A good thing that justifies many bad things. I binge myself into oblivion and write an essay that becomes a hit in *The New York Times*. Validation alters me, confirming the addict as brilliant.

I've only felt good about myself from creative success, but this has only been achieved from substance abuse. I lock myself in a converted closet, writing under self-imposed pressure, abusing drugs and typing nonsense under the delusion this is my destiny. I think I'm giving myself to the craft but am actually giving myself to substances.

I identify as a writer because novelists can be total drunks. Having one essay published makes me an important voice. The speed makes this more likely than being a lucky drunk.

Every Memorial Day, Banjo Bob excitedly announces football preview magazines hitting newsstands. His enthusiasm over *Lindy's* and *Athlon*'s publications is only matched by my dismay at their projections.

I work as a camp counselor in Yosemite National Park. Every night I address a group of children as someone sprays a hose in my face, discovering a new passion with every laugh. Off nights are spent partying, drinking myself into enough of a stupor to ignore the other shoe appearing over the horizon.

A care package arrives from Banjo Bob. Nestled among the sequoias, I pore over expert analysis, getting pissed off. Everyone picks us to finish last, calling us the sport's worst team. Experts are idiots. I'm supremely confident that 2008—like all other years—is the Lions' year.

2008 REGULAR SEASON

College's looming end causes peers to make plans and build futures, but my only care is writing; an ambition without conquer or escape. Friends find entry-level jobs but not me. I gobble pills and swill whiskey, maintaining flow state at all costs.

This delusional self-appraisal is the same I apply to the Lions. Flawed processes steamroll rational thought until only the most optimistic opinions remain.

Our prized acquisition is Rudi Johnson, a capable back from Cincinnati. He leaves his Louis Vuitton luggage outside Millen's office while signing his contract.

Johnson's poised to take carries from incumbent back Tatum Bell. Though it isn't retribution, Bell steals the luggage and is quickly apprehended since NFL training facilities have more security cameras than casinos. Although no charges are brought, Bell never plays in the NFL again. The incident ironically brands him as having too much baggage.

Sterling debuts are rare. Aaron Rodgers takes over as Packers quarterback after a lengthy apprenticeship. With Favre finally gone, we are emboldened by the unlikelihood the successor will live up to standards of the predecessor.

Rodgers opens by dodging contact and throwing a touchdown. He follows it with a 65-yard laser and yet another score. We blink and discover ourselves in a 21–0 hole, once again blocked by a legendary quarterback in our division. Green Bay will beat us forever.

More and more and more losses follow, but we get the victory needed since 1963: Someone stands up to William Clay Ford.

Millen's job security is a black eye on the city rivaling mayoral corruption arrests but WCF lets him linger. WCF's son Bill addresses the press, telling a gaggle of microphones he "would fire Millen if given the authority." These antagonistic but well-intentioned remarks spur WCF from his coma.

Matt Millen is fired. Only seven years too late. A stubborn man will not leave a job he sucks at under a leader who won't dismiss him. A photo circulates of Millen packing up his offices using those boxes only utilized when someone gets axed accompanied by a quote from Mrs. Millen stating he "is finally out of football hell."

Ticket sales skyrocket. The *Detroit Free Press* dedicates an entire page to fan jubilation.

"I haven't been this happy since Saddam Hussein was disposed of."

"The EMS just restarted my heart. Please let this story be true."

"WCF must go before the Lions will thrive. The guy took the team from fans and has given little back."

Detroit loses 34–7 to the Bears, but Ford Field is ecstatic. *Ding dong the witch is dead!*

WEEK 6: OCTOBER 12, 2008.
DETROIT LIONS (0-4) V MINNESOTA VIKINGS (2-3).
METRODOME, MINNEAPOLIS, MN.

Detroit's mired in unmatched *wait 'til next year* mode, but disappointing losses are compounded by the cruel manner in which they unfurl. Unproven young quarterback Dan Orlovsky takes over. Dan goes on to a sterling media career but no broadcasting achievement will outpace the infamy he finds this day.

Detroit recovers a fumble on their one-yard line. Two ineffectual plays pin Orlovsky, in his second career possession, in a desperate position with purple jeers raining down, their volume multiplied by the Metrodome's roof.

Orlovsky drops back. Feared pass rusher Jared Allen breaks free. Orlovsky scurries to freedom but in doing so sprints out of his own end zone. Full, confident strides suggesting internal thought processes of *I can't believe no one's thought of this!*

Allen stops, points, and laughs. The referee has no choice but to agree, co-signing the bullying and awarding two points to Minnesota. The play becomes emblematic of failure—not just with the Lions but for the concept as a whole. It airs on television and circulates on social media to this day. NASA will someday beam it into space to show the universe who we are. Orlovsky cannot outrun his fate or Jared Allen.[5]

Matt Millen's gone but his shadow looms over the "football hell" he constructed. Emotionally invested fans continue watching while Millen quietly retires to his Pennsylvania mansion and beloved cisterns, collecting paychecks for another three years.[6]

The team is 0–8, halfway to history as the first team to ever go winless over sixteen games. The offense has not scored a first-quarter touchdown all season. Their time would be better served volunteering for Habitat for Humanity. Even enjoyable moments feel like a leper spotting a $20 bill on the ground. A blip of joy followed by the dull realization that we lack what's necessary to grasp success. Losing is gravity for the 2008 Lions. Good plays are Wile E. Coyote treadmilling off a cliff. We pursue goals, realize what's next, and plummet.

Recession hits. Concerned professors address classes with ashen faces. Things are tough; the future's no longer promised; I'm nonplussed. Perpetual rebuild is all I've known.

Having no prospects frees me to imbibe flow-state cocktails until words pour. Sundays provide structure and sobriety. It's best to be clearheaded when watching the Lions try to stave off the impossible. The three hours that once affirmed long-held identities are now the only window of clarity. Calvin is a granule of greatness within this pile of horseshit. He's awesome and perfect, a Sunday unto himself.

---

5. I empathize with Orlovsky. I was once fired from a bowling alley for crashing a lane cleaner and cannot imagine the clip running for decades on ESPN.

6. If he had any decency, he would have stayed in Michigan, given out his address, and allowed residents to egg his house whenever they wanted. It's only fair.

Despite it being Marinelli's specialty, the team possesses the league's worst defensive line. Any competent running back moves through our defense unimpeded. The march to a winless season is yet another run we can't defend against.

WEEK 17: DECEMBER 28, 2008. DETROIT LIONS (0-15) V GREEN BAY PACKERS (5-10). LAMBEAU FIELD, GREEN BAY, WI.

There's nothing left to protest. With Millen's sun set there's nothing to do but place a paper bag over one's head and await the next chapter.

I'm back in Detroit, celebrating graduation with friends and family. The party rolls up to kickoff with family huddling around a television in our freezing garage. I'm propped up as an example of someone made good until my answers to "What's next?" questions prove more embarrassing than the team.

"I'm gonna live in a van and become Hunter S. Thompson."

"Uh . . . do you think anything's there with Orlovsky?"

"I think he'll end up in the van."

The Pack open by going 73 yards untouched for a score. Calvin plays Superman, dragging the rest of the team along. They are overmatched but willing to fight, even if no prize awaits.

24–21 Packers

Fifteen games of evidence to the contrary do nothing. I believe the Lions will heroically rally for a defensive stop and 1–15 finish. Rodgers throws a 70-yard score. History is secured. The Detroit Lions have gone 0–16.

★ ★ ★

There's still lower to go: 0–16 is an abysmal record but far superior to the numbers I put up during my job search. Habits deplete dopamine. Failure to find flow state is followed by self-hatred and administering additional doses.

Visiting Bob in rural Indiana is not a great time. He's taken to dressing like a cowboy, perfectly costumed for someone running from themself. We're walking down the street when he takes out a switchblade and hands it to a stranger.

"Why did you do that?"

"He needed a good knife."

My father's love language is taking such poor care of himself that loved ones intervene. I inherit this. Sleepless from speed, I pass out in an antique store, crashing through a table. Descending through the glass, I note the shoddy nature of the antiques, thinking: *They better not make me pay for these.* My father, in AA for 20 years and receiving a message in the language he taught me, says nothing.

I hate this place and vow never to return. I misread my rail ticket and get stranded overnight in the Indianapolis train station, a corn-fed hell that feels like a holding cell with worse aesthetics. I have $100 to my name and give it to Evan Williams, staving off the nip of Midwest winter by passing a bottle around with other vagrants.

I arrive in Los Angeles and walk through Skid Row, reaching the house I can't pay rent in to live a life that doesn't exist. With nothing to fill my days, I fill my glass. There's no money so I steal booze, picking bottles so large and absurd no one would dare have the audacity to shoplift them. Novelty champagnes are pinched from boutique hotel lobbies and boxes of Franzia are carried away in heaping stacks, lending me the appearance of a *World's Strongest Alcoholic* competitor. Standing out enough makes you invisible.

I swallow gin, certain life problems can be binged away. My career is a Skid Row lifestyle. I'm due for a promotion.

MARCH 28, 2009

I feel weak but that doesn't matter. My body's an adversary, an obstacle to the flow state I must perpetually occupy. Skin's pale and head's light but like Barry, I will find my destination. Like Calvin, I will be unstoppable.

I play basketball with roommates in the driveway. I overcome poor conditioning and worse free-throw shooting to win our game of 21. They want to run it back but I'm too tired. I sink onto the living room beanbag, falling into a restless sleep before a cable re-airing of *American Beauty*.[7]

Like the Lions going 0–16, I'm about to achieve the failure that defines me. There's no singular disaster, just a series of Millenesque shortsighted decisions that make me what I deserve to be: winless.

Struggling to my feet is hell. I inch toward the bathroom and fight a nauseous feeling that feels slightly different. The feeling is new because my stomach's contents are not vomit.

All of the blood in my body gets ejected. Blood pours over the toilet and shower. I stagger to the kitchen and lose the rest. I collapse on the floor in a blood puddle in a state rapidly approaching death, a product of addiction.

Near-death states prompt the human brain to release a substance called DMT, a potent chemical reserved for those on death's door or patrons of my neighborhood bodega. A vibrant fantasy plays. In this scenario I need to borrow a hoodie from my roommate.

Nick is like a brother. He followed me to USC from Dearborn only for me to treat him like shit for not following my terrible choices. The decisions I ridicule him over leave him sitting quietly upstairs, close enough to hear me gurgling his name in blood.

"Nick. Nick. Hoodie."

Nick finds me on the floor in a pool of blood as a Roy Williams Fathead looks on. I pull pranks in this room—once reenacting the Abu Ghraib

---

7. The film ends with a character killing himself because of who he is. I apologize for the spoilers, but the movie is nearly three decades old, and I need to evoke the ending as a device to frame the next five minutes of my life.

photos for a cinematography project—but he believes me based on the whiteness of my lips.

I wake to his screams but am unconscious by the time he phones the ambulance.

The chemical cocktail that pulls me into flow state erodes my intestines, filling them with blood and killing me—at least temporarily.

The paramedics load me on a gurney and revive me in the back of an ambulance. We speed toward the hospital and the fourteen blood transfusions needed to save me.

It's hard to sleep with these loud fucking sirens. I wake up. Locking eyes with the paramedic, he chastises, "You need to stop drinking."

"Why? I'm fine."

GAME 10

FRAT BOY FINDS HIS WAY

• 2009-2011 •

One Wild Card Loss—Better Than It Sounds

2009	2010	2011
2-14	6-10	10-6

There it is: the greatest right arm to ever throw a football. It's attached to John Matthew Stafford.

In service of the first overall pick, a new leadership cohort—Coach Jim Schwartz and General Manager Martin Mayhew—travel to Georgia to affirm suspicions. They don't merely watch Stafford's throws, they hear them. *Whistling* through the atmosphere, *popping* into the shoulder pads of receivers strong enough to leave a bruise. It's not an arm. It's a howitzer.

Gridiron intelligence is tested. Lions brass tries confusing Stafford with complicated coverage quizzes, but he passes every test. Matt's robotic focus seems like "notes being written on his brain wave."

Schwartz mandates the obvious. "It's time to find a replacement for Bobby Layne." Stafford already replaced Layne once, winning a state championship at Highland Park High School in Texas where Layne once starred. Perfect pedigree sparks *woo-woo* ideations. This man-child is the chosen one.

Most importantly, Stafford wants the challenge. "I knew what the 2008 Lions were. This was something I wanted to be part of."

The commissioner calls his name. Matthew walks to the podium and smiles. Our chubby-cheeked savior has arrived.

Bobby Layne was Detroit's last franchise quarterback, but that was so long ago the concept didn't exist yet. Civic bankruptcy lacerates town pride. Matthew's right arm immediately becomes the crown jewel of a city that sorely needs one.

We live in concert, starting adult lives being asked to bring fundamental change. He's a young quarterback expected to lead Detroit out of a generation's long abyss. I white knuckle sobriety, knowing booze might kill me but still struggling to quit.

Both tasks are difficult but Matt's is more important. He's a football player.

Ideal practices for quarterback development are a debate that will rage forever. "Start versus sit" will be argued until the sun engulfs us all.

Stafford opens training camp with a glorious tight window throw. If he can make throws no other player in franchise history can replicate, what's he to learn from sitting on the bench?

Stafford's career opens with miscues, but mistakes are wrought from confidence and gumption. The young man's promise is clear even if the situation's difficulty is just as apparent.

Washington visits in Week 2, foolishly accepting a third-down penalty deep in their end. Matthew uncoils a rope to his X receiver that puts points on the board. It takes until the final whistle to believe, but it finally happens. The Lions win for the first time in over a year.

Even missteps can bring joy.

With no prospects, I purchase a beaten-down RV with my friend Jeff. I have no money and idiotically adopt two Vizsla puppies that eat RV walls. I'm the Lions and they're my dual Charles Rogers: perfect young creatures I'm unable to support.

Last dollars are spent on drugs. It's enough for months, but I take it in one fell swoop, turning the world into a jittery, melted nightmare as I lock my keys in my car. Convinced I'm the modern Ken Kesey,[1] I start street performing, emerging from the ocean in a green unitard lumpy with balloons, rolling around a tire for tourists. I make four dollars.

Poverty mires the RV in a Vallejo, California,[2] trailer park containing a diverse population of locals, i.e., reclusive methheads and friendly methheads—a depressing reality for two recent grads. Stunned silence is only broken up by the sound of dogs eating the walls.

I start drinking again.

I was always an alcoholic, but a carefree spirit accompanied the era before acknowledgment. Now, I see my demise every time I grab the bottle but bring it to my lips anyway, downing liquor alongside self-worth. It brings no enjoyment, just darkness. *Why can't I stop?* rings in my ears. I don't realize fixing myself with substances is how my brain has been programmed.

WEEK 11: NOVEMBER 22, 2009. CLEVELAND BROWNS (1-8) V DETROIT LIONS (1-8). FORD FIELD, DETROIT, MI.

Chaos pauses on Sundays for silly little games. The low of drinking myself to death becomes a series of self-worth subbasements but at least there's Matthew.

---

1. Wrote one brilliant book, one okay book, and was amazing at taking LSD.

2. I feel at home in Vallejo because it's one of the few cities besides Detroit to declare bankruptcy.

The Browns game is revolutionary in that it won't be televised. Isolated in the RV, methheads circling the perimeter for something to steal like sharks in chummed waters, I escape reality via illegal stream. Two 1–8 teams facing off in a throwaway game is everything.

The awful Browns storm to a 24–3 lead before Matthew—for the first time of many—puts the team on his back. Stafford repeatedly finds Megatron in stride, tying the game in minutes.

Matt grows up in a single afternoon, progressing through reads and making intelligent decisions to wrest a 31–27 lead. An intentional grounding in the end zone gives the Browns two points, and they score on the following possession. Matthew throws a pick, but the defense holds. Hurdles exist to be vaulted.

Fourth Quarter, 1:46; Cleveland 37, Detroit 31

Calvin takes us out of the end zone's shadow, then grabs another at midfield. Stafford spikes the ball, finds the tight end, and spikes it again.

Fourth Quarter, 0:08

Matthew evades the sack, uncorking one to Calvin for the win. He's tackled before the ball arrives. *FLAG!* Pass interference penalties bring momentary relief but Matthew is hurt, writhing on the ground in pain.

Trainers come to his aid. Matthew shakes them off and goes ballistic, desperate to play. We've had great players but never one so willing to fight for us. One play remains, an untimed down. Matthew sprints in, favoring his shoulder and looking like the city of Detroit became a person.

Stafford takes the snap, fakes the handoff, and throws the winning touchdown. The stadium erupts in jubilation as Matthew collapses in pain. Our leader aligns with our spirit.

Matthew fighting off pain to provide a win is inspiring. Sitting in a hell of my own creation, the best hope I've got is our fortunes rising together. He'll lead the team to glory as I become, uh, anything but this? It's a flawed, silly notion but my sole silver lining. I go to bed in the disintegrating RV, but for one night it feels like a five-star hotel.

LIONS 38, BROWNS 37

Banjo Bob has a massive heart attack. It's no surprise. Smoking and eating salami like he does, his lifestyle is seemingly in response to someone challenging, "I bet you can't induce a coronary." He lingers on the precipice, inducing what-if sadness but pulls through. A doctor calls.

"Your father's extremely depressed."

"What should I do?"

"Do you love your father?"

"Sure?"

"Then you know what to do."

I get drunk on Thanksgiving, watch the Lions lose, and board a plane for Indiana. Life is abandoned to care for my father. I think it's a onetime deal, but it's the theme of the following decades.

I return him to his "estate" from the hospital. Banjo Bob sleeps away the days, leaving me with addiction's close companion: complete isolation. I start the day with speed and end it fixating on Bob's oxy. Aunts and uncles preached its promise. The addict rationalizes it'd be a shame for Bob's recovery to waste this buzz. Banjo Bob knows but says nothing. He hides the pills, I find them, swallowing a few to celebrate winning our demented scavenger hunt.

Banjo Bob's farm becomes my burden. The llama breaks a leg. Putting down the animal is my duty, but I can't bring myself to do it. I ask a neighbor to shoot the beast as plainly as I'd request to borrow a cup of sugar. They do. An ice storm freezes a goat to death. I dig a hole in the hardened ground and cremate the animal. Other creatures, sensing the loss, bray mournfully into the night.

Banjo Bob and I exist in amicable quiet. He puffs and tinkers with the banjo while I pill out and compulsively write. Our only normal interactions are on Sundays. Kickoff sees him adorably nestled in his chair holding a football, anticipating the games.

Matthew and Calvin fall short but their struggles are worth watching. Throws leave Matt's hand at unmatched velocities only to be grabbed by Calvin at impossible altitudes. We don't win any games, but each week concludes with Banjo Bob patting his football, solemnly declaring, "I like Matthew." The Lions finish 2–14, but as an addict who gets pink eye shoveling manure, it's impossible not to consider them the best thing in my life.

Detroit picks second in the draft. Sometimes you pinpoint the problem and receive the perfect solution. Ndamukong Suh, a Nebraska defensive tackle with unmatched strength and an unparalleled mean streak, is the best defensive prospect in years. Suh is nasty, skilled, and inexplicably mentored by Warren Buffett.[3] He breaks the mold so emphatically that future scouting combines will demand prospects explain compound interest.

Calvin, Stafford, and Suh give the Lions an unmatched young core of complementary talents. During any other NFL era, this roster would support a contender for a decade. However, for the Lions—the team that can never win—the peak of our youth movement could not have worse timing.

A hard salary cap orients the league toward parity but grants additional influence to sports agents. Attaching themselves to top prospects like remora, agents use hard-fought negotiation tactics to make top picks some of the league's highest-paid players before playing a down. The Lions' youth is the team's greatest asset, but we lack the financial flexibility to build around it. We finally have the young talent to contend, and it cripples us.

I spend winter in Indiana facing the uncomfortable reality of having no next move. A brief visit to New York City gives a taste of city life doing open mic comedy. It feels like home while making Indiana seem even bleaker. I plot ways to leave but I'm stuck.

---

3. Also, Suh once saved comedian Louie Anderson from drowning on the set of a reality show.

Bob and I drive in a blizzard. The car *chugs* up an icy incline, shuddering to a stop. Turning the engine causes flames to shoot from beneath the hood. We pop it open to inspect the damage, but the influx of oxygen feeds flames, shooting fire to the heavens. We try containing the fire but it's too large. We watch from a safe distance as prospects burn to a crisp. I put my arm around my father.

My hoarder aunt is the keeper of the car's title because she's the keeper of everything. She searches the familial hoard for the document, navigating her compromised frame around dead cats and McDonald's toys, finding the paperwork inside an old cigar box. An envelope next to it has my name written in my grandmother's handwriting. Five thousand dollars is inside. Reparations for trauma.

I move to New York. I don't know a thing except the need to express myself. I don't consider building a career or a long-term plan. I do comedy.

Doing comedy is transformative. It provides community and structure. More importantly, I learn stand-up is something I can't do on Adderall. Being speeded out makes an art form predicated on human connection clunky and forced. I realize this is how speed makes the world feel all the time.

I stop taking Adderall. It's an impossibly seismic shift that scares the shit out of me, but I do what it takes to support the singular, perfect thing that is comedy.

The Lions do the same with Matthew, magnifying hopes until they can set an anthill on fire. Signing Nate Burleson, a sure-handed second receiver, placates the chorus demanding "Matt needs help." The annual search for Barry's replacement is renewed by selecting Jahvid Best, a gifted runner with lingering injury concerns from a harrowing concussion. Both players will be afflicted by star-crossed luck but bounce back with inspiring second acts.

2010 REGULAR SEASON

We still suck but there's enough evidence to think we might not suck forever.

WEEK 1: SEPTEMBER 12, 2010. DETROIT LIONS (0-0) v CHICAGO BEARS (0-0). SOLDIER FIELD, CHICAGO, IL.

Fans can be responsible for losses. If we forget to wear a lucky shirt or neglect a vital pre-game ritual, the loss is on us. Others console saying, "it wasn't your fault," but true fans know better.

This roster inspires unmatched levels of "waiting for next year." Detroit spent decades wandering the desert; this team will be the Gatorade.

A lifetime has merely killed time before these snaps, but I need $11 per hour and am stuck working retail on Sunday while the world revolves around whatever happens at Soldier Field.[4]

I step into an employee bathroom every five minutes, phoning friends for updates. A furious manager demands I stop taking such frequent breaks, but my excuse of diarrhea is buoyed by his knowledge that I can only afford to eat at halal carts. All is well in Chicago and ultimately the world. Jahvid Best breaks two early touchdowns, fulfilling promise from his first touches.

Bears edge Julius Peppers gets a clean hit on Matthew, severely injuring his shoulder. Hope that amounted for months is extinguished by a single blow.

Fourth Quarter, 0:18

The Bears pull ahead, likely winning, but Jim Schwartz breaks the glass on the Greek god playing receiver. Calvin's acrobatics lead us down the field with a chance to win as time expires.

Calvin hauls in a pass, sliding through the end zone with the ball completely secured. Upon landing, he takes the ball with *one hand*, firmly places

---

4. Unable to pay my bills, I join the proud lineage of thieving retail workers. I memorize every item's price, hand customers products without entering anything in the register, then take their money before coaxing them to leave with subtle suggestions.

it on the turf, and joins the celebration. It's a wondrous, game-winning touchdown . . . the NFL overrules on a technicality.

It will become known as "the Calvin Johnson rule." Bureaucracy robs us of our moment in the sun. It's one thing to lose by your hand, but having it taken away like Al Gore's hanging chads embodies the Detroit fan experience. A moment of happiness before returning to a reality that's somehow worse than before. This pattern of administrative screw jobs will be in place for Calvin's entire career.[5]

Officials are blamed but that's not the case. It's my fault for missing the game.

With Stafford injured, a losing streak begins. Concentration laser focuses on finding silver linings. The team will not win, but what else is new? Fun must be had and new traditions must be established.

Williamsburg, Brooklyn, gentrifies amid the bloom of boutiques and coffee shops. The Turkey's Nest, a dingy sports bar that takes pride in never getting any nicer, is the sole holdout. Patrons drink heavily, gamble profusely, and know less about football than my mother. It's heaven.

Banjo Bob once shared his rituals, but adulthood is about cultivating our own. I faithfully visit the Turkey's Nest each Sunday, bringing along Lions fans and comedians that turn Sunday football into a social circle foundation. The season is a set of training wheels, an attempt at establishing my definition of who I am and what I enjoy.

We join a group of septuagenarians stuck to barstools for decades like dated upholstery. Big Dog, so described because he has "Big Dog" sewn onto his jacket, curses his Packers, win or lose. It's a fandom rooted in hatred. I suspect most football fans want to lose, to express justifiable disgust, but that sentiment belongs to us.

---

5. The only explanation is that NFL Commissioner Roger Goodell caught Calvin doing the horizontal boogie with Goodell's old lady.

After every touchdown, especially when being blown out, I belt "forward down the field."[6] Initial responses are side-eyes and giggles, but fifteen years of singing the same song in the same bar makes it my home. Not a geographic place but the joy in my timbre accompanied by drunks clapping off beat.

WEEK 8: OCTOBER 31, 2010. WASHINGTON {REDACTED} (4-3) V DETROIT LIONS (1-5). FORD FIELD, DETROIT, MI.

Matthew's return on Halloween spurs a strong reaction, a stunning display of positivity accompanying such a cruddy record. The young core fires on all cylinders. Calvin catches a ball at the five, thwarting attempted constraints from three defenders while spinning toward the goal and extending across the plane. It's not the sort of thing human bodies do—except for Megatron.

Washington makes it a seesawing battle. Matthew's game for it, threading balls through triple coverage to Calvin for their third score of the afternoon. Washington is set to answer, but Ndamukong barrels into the backfield, bullies the ball loose, and scoops it up for a score as serenades of "SUUUUH" boom through Ford Field.

Young pieces coagulate into position for a day. For Halloween we dress up like a good football team. The challenge for the Lions—like many of us—is being their best self on all days, not just one.

The Lions falter, Stafford gets hurt again, and the once promising season mires the team at 2–10. A silver lining is Suh, standing out among NFL monoliths with WWE aggression. He's frequently called for ticky-tack penalties like roughing Jay Cutler, a man defenders should be allowed to beat with sticks. Apologizing for Suh's behavior becomes the exhausting norm. His positive on-field presence makes us accept the unacceptable.

---

6. After field goals we tickle a man named "the WaeltDog." What can I say? Rituals are important.

I attack the open mic circuit. Onstage joie de vivre allows good sets from dogshit material. Offstage, I ply myself with alcohol, telling myself it's part of being a comic. At one mic I get drunk enough to fall off the stage. It's 6:30 PM. At another, I'm so inebriated I pass out in the street. A man picks me up and puts me in his car. Thankfully, he drops me off at home.

The Lions become a good football team, just too late for it to matter, ending the season on a winning streak representing an inspiring amount of progress. Questions about Stafford's durability persist,[7] but if he can stay healthy, contention will follow. Sometimes a plan works but fails anyway. The achievement one strives for does not guarantee success.

The young roster's already a ticking time bomb due to rookie salary structures. The Lions pick Nick Fairley, another massive DT, with the vision of pairing him with Suh to decimate opposing run games. The plan works but even this is a trap. Acquiring so many talented tackles puts a lien on decision-making, steering the team away from best outcomes. Stocking the pantry sometimes ruins grocery shopping.

Also added is Titus Young, a talented receiver from Boise State intended to take advantage of attention paid to Calvin. Yet again, a brilliant pass catcher lands in an organization lacking infrastructure to protect them from themselves.

2011 REGULAR SEASON

A brilliant start sees the white-hot Lions win in nearly every conceivable way. Even our mascot Roary contributes.

Kansas City back Jamaal Charles takes a handoff out of bounds directly into the mascot's leg. Roary pops up but Charles stays down, writhing in pain with a torn ACL, a victim of furry fury. If your mascot takes out a player, you've already won.

At Dallas, even a 27–3 deficit is no challenge. Stafford lobs to Calvin, levitating over the end zone like some yogic deity. Add in the efforts of Best,

7. He'll shrug these off and become the most durable quarterback of his era.

Suh, and Burleson, and Detroit possesses their most winning formula since the Model T.

WEEK 5: OCTOBER 10, 2011.
CHICAGO BEARS (2-2) V DETROIT LIONS (4-0).
FORD FIELD, DETROIT, MI.

Monday Night Football comes to Detroit for the city's first prime-time game in a decade. Ford Field is explosively loud, teeming with raw-throated fans desperate to confirm that the Lions are for real.

Matt finds Calvin for 73. Ford Field screams so loud it is no longer a dome.

Clinging to a four-point lead at their own 12, Jahvid Best zips through a hole and *poof!* off he goes, teleporting into the end zone, making our lead insurmountable. It's a magic moment, a clear distillation of Best's tantalizing abilities. This run is the exclamation point marking the end of cellar dwelling. Tolkien's lore seems more realistic but it's happening. The Detroit Lions are 5–0!

Jahvid Best's 88-yard run resides in the pantheon of the great Lions moments. It's also his last significant moment on a football field.

COLLEGE FOOTBALL WEEK 10: NOVEMBER 7, 2009.
OREGON STATE BEAVERS (5-3) V CAL GOLDEN BEARS (6-2).
CALIFORNIA MEMORIAL STADIUM, BERKELEY, CA.

The severity is not yet widely known. The afflicted understand, but Will Smith had yet to put on a bad accent in a family film about head trauma and preach the truth: Concussions. Are. Devastating.

Jahvid Best stars for the University of California Golden Bears, powering them through conference play. A hard hit against Arizona State concusses him. His brain clatters against his skull, but with no outward sign of injury it's considered minor.

Best is cleared to play the following week—just eight days after a concussion. This is football. Better to be dead than soft.

Jahvid's the best player on the field. He approaches the end zone, hurtling through the air, soaring past the Rubicon of six points. A defender catches Best but only manages to push him a bit higher in the air, just enough to make him lose control.

Clattering to the ground, Best lands on his head forcefully enough to pop off his helmet like a champagne cork. Teammates rush to celebrate, notice his arms stuck in a stiff position, and realize something is drastically wrong. Medical staff rush onto the field. Best is given oxygen and removed on a stretcher.

Concussions are a concern during the draft evaluation process but not to Jahvid, not outwardly. "Why would it still be a problem for me? I don't even remember it."

The Lions draft him. On *Monday Night Football*, Best announces himself as an ascendent star.

Best gets another concussion the following Sunday—his second of the season and fourth of his career. Jahvid publicly insists he's okay while privately conceding his football career is over.

Best retires. The Detroit Lions call it a sad story but Best corrects them, making the most impactful pivot of his quick-twitching career. He became a sprinter, making the 2016 Olympic team and competing against Usain Bolt in the 100-yard dash. Best's time is .32 seconds behind the gold medal but far ahead in perseverance. His story is the inspiring sequel to *Cool Runnings* the world needs.

Jim Schwartz turns the team around by infusing it with his personality. The 53-man roster borrows enough aggressiveness to scratch their way out of 0–16 depths. In his third season Schwartz's intangibles are an asset—if properly harnessed.

A win against the 49ers slips through the squad's fingers. Opposing coach and famed eccentric Jim Harbaugh ebulliently celebrates, blowing off a handshake with Schwartz. The hotheaded Schwartz goes ballistic, chasing

Harbaugh down like an aggrieved shih-tzu as the two khaki-clad men exchange shoves. This emotional outburst foreshadows the quick-trigger anger that will assist Schwartz's undoing.

Cheering for a supposed contender is not unlike stand-up comedy in which self-image and social standing shift based on the most recent performance. A conquest makes one champion, but a single falter spirals one into self-doubt. Cheering on *this* team is not unlike the interior life of a 25-year-old man earnestly standing on his own for the first time. The most exciting thing will be finding out who we actually are.

WEEK 12: NOVEMBER 24, 2011. GREEN BAY PACKERS (10-0) V DETROIT LIONS (7-3). FORD FIELD, DETROIT, MI.

A nerve-racking obstacle for a young comic is getting booked on a prestigious show. Opportunity produces self-doubt. This fear is not generated by crowds or self-sabotage. Rather, the idea of belonging brings imposter syndrome, reducing one to a watered-down version of themselves. Such is the case on Thanksgiving for my proxy Lions.

The Packers roll into town with shiny new Super Bowl rings and an undefeated record. The Lions are obsessed with validation; concern over external opinions shifts focus away from the task. This recipe for failure applies anywhere.

Best's absence renders Stafford one-dimensional against a staunch Packers defense. We crumble down the stretch, losing 27–15.

True to the team, I fall apart. Banjo Bob imposes his new holiday ritual. He refuses to make plans or pick up the phone. Left with the image of him patting his football and conducting loneliness for sport, I get blackout drunk and see *The Muppet Movie* in Manhattan.

I do not remember the film but wake to a seven-foot promotional statue of Simon from *Alvin and the Chipmunks*. I'm informed that while leaving the theater I picked up the hulking statue and had a friend help carry it down the stairs, onto the subway, and into my apartment.

This is funny. It's so funny the NYPD decides to solve the crime. I bought my ticket with cash, impossible to track. My accomplice, who paid by credit card, is tracked, jailed, and forced to bring Simon along for the perp walk.[8] Someone is imprisoned as a by-product of my substance abuse and inability to process emotions. That doesn't mean it isn't very, very funny.

We play the Saints on Sunday night. I drop acid under the logic that everything's improved under the influence, a textbook example of addictive behavior. Abstaining from Adderall has not made me less of an addict, I abuse whatever else is in reach.

The team follows Schwartz's domineering personality. Titus Young commits a personal foul penalty after a pivotal first down. This infraction costs us dearly but there are no corrections. Ensuing dirty plays and trash talk reflect poorly on Coach Schwartz's locker room.

Hopes of true contention are abandoned but the bar is low. A wild card appearance unquestionably ends dark days.

A road trip to Oakland has playoff implications for both sides. The Raiders score off a Matthew strip sack late to make it a two-score game.

Dwindling hopes consistently spark the best from Matthew. He converts a gutsy fourth and 2 before finding Titus to cut the lead to six.

Fourth Quarter, 1:38

Pinned back deep and needing a touchdown, Matthew finds Calvin, Calvin, and Calvin again. Everyone in the Oakland Coliseum knows what's next but it's too late. Megatron is unstoppable, defying double coverage to bring Detroit the win. He conjures the rare combination of transcendence and reliability to keep playoff hopes alive.[9]

---

8. It is unfair for Simon to be jailed. He did nothing wrong.

9. Even if Detroit occupies the ignominious position of becoming the first team to have four (!) comebacks of thirteen points or more in a single season.

WEEK 16: DECEMBER 24, 2011. SAN DIEGO CHARGERS (7-7) v DETROIT LIONS (9-5). FORD FIELD, DETROIT, MI.

We're on the precipice of clinching the team's first playoff spot of the millennium. What feels new is actually well-trodden precedent. A Christmas Eve game determines the holiday spirit.

I travel to Detroit to "see family," knowing full well Banjo Bob will stay on the farm and ignore hourly phone calls, sadness growing with each ring. I am Ebenezer Scrooge, visited by ghosts of Paul Edinger and greeting Christmas with the epiphany that winning will be enough.

Honto, a charter member of the Turkey's Nest crew, picks me up in her father's American-made automobile. We conduct our lifelong argument as to whether Dearborn is in Downriver,[10] as we drive into Detroit and pull into a Michigan Avenue liquor store for whiskey and Faygo Rock & Rye. It's a huge day for Detroit sports. It'd be a shame if we weren't trashed for it.

Festive moods fill the air. Fans desperately cheer on a team outwardly reflecting Schwartz's interpretation of the city's psyche. We breathlessly wait for our heroes to take the field while they spar with the Chargers in the tunnel.

Calvin makes it look easy, opening the game with a 46-yard reception that kick-starts celebration. We aren't screaming, we aren't cheering; we're manifesting. A 7–0 lead feels like a blowout as Ford Field breaks into song as Honto slurs undying support for her "chubby quarterback."

The Chargers are backed up deep. Star end Cliff Avril picks off a pass and walks in for the clincher. The stadium celebrates like the Super Bowl was just clinched. The final whistle blows but no one leaves. Detroit's stuck in stadium seating, staring at the scoreboard in befuddled glee. The Lions have made the playoffs!

---

10. I'm not. Dearborn is not Downriver. Honto, from neighboring Allen Park, is from Downriver.

Success can be savored but never dwelled upon. The surest way to fall short of long-term goals is deriving too much joy from milestones along the way. Schwartz is a borderline brilliant coach blamed for the culture. He inherited toxic conditions and made them palatable, but the approach that brought improvement will not be enough for a Super Bowl.

NFL football's complexity requires more than the right players, coaches, and scheme. Excellence is also needed in daily operations. Support systems must extend tendril-like throughout the organization, affirming successful foundations. Measures like rehab equipment, player outreach programs, and masseuses let players know they matter. They weren't provided by an ownership group clashing with labor relations across multiple verticals.

What's left is emotion. Schwartz charges through the org like a one-man vision quest, rallying players around his own passionate fulcrum. It's unsustainable. The same reasons for lights-out play fuels letdowns against lesser opponents. Emotion can only be fuel for so long before succumbing to its natural half-life.

The overhaul needed since 1963 was unlikely to stem from a first-time head coach. The best coaches don't just win but usher in a manner of conducting business that supports winning. The way out of the cellar is not also a path to the mountaintop.

WEEK 17: JANUARY 1, 2012. DETROIT LIONS (10-5) V GREEN BAY PACKERS (14-1). LAMBEAU FIELD, GREEN BAY, WI.

A trip to Lambeau remains. Despite the environment's hopelessness, Green Bay, assured of the one seed, will rest starters against a desperate Lions team. A win sends us to play 9–7 New York while a loss sets a date with the 13–3 Saints that we plainly cannot beat. It's unreasonable to expect a victory over Aaron Rodgers on his own turf, but besting backup Matt Flynn is doable. He holds clipboards for a reason.

My mother's side hosts a family Christmas party. A meaningful, late-season Lions game is rarer than the holiday but, for this devoted

Catholic clan, our team takes an unfortunate back seat to Jesus Christ. I slink to the garage, steal my uncle's whiskey, and partake in the worship of insular obsessions. The team connects me to the populace and infuses life with ritual and reverence. This is all a passion needs to justify emotional investment.

A perfect start awaits. Flynn fumbles, Titus scores, and Green Bay botches a kickoff into a safety. Stafford's at his best, perfectly executing the offense, but our defense is at its worst. Every painstakingly perfect drive is answered by home run swings from Packers backups.

What feels like karma is actually sloppiness. Detroit fumbles twice on the heels of big plays, and a Titus score is called incorrectly only for Jim Schwartz to realize he's out of challenges. The game's cursed status is cemented in the second quarter. Titus drops a score, Calvin uncharacteristically drops another, and Jason Hanson whiffs an easy field goal. If God is real, they're punishing me for not being in the house with the true believers.

Throughout the second half Stafford and Calvin win the game on at least three occasions. Unfortunately, the defense loses it four times. Matthew throws for 520 yards and Calvin receives for 244, but these Herculean contributions aren't enough to beat Green Bay's second string.

I learn. Losing isn't an outcome. It's something in our DNA—a destination we were fated to arrive at. We're not a football team. We're Buddhist monks spending weeks building sand sculptures and dismantling them upon completion. We don't lose. We do what we're supposed to. This damning realization is accompanied by the lesson that a season is enjoyable regardless of how it ends. Ignoring my clan to be let down by the Lions solidifies their position as my beloved. I compartmentalize the loss, go inside, and have a lovely time with family.

New Orleans is the better team. I go to the Turkey's Nest like an inmate bounding toward the hangman's noose. The Lions are going to lose . . . a playoff game!

Stafford steals an early lead but a fumble recovery deep in Saints territory yields no points. Our chance at winning is squandered. We possess a halftime lead but lack the run game to protect it. We return a kick for a score, but the play is mistakenly blown dead. Schwartz is furious. The team follows his emotional lead into the void, failing to score on their next drive and dropping two interceptions.

The Saints pull away, relegating Detroit to also-ran status. I walk to the subway platform and run into a friend.

"Who won?"

"We did. Simply for being there."

GAME 11

JEKYLL AND HYDE (IN AN AT&T STORE)

• 2012–2013 •

Meh.

2012	2013
4-12	7-9

Collective wisdom, gleaned across industries, dictates that an organization's most difficult achievement is going from good to great. NFL schedule makers believe, showcasing the Lions on national television five times.

Curses are the only entity capable of stopping our ascent. Vexes from Bobby Layne and Moon Baker are annexed by the Madden curse. Calvin Johnson is chosen as cover boy for the popular video game series. Previous poster children snapped fibulas like Garrison Hearst, disappeared like Peyton Hillis, or retired early like beloved Barry. Calvin's too talented to fail, but his employer ain't.

Coach Schwartz's only blemish is his fiery nature impacting the team. Infractions like unnecessary roughness penalties and Suh's violent actions are an alarming but ultimately harmless subplot reserved for the field.

This evolves during the 2012 offseason. Lions players get written up for conduct unbecoming a member of the NFL, or arrested at alarming rates for various offenses. The team finally leads the league in a stat but it's not positive—Detroit is responsible for 25% of the NFL's arrests.

None of the jailed players approach the designation of most unstable player on the roster.

Organized team activities build chemistry for the upcoming season. In this setting, trash-talking your coworker is a good thing, instilling an iron-sharpening-iron paradigm. Louis Delmas, a promising young safety, has a great day of practice and lets Titus Young know about it. Rather than let his game do the talking, Young allegedly sucker punched Delmas in the face.

Young is banned from voluntary workouts. It's difficult to be sent home from something you're *volunteering* for. Imagine what it'd take to get expelled from ladling out stew at a soup kitchen. That's the energy Titus Young brings.

★ ★ ★

Banjo Bob loves that I do comedy. It's my rarest achievement: a subject he'll talk about. Life revolves around comedy. Work, romantic partners, free time, etc., all orbit social standing and bits.

I work my way up the hierarchy. The pipeline for comedy success is:

1. Start a bar show.
2. Get the scene to support the show.
3. Perform at Kabin—the city's best showcase—the NYC comedy equivalent to a Pro Bowl appearance.
4. Appear at Just for Laughs: New Faces at the Montreal Comedy Festival before agents and TV offers roll in.

Much like Stafford-to-Calvin is the only winning strategy, getting booked on Kabin is the only way up. It takes years to get booked, but I finally perform on a steamy July night. I have the set of my life, soaring reputation, and justifying a blur of drunken celebrations.

Crushing Kabin is an accomplishment but a nominal one. I have no long-term plan or idea how to build off it. I dedicated two years of my life so my dad can compulsively rewatch and memorize tape of a good bar show. I'm the 2011 Lions spraying champagne after clinching a wild card. Celebrating relevance stops us from realizing the extent of the competition. Sustainable planning is needed, but we grow complacent, expecting next steps from inertia alone.

2012 REGULAR SEASON

Matthew, on the heels of a 5,000-yard passing season, plays like a man bought into his own hype, throwing three turnovers on tight window throws that weren't open to begin with. He conjures his magic to throw a winning score, but it's false assurance.

Three straight losses. The only victory is Jim Harbaugh and Schwartz successfully executing a pre-game handshake. The 2011 Lions were a fun, young team that couldn't quite compete with heavyweights. The 2012 iteration removes "fun" and "quite" from the equation.

At least our failures are memorable. Detroit loses "the greatest game no one remembers" to Tennessee—a rollicking defeat featuring everything about the sport worth loving: trick plays, miracle highlights, a Hail Mary forcing overtime.[1]

Unlike previous failures, 2012 is cutting with the disappointment of wasting something special. The thing you spent existence longing for is there for the taking, but you can't get out of your way long enough to grasp it. This shit sucks.

---

1. The highlights are absolutely delightful. The only way YouTube could contain a more enjoyable video is if the Rizzler showed up in a Russian dashcam video.

Glimmers of hope provide the same emotional experience as a kicked puppy coaxed to return with a treat. The Lions' start is so galling the only reasonable reaction is to write them off. That's when the kitties answer the bell.

WEEK 8: OCTOBER 28, 2012. SEATTLE SEAHAWKS (4-3) V DETROIT LIONS (2-4). FORD FIELD, DETROIT, MI.

The game's slipping away when Titus Young steps up. Calvin puts up eye-popping stats but fitting perfectly next to him is nearly as important given the NFL's emphasis on passing.

Seattle hangs tough. Hard-nosed receiver Golden Tate steals a late lead.

Fourth Quarter, 5:27

Stafford milks the clock, advancing the ball to the Seahawks' one with time expiring. Detroit does something Seattle can't in this situation: complete a pass.[2] With the game on the line, Stafford goes to Titus. *LIONS WIN!* Titus goes for 100 yards and two scores, catching every ball thrown in his direction. Unfortunately, he refuses to accept being valuable without being the star.

Early season struggles are shaken off to climb to 4–4 but the .500 record is not a springboard. The 2012 Detroit Lions—a team with three Hall of Famers—will not win another game. Losses accumulate so frequently the only way to comprehend them is via heuristic organization.

We lose in the following ways:

1. The Fix Is In. We crumble when calls go against us, which coincidentally happens in key moments against big-market teams.

---

2. Seattle loses a Super Bowl with an interception at the one-yard line.

2. The Landmine. We convincingly outplay the opposition only to lose on a single, vital misstep.
3. The Cinderella. The Lions face a beatable backup and turn pumpkins into carriages for a three-hour window.

WEEK 12: NOVEMBER 22, 2012. HOUSTON TEXANS (9-1) V DETROIT LIONS (4-6). FORD FIELD, DETROIT, MI.

Suh's borderline on-field assaults are covered by the media like he's running for office. Holiday dinner conversations hotly debate whether Suh is a good person. My mother defends him like one of her beloved rescue pit bulls.

"They startled him."

"He doesn't know his own strength."

"They were asking for it."

Suh's the subject of criticism but the target is Schwartz. How can he be expected to provide emotional balance while outwardly grappling with his passions?

Up 10 in the third, Detroit closes in on the first Thanksgiving win in nine years when bureaucracy targets us again.

Texans running back Justin Forsett is tackled for a short gain. Forsett, acting like an annoying try hard, gets up and sprints to our end zone. It is a waste of everyone's time, but refs irritatingly allow the play to go on. There's nothing to worry about. The NFL reviews all scoring plays.

Schwartz throws his red challenge flag on the field. This action is completely understandable from the perspective of anyone with human consciousness but violates precious protocol. Schwartz throwing the flag somehow makes the play impossible to review. It's a bureaucratic oddity, something never previously called in an NFL game. Once again, the NFL dusts off archaic rule-book legalese to make us suffer.

Ford Field's sudden toxicity makes losing inevitable. The Texans get on top but Stafford responds, willing a victory his teammates squander. Pass catchers fumble away winners in regulation and field goal kickers whiff in overtime, doinking triumph off the crossbar. Watching this defeat makes one conclude the loss as written in the stars, but that isn't true. It was written in the rule book.

WEEK 16: DECEMBER 22, 2012. ATLANTA FALCONS (12-2) V DETROIT LIONS (4-10). FORD FIELD, DETROIT, MI.

With the season lost, Lions fans embrace the familiar coping mechanism of rooting on individual excellence, acting like tennis fans once again. Calvin Johnson has the single-season receiving-yards record within his sights. Instead of focusing on the team's faults, we dwell on Calvin's achievements.

It's a viable harm-reduction method. The team is infected. In a loss to Green Bay, Titus Young lines up out of position, telling reporters: "If I'm not going to get the football, I don't want to play." Outward insurrection is actually taboo in most workplaces. Titus is benched for the season and cut from the team, never to play in the NFL again.

Paralleling Barry Sanders's career, Calvin Johnson is all that remains. These all-time greats possessed unmatched skill and achieved *in spite* of their employers. The Lions use them as catchall solutions instead of building blocks deserving support. Barry never had a quarterback; Calvin never had a running back. It's a yin and yang of failed support systems.

Banjo Bob drives up for the game. He doesn't acknowledge Christmas but tells me he's excited to see Calvin break the record. It doesn't matter if the Lions win. Calvin needs 182 yards.

I work as an under-the-table furniture mover and purchase the tickets. We're walking to the stadium when Bob asks, "Hey, Slick. Can I get some money?"

I withdraw $400 in cash and hand it to him, illustrating how low the bar is. Doing manual labor is considered making it. This money was backbreakingly earned but I give it to my dad.

We enter the game. Banjo Bob buys $400 worth of 50/50 tickets.

There's an anticipatory silence hours before kickoff. Down below, players stretch hamstrings and say hello, but father and son are nestled in the nosebleeds, far enough from the action to share quiet. I ask the question.

"Do you care if I have a beer?"

Banjo Bob has been in AA for decades. He must know about urges, how strong an argument oblivion consistently presents. I'm not asking for his permission; I'm begging for his disapproval.

"It's your decision." This would be the right response from anyone but him.

Calvin Johnson fires on all cylinders. Midway through the third, he takes a mundane catch up the middle and into history. The game is paused and Calvin is rightfully given his flowers, but his standing ovation is rooted in the same delusion as alcoholism. We do what's easy and enjoyable while ignoring better possible outcomes. Sometimes it feels just out of reach. Other times it's hard to know what we're looking for.

The season ends. Only one player excels. The damning thing is knowing one good thing is enough.

★ ★ ★

Honestly? Same. I tell myself everyone drinks in New York. That no one's sober here. Active addiction is ignored to be king of the open mics. I don't branch out or develop. I perform (and drink for free) at *The Creek and The Cave.* Gatekeepers will elevate me when I'm ready. Talent is enough.

I'm a loser but it's enough to be the golden boy in a family of black sheep. I drink to black out, touch subway tracks on dares, and eat cigarettes onstage. There's so much mental illness in the family. I'll always be the normal one by default.

Mental illness is a hard opponent to defeat.

★ ★ ★

Titus Young's demons surface with alarming regularity, securing his NFL exit, but ramifications don't impede behaviors.

Off-field incidents start in midseason. Young approaches a closed AT&T store demanding they open. When employees refuse, Titus literally plays the *do you know who I am* card, showing them a Topps football card as identification. Once inside, he demands free stuff and falls asleep on a bench so soundly employees can't wake him up.[3]

Titus outwardly mutinies against the Lions, bristling at the well-intentioned efforts of assistant coaches.

Young is released on the first day of the league year. The gesture is intended as a wake-up call but, as AT&T store employees can attest, it's hard to wake up Titus Young.

Titus relocates to Southern California and gets arrested twice in a single afternoon—DUI and attempting to steal his own car from a tow yard, respectively. Two weeks later, he's arrested again. If jail had a punch card for repeat offenders, Young would get a free sandwich.

Young's NFL career is over but life contains more chapters. He enters the prison system, throwing a series of knockout punches that awe staff. "You rarely saw someone throw a closed fist punch on a mental health floor . . . until Titus was admitted."

Violence ebbs. Young journals to quiet voices in his head and quell shame from previous infractions. The ambitious question of "What will Titus Young become?" becomes the concerned query, "Can CTE cause mental illness?"

Young is released from prison in 2018. Since release, he has avoided controversy and the law. Sometimes simply living is the greatest victory.

Not everyone gets on track.

---

3. I will not judge. I did the same thing (minus the football card identification) to a Napa Valley bookstore at the height of poverty while wearing a purple tracksuit.

★ ★ ★

I decide that I won't. It isn't a conscious decision but the net result of all my choices. My love of substances will run my life. I do not resign myself to this reality but cheerfully accept it. I'm a drunk, a pill head, a "fun boy." If any nagging voice pipes up to disapprove my habits I will drown them out by numbing myself with a sip or puff or pill or whatever's in reach. Whatever will make me feel different. Whatever distances me from myself.

It's hard to become a person. The path toward addiction is much more appealing. Never feel anything but fucked up and get remembered by glimmers of potential exhibited before following the path to oblivion.

I can't get sober. If I do I will become just like my dad. Locked in a room of my own volition, not using but never feeling anything else.

To be around my father is to contemplate my own fate. Will a substance define my life? Will I ever be able to truly live outside its grasp?

"My biggest fear is ending up like you."

"That's too bad," he replies sweetly, returning attention to his leatherwork.

I love Titus Young. It's no different than my love for Joey Harrington and Charles Rogers and numerous other prospects who could have made a difference but didn't. I don't want to achieve in my life, I just want to do enough to wonder what might have been.

These players are simply totems, cautionary tales I aligned to my psyche during cognitive development. Titus never achieved his potential and transformed the offense of my favorite football team but that doesn't matter. Not with the highlights, a handful of breakthrough moments that illustrate the future that never arrived.

Catching a Hail Mary against Tennessee, beating Seattle at the last gasp, the sensory memories are no different remembering what it was like to exist before chemical urges governed my mind and directed my choices. Even in the darkest moments it's impossible to dwell upon anything but the handful of times we became who we could've been before shrinking back into the reality of who we are.

2013 REGULAR SEASON

A 4–12 finish wrecks long-term expectations. Desperate to save their jobs, Schwartz and Mayhew pounce on Reggie Bush when free agency opens. Having already failed to live up to the expectation of becoming the next Barry Sanders, Bush's presence in Detroit feels preordained.

The Lions get off to a strong start, beginning the season 2–1 powered by Calvin and the performance of Nate Burleson, an invaluable contributor in the passing game and locker room.

In true Lions fashion, the strong beginning is sullied by bad luck so silly it becomes comedic. A celebratory hang is organized as the team gathers to watch *Monday Night Football.*

Burleson drives back from the event with two pizzas riding shotgun. Burleson fiddles with the aux cord while driving along I-696—Michigan's most treacherous highway. The pizzas slide forward. Nate takes his eyes from the road to save the pies. The moment feels borrowed from folklore wherein a momentary lapse in concentration assures one's doom.

Burleson crashes. Concerns over intoxicated driving give way to the most relatable injury in league history. Burleson has broken his arm and misses the remainder of the season because he likes pizza. His injury prevents the offense from reaching their potential but is the spark igniting Detroit-style pizza's ascent over the coming decade.[4]

WEEK 8: OCTOBER 27, 2013. DALLAS COWBOYS (4-3) V DETROIT LIONS (4-3). FORD FIELD, DETROIT, MI.

With so many standout performances it'd be unfair for there to be a Calvin Johnson rule without a Calvin Johnson game.

---

4. If you haven't had the square delight known as Detroit-style pizza, it's emphatically worth losing an NFL season over.

A matchup against the Cowboys pits two great offenses and bungling coaches against each other like a teenager practicing kissing their reflection. The only difference is Calvin. His presence creates a delta so galling the Cowboys deny its existence, insisting the world's best receiver would be third on their depth chart. It's a flat-earther starting a globe manufacturing business.

The game takes its first step toward classic status when Calvin zips a short screen 87 yards to the end zone. Dez Bryant, a vaunted Dallas receiver, hauls in an impressive score of his own to make it 10–7, lending the atmosphere of two heavyweights sizing each other up.

Calvin fumbles in the third, cueing a Dallas field goal, but short-term impediment is a bargain for the fire it lights underneath Megatron, who then makes grab after grab until it's 20–17.

Dez makes an annoyingly impressive play to seemingly put the game out of reach. The worst part about Dez's big game is that it validates the perception of him being on Calvin's level.

Stafford lofts a 45-yard moonball. Calvin floats through the interference of multiple Dallas defenders to wrap his paws around the ball. The impressive feat feels gentle and expected.

Suh swallows up three straight Cowboy rushes to hold them to a field goal and give Detroit a chance.

Fourth Quarter, 1:07; Dallas 30, Detroit 24; No Timeouts

The entirety of the football-watching world knows where the ball is going but it cannot be stopped. Bursting downfield, Calvin gets popped by two defenders and nabs another frozen rope, getting unfairly tackled at the one-yard line.

Detroit sprints to the line of scrimmage. Matthew fakes the spike and sheepishly sneaks the ball over the goal line, stealing a win in a manner borrowed from *The Little Rascals*. Calvin ends the game with 329 receiving yards, another record. Trading a lifetime of shortcomings for a handful of perfect Sundays feels like a fair trade.

The end is never pretty. After guiding the team to a 6–3 start, Jim Schwartz short-circuits. His decisions submarine a talented team, punishing the fan base for daring to dream. Detroit fizzles to a 7–9 finish, confirming the worst suspicions about Schwartz's coaching.

It begins in Pittsburgh. Holding a late game lead, the team runs a fake field goal to the punter. The friggin' punter fumbles. Great idea, Jim!

Detroit loses to Philadelphia in a blizzard. No one remembers the details of the Lions' collapse aside from it happening in the snow. Calvin's face mask fills with frost as Lions slosh around the tundra in all-white uniforms like a more athletic yeti.[5]

Another disheartening loss follows against Baltimore. The Ravens exclusively settle for Justin Tucker field goals. Surely no kicker, not even the best to ever do it, is enough to beat us with leg alone. Wrong. Tucker kicks a 61-yard field goal as time expires. Getting dominated by a kicker is worse than a forfeit.

A Giants team with nothing to play for visits Ford Field. The Lions are still alive for a wild card. The game is a referendum on Schwartz. This singular outcome decides his fate.

Fourth Quarter, 5:06; Lions 20, Giants 13

We're driving for the clinching score when that pesky other shoe appears. A perfect Stafford pass clangs off a receiver's hands, gets intercepted, and is returned by New York for the tying score.

Fourth Quarter, 0:22; Lions 20, Giants 20

Detroit gets the ball. The team with the league's strongest-armed quarterback and most athletic receiver elects to take a knee and play for overtime. Torrents of boos target Schwartz. It's not desire to make the playoffs but

5. AthlYeti.

to let our blue-chip quarterback act the part. The Giants win in overtime, closing the door on a once-promising season and once-promising coach.

Schwartz is fired. Someone can do a great job without achieving their ultimate goals. Schwartz changes winning from abstract ideal to expectation. Questions persist. What could've been with Jahvid Best? Why did the red flag get thrown against Houston? Why was the fake punt called against Pittsburgh? Questions linger but the truth is Schwartz led the franchise out of the darkness.

The only local media voice with the stroke to call things out is Mitch Albom, the *Detroit Free Press* columnist turned bestselling author of *Tuesdays with Morrie*. His column on Schwartz's firing says the quiet part out loud: The only way to lose and keep your job is to be the person signing the checks.

Seismic movements continue in March with the passing of William Clay Ford. Under 50 years of his ownership, the team experienced a single playoff win. WCF wholeheartedly loved the Lions but kept them ill, treating his beloved like an overly doting mother with Munchausen syndrome by proxy.

Ford's passing spotlights the next generation and the particular way football is consumed. It isn't a sport so much as connective tissues between generations. Fandom is criticized as "cheering for laundry." I don't consider this a takedown. Being dyed in the wool makes us who we are. How much identity do humans need? We yearn for community in nation, religion, schools, and sect. Sometimes it's only found in our teams.

JULY 2023

I write this in Banjo Bob's shack. Helping someone die is a 24/7 task with lots of downtime. I work on this book, diligently plowing away to a soundtrack of snores. My pen runs out. I tiptoe around the hoard, crashing into clutter because all windows are blacked out. I open a kitchen drawer. It's filled with whoopie cushions. Hundreds, possibly thousands.

"Bob. Why do you have these?"

"In case of emergency."

I do the math on these purchases, comparing it to the amount coming out of my pocket to support him financially. Woof.

It's good to love what disappoints—even if it only ever disappoints. Bob's tethered to oxygen tanks, panting, "I've never been so happy" before slinking out of his darkened room for a cigarette. He loves the cigs even though they've already killed him. I wonder if he loves them because smoking is the only time he sees the sun.

"Bob, would you rather smoke cigarettes or meet your grandkids?"

"Grandkids," he grumbles, but actions—a loop of shuffling outside for smokes—scream *CIGARETTES!*

Can I *only* love what disappoints me? Knowing I'll be let down by these entities makes me look at them in a way that makes them enough. In time this perspective becomes my worldview. An existence spent straining to see the positive leads me out of darkness.

I leave for the airport. Flights are canceled.

"Should I come back?"

"No."

"This could be the last time we see each other. You sure I shouldn't come back?"

"I don't care."

You don't need to achieve it all. Sometimes you just need to see the light. Jim Schwartz did that for the Lions so he did it for me. I look at him as a great coach. It's a matter of perspective.

GAME 12

SOME APEXES ARE SHITTY PLATEAUS

• 2014 •

Almost . . .

2014
11-5

The Lions pull off the upset.

William Clay Ford Jr. had been groomed to run the Lions but doesn't receive the brass ring.[1]

Ownership passes to Martha Firestone Ford, his mother and WCF's widow. It's a tall task. NFL ownership regularly exposes global magnates and hedge-fund pioneers as incompetent.

---

1. Publicly saying he would fire Millen if he was in charge.

Martha's rejected by the fan base. It's not misogyny. Nor is it resentment toward a silver-spoon lineage featuring considerable market share for *two different industries.*[2] Reservations are based on age.

Martha Firestone Ford, the new blood, our fresh-eyed invigoress, is 89 years old. Do you know what an 89-year-old looks like? Like an 88-year-old but worse![3]

Martha shows aptitude early into her regime by addressing the recurrent problem with ownership: a famed surplus of loyalty. A disappointing start in 2015 pisses Martha off. She issues a statement about her desire to field a "consistently" winning team, rolling through the practice facility in her wheelchair, firing anyone who draws her ire.

After being rejected by hotly pursued coaching candidates,[4] Detroit settles on Jim Caldwell, a respected player's coach known for assisting Peyton Manning's development. Most importantly, he's chill. It's not a great hire, but it's certainly not a bad one. That's Jim Caldwell.

Apart from demeanor, Caldwell's core competency is quarterback expertise. Bringing in a portion of Manning's support system communicates how high the bar is for Matthew. Stafford can't overpower opponents with sheer talent; he needs Caldwell to make his head as deadly as his arm.

Pizza-loving Burleson is replaced by Golden Tate, who approaches the finesse receiver position with a blue-collar mentality that makes him beloved in Detroit.[5] Even more impressive are rumors of him wandering into a closed donut shop to eat sweet treats. It's an intangible, not a blemish. A man who goes after what he wants so doggedly will certainly come down with 50/50 balls.

---

2. Tires and cars. Once upon a time the tire princess married the prince of cars.

3. Joke borrowed from wonderful Detroit comedian Nate Fridson.

4. Who actually all go on to suck.

5. Don't worry about Burleson. He goes into broadcasting and becomes the modern Katie Couric.

Ndamukong Suh is the team's most important player but they can't afford him. Suh's play warrants a raise, but his high rookie salary makes a long-term extension impossible. The team remains optimistic, but the stark reality is that Suh's unlikely to take another hometown discount. The tough truth is that Detroit would be wise to pur-Suh[6] his replacement.

Aaron Donald is available in the draft. Donald becomes the standard bearer for defensive tackles, redefining the position. The opportunity cost of false hopes in Suh's loyalty and Nick Fairley's development will cost the Lions dearly.

Donald will make any team he lands on a Super Bowl contender, but we pass on him because we have one at home.

The Lions select Eric Ebron.

Many high draft picks are taken because they're good at college football. Ebron is not a good football player, but athletic testing reveals traits that could potentially make him one. The selection is born from what Ebron might be, not who he is.

Ebron is riddled with immaturity and prone to drops. I could watch Ebron try catching a single ball and recommend he get a case for his iPhone. He stinks!

2014 REGULAR SEASON

WEEK 1: SEPTEMBER 8, 2014. NEW YORK GIANTS (0-0) V DETROIT LIONS (0-0). FORD FIELD, DETROIT, MI.

Optimism is rational. Jim Caldwell's stability will act as an SSRI for an emotionally reckless roster.

An entire offseason spent arguing over Caldwell's ability to induce Stafford 2.0 pays immediate dividends. Backed up deep in his own end, Stafford evades a pass rusher. The maneuver gives Calvin time to cut upfield,

---

6. I'm so fucking sorry.

causing two Giants defenders to crash into each other, creating an easy score. On the next drive, Stafford once again ducks a rusher to find Calvin for a long score.

We don't just win, we dominate, causing Giants fans to complain about a team that won two championships in five years. The moment losing begins, fans fixate on how terrible their teams are. It's not about outcome but how it's centered in our minds. Fans don't always want wins. Sometimes they want something to piss and moan about.

Week 3. Detroit beats Green Bay, affirming suspicions that the 2014 Lions are really, really good. A staunch defense stifles the Packers, standing out as the best unit on that side of the ball in my lifetime.

Of course, this is Detroit, where even success cues failure. Star linebacker Stephen Tulloch sacks Aaron Rodgers. Tulloch leaps in celebration, theatrically unsheathing his claws a la X-Men's Wolverine.

He tears his ACL. Since Tulloch's DNA is sans adamantium, he will miss the rest of the year. Hot[7] on the heels of pizza derailing the previous season, it's fair to believe in curses.

★ ★ ★

Comedy is a beautiful thing. It's the only thing. I still drink in the only manner I know how: pounding booze until oblivion. I wake up on the L train so often that it feels like a bedroom I sublet.

There are many delusions behind pursuing a dream. Ignoring addictions is just one of them. It's all worthwhile.

I do well in New York and work the road. Milestones that matter to a young comic are secondary to me. Banjo Bob loves comedy. He drives to any show in the Midwest, beaming with pride in the front row, silently mouthing every punch line ripping him to shreds.

We celebrate my first headlining gig by driving back to his shack and sitting in his backyard in the rain. I chug a six-pack and let liquid courage

7. And ready. Sorry again!

ask unanswered questions. I need to know about the skeletons someone else put in my closet. He gives me my answers. They're horrifying.

For the first time, I understand him. Heck, I respect him. Evil puts him in stasis, but keeping kindness in his heart is an accomplishment.

"I'm proud of you," I say.

"Thanks . . . I like your comedy."

"I can tell."

"It makes me happy."

"I can tell."

The downpour begins but we can't end the moment. We stay in the rain. He watches me get drunk.

WEEKS 5–10: HUMILIATIONS AND PRAYERS, COMEBACKS AND BREAKTHROUGHS, NEW ORLEANS, AT ATLANTA (IN LONDON), MIAMI

There are downturns. A frustrating loss to Buffalo—where Jim Schwartz is now defensive coordinator—sees Jim carried off on players' shoulders. The boos that exiled Jim fade into a soundtrack to his moment in the sun.

Delightful human-interest stories accompany winning. Joique Bell seals a win against Minnesota, ascending to folk hero with a pro wrestling style postgame interview that gives credit for the win to praying with his mama.

Bell's a powerful totem. A collegiate career at nearby Wayne State University created no pro football opportunities aside from a job working security at Ford Field.

Bell works his way onto the roster and shines. The team's performance goes hand in hand with the city's self-image. Featuring a native Detroiter with Joique's narrative feels like we are proactively combating fate.

Matthew 2.0's dominion is demonstrated with a feisty comeback against New Orleans. Detroit gets the ball down 13 with five minutes remaining while traffic-averse fans exit. Tate catches a conservative throw on third and 13, but absolute dogs don't settle for checkdowns. He finds the end zone to give us a chance.

Glover Quin—a culture-defining member of the secondary—picks off Drew Brees on his next drive. Matt takes us to the promised land. It isn't just a win but further illustration of who he is. No one's better when the chips are down.

A London game against the Falcons proselytizes the NFL's wares before battalions of confused Englishmen. The 9:30 EST kickoff forces my active alcoholic ass to shudder into consciousness in time to see the Falcons race to a 21–3 lead.

A third and 25 ought to affirm outcome and return me to a hangover's throes, but Tate reels in a 50-yard rope to make it competitive.

It's 21–20. All Atlanta must do is run out the clock. They foolishly pass. *Dropped!* Matthew is backed up to his own five with no timeouts but shines again in the land of minuscule probabilities. He seamlessly moves us into field goal territory, allowing new kicker Matt Prater to boot the winner.

Next week a few bad breaks squander a lead to Miami but there's no doubt—not with the ball in Stafford's hands.

Fourth Quarter, 0:29; Miami 16, Detroit 13

Stafford scrambles left and uncorks a daring sidearm. It's an illogical throw, unable to be completed by anyone else in the world, certain to draw a brow-beating from coaches at any level of football.

Stafford completes it. His idiotic, stupid throw lofts over multiple defenders to Theo Riddick in the end zone. A special play from a special player. The string of heroics marks three straight comeback victories, announcing in ALL CAPS that this team is different.

WEEK 17: DECEMBER 28, 2014. DETROIT LIONS (11-4) V GREEN BAY PACKERS (11-4). LAMBEAU FIELD, GREEN BAY, WI.

Christmas in Detroit. A showdown for the divisional crown looms. The city's locked in, fixating on the chance to be a hero.

My Aunt Jackie is declining. We stay close, sharing laughs and pain pills. My first stop from the airport is always her home. On this visit I notice her car—an emerald-colored Jaguar emblazoned with the Hello Kitty logo—is missing. Her caretaker has stolen it. There's something especially evil about taking mobility away from a handicapped woman.

I show up at his house on Christmas morning. An exasperated woman answers the door while a stressed male face peeks around a corner. My message is simple: The car needs to be returned in 24 hours or I'll come back.

It's in the driveway the next morning. Sometimes a Christmas miracle is just a big nephew being imposing.

The season peaks with a road game at Lambeau. The Lions are dealt ideal conditions for an exorcism.

Detroit possesses a winner's componentry but exhibits fatal flaws. They fail to close out lesser teams and, given our penchant for heroics, have been conditioned to believe Matthew can conjure wins at will. Miracles foster belief that improbable conquests weave a larger tapestry of winning. There's a thin line between trust and lackadaisical reliance on Stafford's right arm.

There are reasons to believe—even pragmatic ones. Aaron Rodgers has a gimpy leg against our vaunted defense. Our mature offense can take advantage against our longtime tormentors.

Green Bay returns a Lions punt for a score. Brutal. We finally have a defense capable of stopping Green Bay and special teams blows it. Rodgers piles on another score to make it 14–0 before limping off.

Stafford rallies, leveraging Calvin until the score is knotted. The Lions are on the precipice of taking control when Rodgers jogs out of the tunnel. *Gulp.* This is our fate. We aren't heroes or the final boss. We're the underling John Wick defeats en route to greater glory.

The man with the sore calf becomes our Achilles' heel. Green Bay pulls ahead.

The Packers miss a field goal. There it is: *momentum.* Decades of what-ifs coalesce into a sudden realization. The ball's in our hands against a compromised opponent with the wind literally at our backs. We might win this one.

The game resumes, certain to usher in new realities. Stafford hands off to Joique Bell.

He fumbles.

The Packers pounce on the ball, capturing possession and a divisional title that means little to them but would have meant everything to us.

The mistake kills us. It hurts so much more knowing it came from one of us. The Detroit upbringing, working Ford Field security. Factoids suggested it was time for Detroiters to change their fate but the moment of truth only cemented it.

Rodgers gets the game-sealing touchdown. I'm not sad or angry. This is all I've known.

There are meek rationalizations, the pip-squeak hope piping up to remind, "at least you made the playoffs." This defense mechanism dilutes devastation, ignoring how much darker things can get.

WILD CARD ROUND: JANUARY 4, 2015. DETROIT LIONS (11-5) V DALLAS COWBOYS (12-4). AT&T STADIUM, ARLINGTON, TX.

Instead of hosting Ford Field's first playoff game, Detroit travels to Dallas to play the hated Cowboys.[8]

The annals of Lions history and my own lineage have no shortage of downturns. This is not hyperbole: Nothing is as hard to face as this loss. I would give a keynote address on my grandmother's pedophilia, TED Talk on the myriad ways addiction has derailed my life, or swallow a live scorpion. Anything's more desirable than facing what happened: a blatant pass interference committed against our tight end being picked up and discarded.

This play stands on the podium of inherited shame, addiction, and poverty as part of my trauma. On one hand, this is somewhat embarrassing to say. On the other hand, the call was that bad.

---

8. The Cowboys are not our rival. The Cowboys are the rival of good, decent people everywhere.

Playoff football has a bounce to it. Fears and expectations swirl in equal measure with nothing else worth thinking about.[9] This is the pressure system of truly wanting something.

Detroit plays the early going with the singular focus of a man on fire pursuing water. Stafford finds Tate for 51 to open scoring.

Suh shuts down the Dallas run game. Stafford piles on, orchestrating a 99-yard drive demonstrating every lesson learned. The unbelievable is upon us. The Lions have a double-digit lead in the playoffs.

Our lead isn't just a cushion, it ushers in conditions necessary for our ideal style of football: The offense plays from in front as the defense pins back their ears to pursue the quarterback. We dominate until a blown tackle sets up a score, giving Dallas life. Still, we go into halftime up two possessions and are due to receive the second-half kickoff. Life is wonderful.

Stafford's first pass is deflected and picked off. This is where we usually fold but we don't. The defense holds, forcing a missed field goal. We tack on a successful attempt of our own to go up 13.

Dallas stalls in the red zone. A fourth and 1 stop would secure victory but Dallas converts. The perfect day is suddenly a one-score game with breaks piling up in the Cowboys' favor.

A couple more points or a few more first downs. It won't take much to ice it. The first playoff win in 23 years is right there.

Third and 1, Midfield

A surprise passing attempt in a situation that suggests the run. The tight end is open on the sidelines. Stafford finds him. A face-guarding linebacker crowds the tight end's personal space, sending him to the ground.

Flag! Referees announce the obvious penalty.

---

9. The only diversion is defending Suh for stomping on Aaron Rodgers the previous week. He excuses himself by saying his "feet were cold," but if he'd just waited a few years the action would have made him a hero.

Dez Bryant, Dallas's Temu Megatron, runs on the field sans helmet to protest. Rule books dictate that this gesture automatically triggers a 15-yard penalty, but that won't be called. Not against a crown-jewel franchise. Bryant's infraction goes uncalled and the tantrum works. The referees reverse the penalty against Dallas *because they asked*.

Two clear penalties ignored. Fairness favors large-market teams with national fan bases. One would expect flagship teams to be popular because they win, but the inverse is true. They win because they are popular.

The sequence rattles us. Everything goes wrong. Caldwell makes the wrong decision on fourth and 1 and decides to punt. Our otherwise-reliable punter shanks it and Dallas is in business. Cowboys take the lead.

Stafford has a chance to answer, just as he's done all year. His offensive line does not hold. He hangs in the pocket and gets hit before receivers get open, including on a game-ending fourth down.

The Lions resoundingly win this game but ultimately lose.

This is the big loss, others paling in comparison. I ply myself with liquor to stop the pain, but truthfully? Being cheated out of a playoff win *should* hurt. Nothing could or should dampen this sting. It's part of life. To dull these emotions is to be less alive.

I end up weeping in a pizzeria, chewing soggy slices.

★ ★ ★

Drinking is a way of dealing with disappointment because it's a way to deal with anything. The two core facts of my existence are loving this team and solving my problems with substances.

There's no escaping the lesson: What's earned is not always received.

I'm a competent comedian. Years of beelining from crappy day jobs to the stage pay off in the form of seasoned presence and 30 minutes of decent material. I think of comedy as who I am, not what I do. It's an addiction like everything else. A new joke hitting spikes dopamine levels while bad sets torpedo self-worth. Either outcome is an excuse to consume.

The comedy fraternity is a wonderful thing imposing all-encompassing rivalry. There aren't enough breaks to satiate the bloated middle class of good, but not great, comedians.

Success is getting a credit. Next to every name on a comedy show lineup is a set of parentheses. What sits in this space defines our worth.

(Conan)
(Late Night)
(JFL: Just for Laughs)

The only way to have value is to fill the void. Not in ourselves. The void that counts is the one between the parentheses. I have my chance to fill it. I'm up for New Faces at the Montreal Comedy Festival or "JFL."

Here, thousands of comedians perform their best five minutes for a chance to be formally welcomed into the industry. Even the most talented and self-possessed are anxiety crippled by this process, performing mental gymnastics in pursuit of the approval of a single booker who happens to be a middle-aged man in a fedora.

My tight five cover tales of Banjo Bob's eccentricities, polished to the point where I could do them in my sleep. I crush at my home club—the difficult-to-perform-in *Creek*—advancing to the next round of my own personal playoffs.

My community lives in competition. The prize is inside the parentheses. I want to win and have never been so close. The only way to live is to kill.

Final auditions are at *The Stand*, a great club with low, punch-line-exploding ceilings. The room pulsates with neuroses save for an oasis where the fedora man receives hellos like a little, feckless king.

Some rise to the occasion. Others falter under the pressure. Comedy is tension and release. The comic manages it internally to manipulate it from the audience.

I take the stage.

Stafford gets the ball.

An improvised opening riff gets a laugh. The first hit shapes disparate individuals into an audience. Once they like you they're yours.

Every joke lands. Every tag expands the bit. I've been a comedian for years but now—when it finally counts—I'm the best I've ever been. I kill.

Stafford to Pettigrew. Flag on the play!

I get offstage. Comics start congratulations, offering advice ranging from next career steps to where to get a passport. I shake the fedora's hand, thanking him for the opportunity. He tells me, "We'll see each other soon."

Dez Bryant throws a tantrum, refs rescind an obvious penalty.

I never hear from the festival again. I don't even get a rejection. Someone high up on the ladder decides I don't belong so I languish in obscurity.

Lions lose.

GAME 13

EXITS AND MIRACLES

• 2015-2017 •

One Wild Card Appearance, Many Cathartic Comebacks

2015	2016	2017
7-9	9-7	9-7

Suh leaves in free agency. The cap-constrained Lions don't secure him short term with the franchise tag or long term with an early extension. Optimism causes the Lions to let the franchise player depart after turning down a generational replacement. Lack of foresight can't be overcome until it's too late.

Detroit would have made Suh the highest-paid defender in league history, but Miami offers more. Loyalty doesn't matter when Warren Buffett's whispering in your ear.

Dolphins owner Stephen Ross, a Michigan alumni, pitches Suh on the relocation, telling him, "I hope it's as worthwhile for you as it was for me."

The Lions were historically bad when adding high-value rookie contracts was disproportionately punished by the league's rigid salary cap, making it impossible to secure our core long term. Multiple contract restructures bungle Suh's finances so badly Detroit pays him $10 million during a 2015 season he plays in Miami.

Suh's remembered for dominant plays, dirty moments, and huge paydays but no fan base loves him. A few million dollars was worth more than a legacy. This is the advice one gets from Warren Buffett—someone respected but not adored.

The biggest loss isn't Suh. It's belief.

All I think about is quitting drinking, making promises du jour of lifelong changes. I quit each week but lapse within days. There's always justification. I'm controlled by urges.

Everyone knows I have a problem. I tell myself addiction doesn't exist in New York, but I do so the problem persists.

Moderation is exhausting. Limiting myself to eight drinks requires the same effort as sobriety. Every thought is of booze. Any lull monitoring consumption lifts restrictor plates and I slip into belligerence, convinced booze isn't derailing my life. I do not know I'm a loser.

Partying blurs the line between person and performer. "If you aren't drinking with Joel you aren't getting carried around a room." I go harder than everyone else because I'm expected to. I don't consider how I feel about this; feelings are the right chemical balance. Wonderful nights I don't remember are worth everything.

A familiar feeling enters my abdomen at a bachelor party. I'm bleeding internally. I power through. You can't die of alcoholism when you're going streaking.

Monday morning. I'm weak, pale, but scheduled to work. I commute on my bike but can't find strength. *Must be dehydrated*. I go into a bodega,[1] buy water, and chug.

I vomit. I don't need to look down to know what I'll find. Familiarity breeds calm. I lock up my bike and call 911. I eject another puddle before passing out in my own blood. *An ordinary inconvenience.*

---

1. If you aren't a New Yorker, a "bodega" is where you buy Pringles from a Yemeni teenager while a cat watches.

I get blood transfusions for the third time. They don't save me. I'm saved by thinking the thought, notions simmering from my first solitary sip: *I'm an alcoholic.*

I quit drinking.

Big deal. I've done this dozens of times.

This time—on September 1, 2015—it sticks. I haven't had a drink since. Part of me is still surprised.

There are stages of change. It takes years to create a problem, more to realize it, more to make a plan, and more to take action.

With no guidance, routines go unaltered. I power through, rejecting alcohol until it's muscle memory.

Knowing you're an addict and identifying as one are different things. I don't tell anyone. People ask why I'm not drinking. "Stomach problems."

Life revolves around alcohol the same way the Lions revolve around Calvin. We demand this powerful thing make us who we deserve to be. We don't need to do the work. Calvin would score. The buzz would insulate me from me.

There's a difference between sobriety and recovery. That delta is why good teams don't always win.

2015 REGULAR SEASON

Detroit has a decent coach, able defense, and—most importantly—prime Stafford and Calvin.

They start 0–5.

The 2014 season should be a stepping stone to greater success. Even sans Suh, Detroit possesses five of the NFL's top 100 players.[2] Talent doesn't stop a backslide into oblivion. A wild card loss will be this era's high point.

---

2. NFL players annually vote on the top 100 players. Glover Quin, Calvin, LB DeAndre Levy, Suh's replacement Haloti Ngata, and Golden Tate. Stafford's absence is the worst thing to happen to the Great Lakes since the *Edmund Fitzgerald* sank.

WEEK 4: OCTOBER 5, 2015. DETROIT LIONS (0-3) V SEATTLE SEAHAWKS (1-2). CENTURYLINK FIELD, SEATTLE, WA.

One last chance to hop out of the grave.

Game on the line. Matthew's playing lights out. The ball moves and the clock ticks. Efficient operations ensure Seattle won't have a chance to answer.

Fourth Quarter, 1:51

Calvin gets the ball and sprints toward the pylon. Defenders converge, knocking the ball loose.

Fumble!

The ball tumbles into the end zone. Only two Boolean outcomes are in play. Either Detroit will recover for victory or Seattle will snag it, preserving theirs.

Mathematical laws are violated. Neither outcome happens. A Seattle defender approaches, batting the ball out of bounds for a Seahawk touchback. It's an illegal play, done directly in front of the official. Refs screwing us again puts Lions fans in the uncomfortable position of receiving consolations from conquerors. Others can't even feel good about beating us.

WEEK 10: NOVEMBER 15, 2015. DETROIT LIONS (1-7) V GREEN BAY PACKERS (6-2). LAMBEAU FIELD, GREEN BAY, WI.

Chris, a congregant of the Turkey's Nest, promises he's telling the truth. His serious tone makes me suspect he's getting married, having a kid, or achieving some comedy milestone.

"Calvin's retiring."

Megatron has good years ahead of him, but this franchise exhausts its foundations. The great one's blood, sweat, and tears are just a finger in the flooding dyke. The jig is up once the GOATs realize the arrangement.

We could build around these assets but we can't. They're too wonderful; we're too infatuated. Fifteen years pass but nothing changes. Calvin leaves for the same reasons Barry did.

Super Bowl champions rarely center around supernova wide receivers. Besides Jerry Rice—who excelled in a specific scheme—few top receivers take home the ultimate prize. Supreme talents imbalance an 11-person offense. It's no different from liking alcohol so much you can't have it at all.

I brace myself for premature farewells to another iconoclast. A 1–7 start extinguishes expectations, but the 0.00% ABV in my bloodstream makes emotions accessible. Preparing for departure makes love bypass impending grief.

A lifelong winless streak in Lambeau makes Green Bay games feel like visiting a loved one in hospice.

Fourth Quarter, 2:00; Lions 12, Packers 10

The Lions play their best but kicking miscues keep Green Bay in it. A huge Golden Tate play should be the clincher, but we miss our second extra point of the afternoon. Instead of a nine-point safe haven, Aaron Rodgers is in a one-score game against a team he "owns."[3]

Omens amount. A fumble recovery is overturned and Rodgers throws a score. The two-point conversion attempt would tie the game but gets knocked out of Davante Adams's hands.

Recovering the onside kick will end the 24-game Lambeau losing streak. The ball bounces off Calvin's shoulder pads into Packer hands. A loss has never been this expertly crafted.

Green Bay lines up for the winner. Jason Jones, a lengthy lineman, perfectly times his jump. The ball strikes his hand, tumbling to the formerly feared tundra. The Lions are 2–7 *but won at Lambeau.* Diminished expectations lower happiness's barriers of entry.

---

3. Apologies to the Bears for taking their identity.

Two more wins follow, including a Thanksgiving thrashing. Calvin Johnson scores three times, headlined by a twisting fade achieving a level of aesthetic beauty rivaling Diego Rivera's industry murals.[4]

WEEK 13: DECEMBER 3, 2015.
GREEN BAY PACKERS (7-4) V DETROIT (4-7).
FORD FIELD, DETROIT, MI.

Another good outcome against Green Bay saves the season. Matt's white-hot, burying them in a 20–0 hole, but they play perfectly, cutting the deficit to 2 as the hourglass empties.

Fourth Quarter, 0:06; Lions 23, Packers 21

We snuff out a lateral, suffocating the last gasp. Rodgers is gently tossed to the ground, preserving the win . . . *Flag!*

A Lions defender is erroneously called for a face mask against precious Aaron. The referee's obvious mistake grants Green Bay an untimed down.

We know what happens next. Aaron Rodgers converts a game-winning Hail Mary. It's the defining play of his career, shown ad nauseum to illustrate his greatness. The wrongly called penalty is never mentioned. That's how propaganda works. We exist to prop up the real heroes: unlovable anti-vaxxers.

* * *

Aunt Jackie's dying. Banjo Bob refuses to visit her deathbed.

I force my father into the room to face the last link to family trauma. It's not about my emotions but him acknowledging his.

---

4. It is not lost on me that both great works contain hidden frustrations with Ford Family managerial practices.

I put my arm around his shoulder and drag him to his sister. He brings a pair of novelty-sized crustacean claws and puts them on the dying woman.

"Why are you so crabby?"

She dies.

Banjo Bob wastes his inheritance on leather and banjos. I beg him to consider the future but tchotchkes are the only thing on his horizon.[5]

"You don't have any money. You should plan for the future."

He spends $5,000 on a buffalo skull.

"You don't have a safety net."

He spends $10,000 on a buffalo pelt. The saying is true. Native Americans use every part of the buffalo. They sell each part to a Polish dipshit.

"You have no money left."

He takes out a bank loan to purchase a banjo made of gold.

The Lions aren't the only ones whose existence props up others.

MARCH 6, 2016

Calvin Johnson retires, citing nagging injuries and a losing culture. The man went to a winless program and used otherworldly gifts to nudge his employer toward relevance.

The cycle of failure never changes. Even the unique dynamic of a legendary player exiting early is frustratingly familiar.

The only notable change is going an entire season without drinking. Teetotaling dovetails with a particularly painful season, but these emotions aren't a reason to drink. They're felt.

Cowardly, I deflect inquiries by embellishing "stomach problems." Honestly answering the question "Why aren't you drinking?" brings up my truth. Answering, "I don't drink because I throw up blood," stops follow-up questions but spark my own.

Am I an addict? Can I use any substance? Did my family impact me?

---

5. Tchotchkes: a Yiddish word meaning cheap bullshit.

Calvin becomes my favorite player by retiring. The bravest thing one can do is move forward and do it for themself.

Grizzled old addicts, having beat Goliath to maintain light in their eyes, love giving advice like, "Not drinking will improve your life." This is true but too granular. The first fact requiring acceptance is that not drinking will *change* your life.

I become the man booze boxed out. It isn't all easy. A relationship ends but is offset by things generally going my way.[6]

I fly to Detroit on my mother's birthday to surprise her. She stifles tears and drives us to training camp. We mingle with undrafted free agents in what she calls, "the best birthday I ever had." What's given to me by my father is regifted to my mother. She becomes a fan.

WEEK 1: SEPTEMBER 11, 2016.
DETROIT LIONS (0-0) V INDIANAPOLIS COLTS (0-0).
LUCAS OIL STADIUM, INDIANAPOLIS, IN.

Drinking is submission. Programmed concepts of fun are accepted, making getting shit-faced the only path to joy. Pinpointing what sober me enjoys, I dedicate free time to pickup basketball.

Friends organize a dry birthday for my thirtieth: a three-on-three basketball tournament complete with anthem, uniforms, and black-tie draft. It's a staggering amount of energy channeled toward me. What eventually develops into The Big Walkowski, a nonprofit and pillar of the NYC social calendar, starts as simple peer support. A group of comedian buddies become my community.

I fly to Indianapolis. The NFL's most underwhelming team starts the season in my least favorite state. I'll be damned if I miss it. Every expert

---

6. The day after a breakup, I attend a Nets game and win an all-expenses-paid trip to Barbados. They show me on the jumbotron and ask, "Joel, you're going to Barbados. How does it feel?" My answer: "Confused and kind of alone." I expect the Nets to be mad but they're glad not to be the saddest thing in the building for once.

picks the Lions to finish last, but 2016 is about realizing miracles come after loss. We are counted out without Calvin. This is when Stafford shines.

Banjo Bob picks me up at the airport. He's older, weaker, but unchanged—handing me a luchador mask and nose-hair trimmers. Road games can be harrowing, but Colts fans are laid back and welcoming. Like Moses playing fullback, Bob's cigarette cloud clears a path through throngs to Lucas Oil Stadium. I hold my father's hand as a bit, but no one laughs. We're home.

Stafford opens with a torrent of scores: 7–0, 14–0, 21–0!

The Colts make it close. Stafford and Indianapolis quarterback Andrew Luck put on a second-half master class, vacillating between deep shots and checkdowns. A late-game Stafford dart puts us up, but a missed extra point makes our 34–28 lead vulnerable.

Fourth Quarter, 0:37; Colts 35, Lions 34

Luck throws a likely winner. The bitter loss is simply more nostalgia for me and the old man.

The stadium blares air-raid sound effects as Detroit takes the field. It's accurate. The aerial attack is on. Stafford completes three throws in rapid succession, capping the flurry by lacing a beam to Marvin Jones Jr.

Detroit lines up for the winner. Tensions from the day and year and life are released by grabbing Bob in a vise-grip hug. I squeeze his lungs worse than any cigarette.

I avert my eyes, knowing the kick will be with me forever whether I see it or not. I kiss my father's head and watch the last play of a football game like it's the bravest thing ever done.

It swishes through the uprights, silencing the air raid. Detroit wins.

Walking back to the car Banjo Bob is exhausted, pausing every few blocks for another life-giving cigarette. At each stop he is older, frailer. Mortality's right there, but I can't be upset when declining conditions provide more chances to replay a perfect day.

Three straight losses follow, affirming the team's low reputation.

General manager Martin Mayhew has been relieved of duties. Mayhew made an awful team pretty good but is blamed for bungling Suh's departure.

In his place steps Bob Quinn, a yes-man from Bill Belichick's Patriots. Bill's genius is exemplified by the fact that no one from his regime ever succeeds outside of the organization. These less-than-esteemed ranks eventually include Quinn, a corporate drone known for poor communication and carrying around a baseball bat.

Quinn's infatuation with New England defensive coordinator Matt Patricia is an open secret. Looking like Santa Claus spawned with a pile of garbage, Patricia wears a pencil behind his ear to write on laminated play sheets. He's irresistible.

Caldwell's beloved, but the hot seat beckons. He'll be fired if the Lions lose their next game. The offense boat races Philadelphia for a 21–3 halftime lead.

Fourth Quarter, 2:41; Philadelphia 23, Detroit 21

A second-half collapse leaves Philly a conversion away from victory.

Darius "Big Play" Slay slices into the backfield, jarring the ball loose. The recovery sets up a chip shot field goal for the lead. The Eagles try answering, but Slay runs under a deep shot securing the ball, the win, and Caldwell's job. Slay's a rare talent but not everyone will see it this way.

Another comeback victory is keyed by one of Matthew's greatest throws. Tantalizing what-if Aaron Donald drags Matthew to the ground. From a sliver of back foot, Matt's loft leads his receiver into the slightest possible window for a stunning score, keying another miraculous comeback.

There have been better, more talented Lions teams, but this iteration is resilient and lovable, a vehicle of joy.

Detroit lacks talent to truly contend, but that's secondary to Matthew fulfilling his potential. The gunslinging mentality becomes an asset, allowing him to play free in stressful situations. Stafford steals another win over Washington, making the fan base the romantic interest in a superhero film. We love this entity a little bit more each time they save us.

The repeated catharsis of unexpected wins is a simple, happy thing securing Matt's place in Detroit's heart. Sabermetrics easily poke holes in our strong record, proving the unsustainability of our approach, but that's the fun part.

WEEK 9: NOVEMBER 6, 2016.
DETROIT LIONS (4-4) v MINNESOTA VIKINGS (5-2).
U.S. BANK STADIUM, MINNEAPOLIS, MN.

Fourth Quarter, 0:23; Vikings 16, Lions 13; No Timeouts

The Lions nudge out front but our exhausted defense gives up a late field goal. Matthew's greatest challenge barely even registers. He does what he has to, forcing overtime. Tired teams trade dillydallied possessions until our offense clicks, working the ball into Viking territory.

Third and 8. Minnesota expects a run designed to shorten the game-winning kick. Matty deals instead, finding Tate streaking toward the sideline. Momentum will surely carry Tate out of bounds, but Tate stops on a dime as a Viking defender shoots past. Safety Harrison Smith rushes over but gets sent to the ground with a brutal slam. Tate sprints toward the end zone, literally front flipping over the final defender to win in the most marvelous way imaginable.

WEEK 12: NOVEMBER 24, 2016.
MINNESOTA VIKINGS (6-4) v DETROIT LIONS (6-4).
FORD FIELD, DETROIT, MI.

Divorced parents come together for the holiday. The Lions' relevance reunites us for a family outing like a knockoff of Disney's *Angels in the Outfield*.

A buoyant Ford Field mood amplifies the holiday's familial aspects. We bound through security, a couple custom T-shirts shy of a true family reunion.

Panic punctures the pleasant mood as Banjo Bob announces, "I've lost my car keys." We search high and low. Steps are retraced, security interrogated, and ushers harangued. Nothing. *Where are the keys?* Thanksgiving is ruined, certain to be spent with elderly parents and a locksmith.

Rule #1: Never leave early! Compartmentalizing the problem, I settle into my seat for the game.

Aretha Franklin, the highest rung on the ladder of Detroit royalty, prepares to sing the national anthem. We dutifully stand and remove our hats.

Jangle!

Banjo Bob's keys fall from under his hat and onto the floor. It's a hoarder's key ring weighing several kilograms *that he doesn't notice resting atop his bald head.*

Aretha gives a rousing performance, one remembered as her last great public act. I laugh through the entirety, pissing off more people with my anthem conduct than Colin Kaepernick.

Stafford has the ball late and does just enough to set up a game-tying field goal.

Sam Bradford, a Viking quarterback who previously stayed in college to avoid playing for Detroit, tries answering. Slay jumps the throw and reels it in. Detroit wins it with a kick at the buzzer, sending the city into bacchanal. Aretha sings, Lions win, but no amount of wonderful competes with Bob being a doofus.

More stirring comebacks produce a 9–4 record. Caldwell, on the hot seat four weeks into the season, is now frontrunner for Coach of the Year.

In Chicago, clock strikes midnight on Cinderella. Matty bangs his hand against a defensive lineman. Our once-injury-plagued, chipmunk-faced youngster has evolved into an iron man of the highest order. He returns to the game. Unable to throw, he uses his legs, bulling through the defense for the winner. Arm is compromised but leadership isn't.

WEEK 17: JANUARY 1, 2017.
GREEN BAY PACKERS (9-6) v DETROIT LIONS (9-6).
FORD FIELD, DETROIT, MI.

Matthew struggles to throw, the team drops two straight, but it's impossible to be anything but thrilled. Detroit hosts Green Bay for the division title.

The Packers roll into town on a five-game winning streak while the Lions are either the league's worst good team or best bad team.

Detroit has seven comeback victories. Instead of expecting more, why not reframe the season and maintain gratitude? We leave stadiums arm in arm with our clan, cherishing moments. No banner is needed to tell us we won.

We lose but outcome is secondary. The metric is not record but moments. The game is our love language. Super Bowl wins echo in time but so does the sound of keys falling from beneath my dad's hat, interrupting Aretha.

The Lions lose a one-sided wild card game at Seattle. It's absolutely thrilling.

Front-running teams bear the weight of expectations. I put this weight on myself. It's the impulse that makes me an addict. Being creative, the Lions winning—none of it guarantees salvation.

Comparing myself to Stafford may seem to be a forced literary device, but it's an authentic distillation of how I come of age. Pushing my chips to the center of the table for anything I do, forever a gunslinging quarterback. The beauty of 2016 is Matthew leading the team as only he could. Anything seems possible.

Intelligence catches up to arm talent as Matthew fulfills the potential carried throughout his career. Lions decision-makers ink Stafford to a record contract but it's not a flex. Routes to improvement are limited by cap space. Quinn whiffs on nearly every draft selection, renewing the unfair assignment: Matthew must drag a terrible roster to wins.

2017

Caldwell is the franchise's best coach since the 1960s but must secure his job each week. Quinn's infatuation with Matt Patricia makes the regime look for any excuse to throw a good coach onto the scrap heap. Bob Quinn dates someone out of his league while desperately seeking reasons to break up.

The team's only meaningful addition is increased tension on the guillotine over Caldwell's head. Stafford wins the opener by repeatedly connecting with lightly regarded rookie Kenny Golladay. There's nothing more optimistic than an unheralded newcomer's shining debut. A single game sparks visions of gold jackets.

The Lions play the Giants on Monday night and I'm stuck working a production job. The director asks me to stay while Banjo Bob's career advice of "take the money and run" echoes through my ears. Careers aren't a network of skill and relationships. They're a scam pulled on someone silly enough to trust us.

I refuse to stay late. I see the Lions and lose my job because my life is so deeply aligned with my principles.[7]

Stafford is as perfect as the warm September night. The Giants close the gap but we answer. Rookie return man Jamal Agnew's strategic spin opens an express lane to victory. Eminem blares on the way home. Life is perfect.

The next game is the one this book opens on—my first official act as godfather. Existence dictates that you'll lose. Not dwelling on it is learning you're worthy, even after failure. Life isn't about winning but about refusing to be the things that happen to us. There's a thin line between "mental illness" and "going through some shit." This attitude is the border. I introduce Julion to the Lions so he can someday drag himself off the mat.

This little boy has the same little brain I had, the same need for a guide. If I'd been drinking, I'd have been hungover at the funeral and unable to be as present with him. Our relationship sprouts from temperance and the presence that comes with it. I'm there to teach him. How to exercise, how to feel, how to lose.

There's a sliver of time where Golden Tate secures a 3–0 start. The perfect day doesn't occur but it's better that way. We finish 9–7, missing the playoffs by razor-thin margins. The bad finish starts a Rube Goldberg machine of shitty events for the team but impactful ones for us. The loss is an ideal beginning.

That's how Detroit deals. It's not an inborn trait but a rational way of dealing with the hand we're dealt.

---

7. Also, I crash the production's art truck two times.

WEEK 10: NOVEMBER 12, 2017.
CLEVELAND BROWNS (0-8) v DETROIT LIONS (4-4).
FORD FIELD, DETROIT, MI.

The 2017 Browns will join the 2008 Lions as the only teams to go 0–16.

We play our past, empathetically giving Cleveland a lead they're simply too bad to uphold. At the first whiff of losing, Stafford sniffs salts and rips off 21 consecutive points to win.

This game's healing. The incompetent, poorly run team in Ford Field? For once they're the visitors. It's impossible not to savor how far we've come . . .

. . . but then why is Caldwell not good enough?

WEEK 16: DECEMBER 24, 2017.
DETROIT LIONS (8-6) v CINCINNATI BENGALS (5-9).
PAUL BROWN STADIUM, CINCINNATI, OH.

I've made it as a comedian. At least in the sense that Triple-A baseball players with a few big league at-bats have made it to the majors. I spend a month touring, playing a different city each night. Banjo Bob follows me around for much of it. Each Sunday, we sit at sports bars, bonding over endless seltzers.

The team collapses but his only response is, "I like Matthew."

Banjo Bob has exclusively witnessed failure but never says a negative word.[8] How does one stay happy while losing forever? Do they learn to enjoy losses or simply experience so much sadness they grow immune?

The comedy marathon closes in Orlando. Week 16, played at 1 PM on Christmas Eve in Cincinnati, is a must win. I need to get back to my life—which means supporting the team.

---

8. Or anything really. This is also the man who excused his mom for being a child molester by saying, "She gave away full-size candy bars at Halloween." That's also a red flag, my man!

I spend days studying the map. It's possible. Not logical or advisable but possible. I wrap up my 8 PM Orlando show on December 23 and sprint to my car.

I start driving. I swallow coffee. I drive for 16 hours straight. My best performance as a fan puts me in Paul Brown Stadium with a half hour to spare. I have not slept or eaten, but the prospect of consecutive playoff appearances is enough.

There are positives in my life. I am not in the process of becoming. I'm me. I sit in the stands alone, radiating positivity toward the team. We can both change, Lions.

We have a chance to bury the Bengals. With his job on the line, Caldwell elects to punt. *Why won't the architect of an effective offense simply trust the offense?* wonders the alcoholic who took seven years to quit booze after it nearly killed him.

The game slips away. The decision that cost us a playoff game in 2015 costs us a spot in 2017. The resilient team that spent two years playing for their coach's job has no reserves of emotional energy. The Bengals gouge us with long runs, ending our season on Christmas.

Once again, it's perfect. The Lions helped me love my dad. From the Lions? From my father? Who cares what I receive in return? True love is unconditional.

A blizzard rolls in. A four-hour drive back to Detroit takes twelve. I should be cozy by a fireplace but I'm too much of a fan. Loved ones let us down on the holidays. Who says the loved ones can't be a football team?

Jim Caldwell is unceremoniously fired on New Year's Day. The fan base endures Mornhinweg's motorcycle and Ross's cowardice begging for a "halfway-decent coach." With Caldwell in place, decision-makers decide what we longed for is no longer enough.

Caldwell never had a chance. Quinn's fixation on Patricia would never be swayed by something as feeble as results.

FEBRUARY 4, 2018. SUPER BOWL LII. PHILADELPHIA EAGLES (13-3) V NEW ENGLAND PATRIOTS (13-3). U.S. BANK STADIUM, MINNEAPOLIS, MN.

Patricia's defense gives up 41 points to a backup quarterback, costing the New England team the Super Bowl.

It's the year's most watched broadcast but apparently no Lions decision-makers tune in.

FEBRUARY 5, 2018

The dark ages are about to return. For both of us.

Matt Patricia is hired as head coach.

GAME 14

VOLDEMORT RETURNS

• 2018–2020 •

The Worst It's Ever Been . . . Again

2018	2019	2020
6-10	3-12-1	5-11

Bob Quinn beams, completely fulfilled. "I wanted to find a leader that could take us to the next level. I'm confident that we've found that in Matt Patricia."

Only 32 individuals run NFL teams. It's a harder job to get than senator. Quinn dedicates this rarefied opportunity to Patricia. Fixating on one thing, placing it on a pedestal, arranging his enterprise around it. It ruins him.

Patricia squeezes into a suit, emphasizing his rocket science background, carefully acting the part of football wunderkind. Media accepts the narrative, positioning him as the man who'll take us to the promised land, praising his character.[1]

1. One article fawns over Patricia for, uh, having a job in high school?

Patricia will tear down anything that doesn't submit. Ambitions aren't oriented around leadership. They revolve around his authority. "I plan to be involved in all aspects of the team," he ominously growls.

Charismatic leadership is a tenet of organizational behavior exemplified by CEOs rallying staff around common goals during crises. This practice serves the collective by ushering in dynamic collaboration. It's not unlike the traits needed to successfully host a comedy show. Disparate individuals become an audience, achieving the shared ambition of enjoyable nights out.

Great hosts are different from great comedians. Thriving as a host requires considering others and a broader goal. What looks simple is harder than headlining.

Authority is given, not commanded. Patricia and Quinn attempt to import Bill Belichick's Patriots culture without incrementally building it. Actions don't consider stakeholders. They only want to headline.

Matt Patricia's introduction as head coach is already marked with red flags when disputed charges of sexual assault dating back to his college days resurface. In 2018, *Detroit News* writer Robert Snell unearths a 1996 aggravated sexual assault charge filed against Patricia while in college. Twenty-two years earlier, a grand jury issued an indictment for aggravated sexual assault—though as Judge Wachter once famously said, "a grand jury could indict a ham sandwich." However, the case never went to trial because the alleged victim refused to testify, concerned about the trial's emotional toll.

Vehement denials are issued. Sticking by the hire, when approached by the *Detroit News* for a comment, the team's president issues a statement saying "everything learned would have in no way changed our decision." Meanwhile Patricia's attorney calls the alleged victim a liar in the local paper, insinuating the charges were brought for "unspecified personal reasons." It's a thrilling start to a new regime.

★ ★ ★

I'm happy. This doesn't come from the highest of highs but pursuing stability. It's normal to believe yourself to be normal. I observe other families painstakingly crafting decisions and moving as a unit and channel these learnings toward my father.

Despite his kindness, his life does not consider others. There's no collaboration or community. I concentrate on what I'm building. The relationships, the people, the activities. Pied Piper energy flows through all threads of my life, weaving them into a beautiful tapestry.

It's taken a lifetime to learn that I deserve more. The current iteration of me isn't my destination. Like the team that fires Caldwell, I decide it's time to level up. Like the team that hires Patricia, I take the wrong route.

Seven years without Adderall allows me to build a life, maintain a healthy relationship, fix my self-image, and live out a number of fantasies rivaling George Plimpton or a recovering sex addict.

I know I'm better off without it. But it gets closer, gaining prominence in my circle. My eyes drift up on the subway, gazing past other straphangers at advertisements for shady start-ups offering medical-grade speed. An extended reunion with my most beloved mistress is only a phone call and half-hour appointment away. I deny the urge but it returns with increased frequency. I deny, deny, deny but it only takes one fuckup to make forever mistakes.

I love my beautiful little life, but when life gets hard I wonder if I wouldn't love speed a bit more.

Patricia makes his presence known at training camp—riding around on an ATV and forcing players to run a homemade hill.[2] It's reasonable to request players be conditioned, but personal accountability is undermined by Patricia's refusal to walk . . . anywhere.

Key young pieces tumble down the depth chart in favor of career journeymen from New England. Ability? Draft status? Those are secondary to being one of Patricia's guys. Instead of building the future, the franchise repurposes Patricia's past.

---

2. It's worth noting that the Lions campus is not particularly large. The only excuse for an ATV is extreme laziness.

WEEK 1: SEPTEMBER 10, 2018. NEW YORK JETS (0-0) V DETROIT LIONS (0-0). FORD FIELD, DETROIT, MI.

Banjo Bob visits New York. He puffs cigs on the sidelines of the comedian basketball tournament, whispering, "You guys are hot shit."

Bob continues handing out switchblades. Like a lot. Basketball players, baristas, strangers on the street. Everyone gets a knife. Stressing over his finances, I compute the net switchblade expense and try uncovering the utility he sees.

"Why are you giving everyone a knife?"

"Everyone deserves a good knife."

The Patricia era kicks off. We watch together at the Turkey's Nest, worlds connected by him bringing a banjo to play "Gridiron Heroes."

It's immediately time to pluck. Heart of the team Quandre Diggs jumps a pass on the first play, returning it for a score. The Turkey's Nest erupts in song and shitty bluegrass.

We crash. New York finds holes in Patricia's scheme. The defense must adjust but refuses for three years. The Jets offense, a subpar unit featuring a quarterback in his first start, puts up 38 points. Stafford looks hopeless. No worries. Genius is at work.

It's stunning. It's shocking but it happens. Detroit outplays the mighty Patriots as Patricia's encyclopedic obsession makes him look like a genius this once.

It feels like a new era has begun. It hasn't. The team drew a lucky dance partner with the world watching.

The team steadily declines each week.[3] Patricia resorts to harsh discipline and ham-handed attempts at replicating the Patriot Way. He's a

---

3. This downturn begins with a loss to Dallas in which Cowboys star Michael Bennett says he holds Matthew Stafford responsible for the Kennedy assassination since he's a Dallas native.

principal brought in to boost test scores resorting to beating kids at the first sign of struggle.

Holding star players accountable is a Patriot Way cornerstone. Patricia clumsily attempts this with Darius "Big Play" Slay, one of the league's best cornerbacks. Gaining a defensive mind at the peak of his career should have boosted Slay's career. Patricia doesn't see it that way. Slay must be torn down.

Patricia tells Slay he isn't very good; that his hard-earned status isn't warranted. Slay, fresh off private practices with other elite CBs, is publicly told he doesn't deserve the invite by his own coach.

Humiliation rituals with no clear motivation continue. Film sessions project Slay's worst plays on loop before the entire team. If this weren't enough, Patricia responds to Slay posting a picture of a friendly rival on social media by publicly admonishing, "stop sucking the man's d***."

Slay recounts the exchange as "disrespectful."

Patricia calls it "constructive and satisfactory."

Trust is gained in drops and lost in gallons. Within a matter of months, Patricia loses the locker room he spent a lifetime striving to govern.

Disrespect isn't reserved for Slay or even players. Patricia's authoritarian approach extends to all.

OCTOBER 16, 2018

Patricia waddles in late to a press conference. A reporter asks a straightforward question. Rather than answer, Patricia demands they "respect the process and sit up straight." It's worth pointing out that the optic-obsessed but slovenly Patricia has ballooned to such gargantuan proportions that he only wears black—resembling the bag of trash he coaches like. Appearances matter. Just not his.

Patricia maintains golden-boy status for his long-term plan while demonstrating short-term thinking.[4] A couple wins shift the team into

4. Tucking a pencil behind one's ear and going as Patricia for Halloween is a very popular costume in Detroit circa 2018.

win-now mode, sparking a trade for DT "Snacks" Harrison. A few losses later see Golden Tate unceremoniously shipped out of town. Apart from inconsistency of vision, Tate's departure eliminates timing throws from the offense. Matt drops back, waiting for receivers that never break open, taking more sacks than an Idaho potato bandit!

Logic dictates teams under new management will improve over the season. This does not happen. The divide between coach and team is not just psychological but physiological. NFL teams normally reserve easy practices for Fridays. This allows a 36-hour recovery window, ensuring the team is rested come kickoff.

Patricia schedules his hardest practices on Fridays. This insistence sparks fatigue and the poor tackling that accompanies it. Players who critique his methods are threatened with release. He doesn't want the best team. He wants obedience.

Achievers have a *why* motivation inspiring drive and pulling one from bed each morning. Personal motivations are especially ingrained in football players pursuing a tumultuous field requiring endless dedication. Patricia aims to replace his team's deeply held, intrinsic beliefs with "because I said so."

Patricia's billed as a defensive tactician but repeatedly makes Bears quarterback Mitchell Trubisky, a bust remembered for being picked over Patrick Mahomes, look like a world beater. Patricia makes Trubisky look so good it's likely he duplicitously works as his agent. The Bears throttle Detroit on Thanksgiving. Patricia ruins the holiday like a red-faced uncle bringing up QAnon.

The season swirls down the drain. The happy saunter to Turkey's Nest becomes a joyless trudge but decisions have been made. This is what I enjoy, I guess.

Knowing the team will not make me happy makes me proactive. I start renting a gym and hosting pickup basketball games on Sunday evenings. Competition and endorphins wash away pangs of tough losses, teaching an invaluable lesson: If defeat is inevitable, proactively plan bouncing back.

2019

A puzzling offseason sees *Quinntricia* sign every Patriot in free agency. They do their damnedest to turn Detroit into Boston, stopping just shy of boarding merchant ships to dump tea into our river.

The team even trades for Patriot star tight end Rob Gronkowski. Of course, the NFL's marquee star has no interest in joining a permanent rebuild. Gronk rebukes the trade in a fashion befitting the Lions by threatening to retire.

Eric Ebron's departure makes the front office desperate for a tight end. Fixating on one position makes Detroit waste the eighth overall pick on T.J. Hockenson. He's a fine player but efforts to keep pace with the offensive revolution that turned a blocking-centric position into a receiving threat miss the point. The tight end's positional effectiveness isn't determined by individual players so much as how it's wielded in modern offenses.

The season kicks off in disheartening fashion, with the Lions blowing a 17–0 lead to subpar Arizona that results in a tie. A common adage decrees that "not losing feels a lot like winning." As someone intimately familiar with losing, let me just say this is wrong.

A Week 2 win blooms as Frank Ragnow, foundational offensive lineman, excels at his natural position of center, keying a tide-turning touchdown run with a devastating block. Darius Slay parks under a Phillip Rivers moonball, once again cementing a win with phenomenal ball hawking. Just don't call him elite.

I travel to Philadelphia to support my toothless but undefeated Lions. I figure Eagles fans—infamous for booing Santa or hurling snowballs at injured players—will accept Detroit's lovable loser designation. Wrong. I spend my afternoon politely declining fistfights.

The Eagles play poorly and their fans are miserable. The team plays better, causing fans to become even more miserable. Their conduct strikes me, *the author of this friggin book*, as unhealthy. Detroit pulls away, and Philly fans embody the surliness they're desperate to reside in.

WEEK 4: SEPTEMBER 29, 2019. KANSAS CITY CHIEFS (3-0) v DETROIT LIONS (2-0-1). FORD FIELD, DETROIT, MI

WEEK 6: OCTOBER 14, 2019. DETROIT LIONS (2-1-1) v GREEN BAY PACKERS (4-1). LAMBEAU FIELD, GREEN BAY, WI.

The hot start boosts Patricia's reputation, pressurizing the next few weeks, as a playoff atmosphere greets Pat Mahomes at Ford Field.

Detroit goes into the half tied with the league's best team. The Chiefs open the second half with a stunning gaffe, fumbling the kickoff for a Detroit recovery.

A new, stable future is there for the taking but we collapse. Still, we won't give up.

A turnover near the goal line inspires the defense. We steal possession from Kansas City. We're so close to icing it. Kerryon Johnson, a likable back, stalls going into the end zone. The play is dead and the ball comes loose as players mill about, making postgame dinner plans. A Chiefs defender gathers up the rock and ambles 100 yards to our end zone. It's a tiresome, theatrical ruse but refs play along, awarding an undeserved score to Kansas City.

The Lions battle back, fulfilling the roster's potential before ultimately succumbing. The best version of us cannot overcome who we are.

Another chance at validation awaits in Lambeau—a direct reprisal of the previous week's letdown.

The Lions have the game in a choke hold, stopping Rodgers on a key third down. *Flag!* A shaky call bails out Green Bay. This mistake isn't a conspiracy. It's human error that occurs four more times in this game.

Fourth Quarter, 10:16; Lions 22, Packers 13

A game-sealing Rodgers sack is reversed on an erroneous hands-to-the-face penalty against Trey Flowers—his first infraction of this kind at the high school, collegiate, or professional levels.

Fourth Quarter, 1:45; Lions 22, Packers 20

The Lions stop Green Bay on third down. *Flag!* Another erroneous hands-to-the-face penalty is called against Trey Flowers. The Lions have experienced plenty of bad luck. This is match fixing.

Detroit spends generations struggling to be capable while the NFL puts their thumb on the scale, ensuring eternal suffering.

The weight of bad breaks submarines our once plucky little outfit. The promising 2–0–1 start takes a Dante-esque route, reaching fiery nadirs of dysfunction. Dispiriting defeats remove remaining bloom from Matt Patricia's rose, exposing him as one of the worst coaches to ever grace NFL ranks.

The losing streak starts. Team captain Quandre Diggs speaks up with constructive criticism. Practices are too physical, recovery times are too limited, the team can't compete against opponents *and these demands*.

Rather than adjust or listen, Detroit ships Diggs to Seattle for a measly fifth-round pick. Diggs serves as Seattle's captain, excels individually, and helps establish culture. Detroit finishes 3–12–1.

The disappointing season finally ends. Quinn and Patricia search for someone to blame. Darius Slay, repeatedly deemed not good enough, is traded to Philadelphia. He'll make three Pro Bowls and help the Eagles reach two Super Bowls.

Patricia inherited a talented roster and strong locker room culture. Two years into his tenure, his ego is all that remains.

Urges can be combated. Delay, escape, avoid, accept, deny, substitute, distract. Many methods must exist. An addict only needs one falter to spiral.

★ ★ ★

I have a fleeting thought of low self-worth on the subway. A passing notion, indicative of the moment and nothing more. Once again my eyes wander up to advertisements for fast, legal speed. I tell myself I'm just looking but my mind memorizes the phone number.

Addicts are taught to name our urges. Upon entering recovery I'll learn to call mine "the Whiner." He won't leave me alone in late 2019, crying for speed at all hours. The rational part of me knows this isn't a good idea, but he's damn loud and fucking persistent.

I'm obedient. It only takes a moment. Like trading Layne, an instant of bad decision-making locks down years of losing.

I make an "appointment" with the "doctor." Patricia's shortcomings make me hate the Lions for throwing away stability and Jim Caldwell. I despise them for this but do the exact same.

The doctor's either too shy or ashamed to make eye contact. I get my fix in 20 minutes, delivered with an urgency that ought to be reserved for real medicine.

The Whiner and I conduct extended negotiations. I tell myself I've changed, that there are boundaries. Speed is a serious substance and can only be wielded in an occasional, intentional fashion.

Within 30 seconds of receipt, the first pill's in my mouth. Before it finishes sliding down my gullet, I'm reaching for the second. The Whiner's in charge and this shit rules. Pills forever.

Self-equilibrium required decades of effort but now feels worthless. Doing okay feels genuinely bad compared to speed's electrified faux euphoria. Submitting to the authoritarian regime, I do as it says. Matt Patricia is hired to run my interior life.

COVID hits. The world takes a scary downturn that registers as convenient. Locked inside with a battalion of pills and surplus of downtime? *How awful . . .*

I tell the Whiner, "There's no point taking Adderall during a global pandemic. Productivity doesn't exist right now." I pack up my car to leave New York, deliberately leaving the pills behind.

Resolution lasts 15 seconds before the Whiner starts his argument. Every addict has a world-class lawyer within them. I'm the jury and I fall for his pleas. I return to the apartment and pocket the pills. I tell myself there are rules but swallow one immediately, satiating the Whiner's observation that "rules shouldn't apply right now." I will be on pills 24/7 for the next eighteen months.

I like the pills more than life. I want to say that it's awful, that I regret debasing myself to be constantly strung out. I suppose that's true but my humanity is a distant second to being fucked up all the time.

I'm technically engaged but my true relationship status is married to pills. I don't tell my partner about the extent of my usage—luckily she doesn't notice. We stay with her parents and I perform manual labor to earn my keep. I load up a truck for the family's relocation, listening to the NFL draft while the Lions load up for their future.

The 2020 draft is rich with quarterback prospects. The third pick's ideally positioned for trade-down bounties, but Bob Quinn publicly declares his intention to stand pat, evaporating the market. There's finally urgency. Not to win but to save Patricia's and Quinn's jobs. Long-term prospects are less important than slightly improving the miserable present.

The hill the Lions choose to die on is loyalty to a coach boasting about his expertise while his squad repeatedly blows leads, essentially killing the franchise with ineffectual fascism. One scout suggests taking a quarterback and trading Stafford. He's laughed out of the room. Detroit selects a CB to replace Darius Slay, the star they chased off.

Life only has room for one value. For the Lions, it's Patricia. For me, it's Adderall. I multiply doses, using the pandemic excuse to ratchet up habits. Eighteen-hour shifts of eyeball-twitching concentration seek an outlet. With no comedy to fill my calendar, I pursue my MBA. What seems upstanding is just another excuse to use. I binge speed and LSD, getting straight A's on papers exclusively written about soil.

The Walkowskis isolate and accumulate. I evolve family traits by making my head my hoarder's den. Anything that occurs, and I mean *anything*—attention from my beloved dog, a sandwich, floating on a river in a tube—is barrier to accomplishing arbitrarily chosen tasks.

What I want is to overdose. I outwardly chase the end. I am selfish. I am bad. I don't identify as these traits, but pills provide this darkness. I have love and support but spit in its face to isolate myself with my drug(s) of choice.

My true partner is pills so everything else withers. I'll give everything to pills. I do.

I can't be vulnerable, only Midwestern.

"Are you okay?" people ask.

"I'm fine."

The only shot at redemption is an entirely new way of being.

Martha Firestone Ford steps aside as team owner, replaced by her daughter Sheila Ford Hamp. It's a familiar battle, unlearning familial ways of doing business just to have a chance.

Sheila knows the fight ahead. She's been team chairwoman, achieved academic and athletic excellence, and—most importantly—knows success is a process.

Quinn and Patricia keep their jobs, but Sheila makes it known that "major improvement" is necessary for continued employment. The doomed regime does their damnedest but desperation is rarely strategic or intelligent. They bring in more Patriots and sign Adrian Peterson even though the running back nicknamed "AD" is so old he ought to be called "BC."

WEEK 1: SEPTEMBER 13, 2020.
CHICAGO BEARS (0-0) V DETROIT LIONS (0-0).
FORD FIELD, DETROIT, MI.

The pandemic-throttled season kicks off in an empty Ford Field. Great care is given to accurate, piped-in crowd noise, but if audio engineers wanted realism they'd play choruses of "Fire Patricia."

Stafford builds a three-score lead and seemingly easy victory but bad omens pile up. A sack leads to a missed field goal, a prized LB gets ejected for demonstrating a maneuver to a ref,[5] and Patricia's scheme continues making Trubisky look unbeatable.

---

5. The ref asked, "Why did Jeffrey Toobin get fired?"

Matt's in the familiar position of keying wins himself. He drags the team into the Chicago red zone with one play to win it. Everyone in the building—cardboard cutouts included—knows he's making the next throw.

D'Andre Swift, a rookie with renowned pass-catching abilities, lets a perfect throw slip through his fingers. The brutal drop in a big moment encapsulates Stafford's Detroit tenure.

"Welcome to Detroit: an uphill battle on flat topography."

Against Atlanta, Matts put up three tight window throws in 29 seconds to claim victory. His situation is so shoddy he has no choice but to evolve. We claim him as a Detroit icon while wondering if he deserves better. Stafford brings his best regardless of circumstances while conducting himself with class.

Stafford is naturally reserved and relatively private.[6] The most widely known fact is that he's an upstanding family man. His difficult season is more treacherous behind the scenes. His wife Kelly suffers from a brain tumor. He carries his family as well as a city.

His magical right arm makes private tribulations public, humanizing our longtime hero. Stafford goes from golden boy to decent man, a far better lesson than Peyton Manning's birthright career. Stafford handling a taxing family situation while navigating a FUBAR-ed workplace resonates with rank-and-file Detroiters struggling to put out their fires.

Allegorical thinking is valuable during active addiction. I go all out at school despite suicidal ideations and a toxicology report rivaling Charlie Sheen's. I am Stafford once more. Spending my pandemic putting up points in a blowout.

Failure's not a crime, but Matt spending the back half of his prime serving Matt Patricia certainly feels like one. I come back to New York but my routine's locked down. The Turkey's Nest is closed and Sunday basketball is canceled. The era dovetails with new apexes of addiction, urges only pausing when the ball is kicked off.

---

6. Photos of him hoisting a keg while at Georgia are mindful and demure.

The Lions remain the only thing I stay sober for. Matthew's wonderful against Washington. The defense falters but Stafford's undeterred. It takes just three plays and 16 seconds to set up the winner. It's his last great performance as a Lion, but the only takeaway is that we don't deserve him.

Patricia operates like an addict, only considering his system built around bad habits. Any asset beyond this scope is discarded, extracting any ability to change or grow. Patricia's brought in to lift all boats but drains the swamp instead. The regime doesn't win arguments with logic or results but by surrounding themselves with yes-men.

WEEK 12: NOVEMBER 26, 2020. HOUSTON TEXANS (3-7) V DETROIT LIONS (4-6). FORD FIELD, DETROIT, MI.

A joyless Thanksgiving arrives. No moments like Johnnie Morton's feud with Jay Leno or Dan Orlovsky running out of the end zone allow us to stare up at the stars while lying in the gutter. Quinntricia blots out the sun.

Banjo Bob knows there is only pain in watching this team. He sends a gift, a homemade leather BDSM whip painted Honolulu Blue and silver.

"What's this?"

"A pom-pom used to root on the Lions."

Banjo Bob refuses to progress—financially or emotionally. It evens out over time. I don't receive a childhood birds-and-bees convo but get a sex whip as an adult.

It's comfortable to lose. I inherit this preference. Winning and stability make me panic, desperately trying to end up in the cellar I'm accustomed to.

I post a picture of the whip. It goes viral, sparking conversation between thousands of football fans and BDSM enthusiasts. Hundreds of people send messages, begging to purchase a whip.[7] Banjo Bob doesn't have a dollar to his name and spends every free second crafting leatherwork. This is salvation.

---

7. Which they probably enjoy doing.

He refuses to sell them. Poverty isn't a station he resides in; it's an identity he desperately clings to. He keeps making whips, giving them as gifts to force uncomfortable chuckles. I witness this dozens of times, knowing the whip will be thrown away. It's not his fault that he is this way but it is his fault he embraces it.

The Texans embarrass us on Thanksgiving. I rationalize my familial mindset, thinking it's best to never have anything wonderful because it'll be accompanied by fear of losing it. That's how bad this season is.

Certain memories become seared into long-term storage. These moments will always be fresh, vibrant, a part of us. The firing of Quinn and Patricia is one of these for me.

I walk the produce aisle of my local grocery. *Buzz, Buzz, Buzz.* My phone's flooded with congratulatory texts. They're gone. *GONE!* We wished on a monkey's paw for these men to transform the franchise. They took us to the bottom with the likability of the Spanish Inquisition.

Adderall's my Patricia, running me into the ground, insisting it's the only way. I negotiate each fix at the expense of all else. This happens so frequently that the real me is merely a concept. I am but a tumbleweed of interconnected urges masquerading in a flesh suit.

I start speeding the moment I'm alone. I don't hide it because I have a problem. I hide it to have an intimate relationship with my drug of choice. *My dear speed. Nothing exists in this world but you and I . . .*

I go lower than my lowest.

My only thought is the need to quit.

I go to bed each night believing tomorrow is the day. I fail the moment I gain consciousness and spend the rest of the day fixating on failure.

The Whiner commands. I give in. The devastating cycle of terrible behaviors resembles the act of feeding a begging cat. It's over as soon as you give in. They know your weak points, expertly asking until life becomes one long loop of repetitive pestering.

Control is lost. I take a cocktail of speed and LSD with my morning coffee and chasers of gambling, sex, scams, and inventing weed edibles made from Japanese algae that pop like new-age gushers.

There's a real me but the sweet boy is just a passenger.

I vow to be sober for the rest of my life but don't care how long that span is.

Active suicidal ideations spring from the realization that getting high is what's important to me. I'm exhausted but never tired, spending hours wide awake in bed, jealous of my snoring old dog. I've put an evil thing in charge, and it's holding me in lockup.

There's one way out: an acknowledgment of the facts I've never spoken. One powerful phrase will change everything. I speak the truth for the first time. These words were the subtext for almost every action I ever took but did not realize that until I say them out loud and kick my Matt Patricia to the curb.

"I'm an addict."

GAME 15

REBUILD DONE RIGHT

• 2021-2022 •

2021	2022
3-13-1	9-8

Other men made promises at this podium. They were more highly regarded, possessing preferable pedigrees. Others had *it* but the definition of *it* changed to fit each one. They knew analytics, scheme, or Bill Belichick. Each was deemed the one—the individual to lead Detroit to greatness.

None of them would.

This one's different. He's an idiot meathead.

A press conference introduces the blocking tight end as our leader. He promises no victories, speaking to the bleakness of our town with unvarnished, authentic, raw truth. Coach Speak is dead.

"This place has been kicked, it's been battered, it's been bruised. This team's gonna take on the identity of this city, all right? And this city's been down, and it found a way to get up, all right? And when you knock us down, we're gonna get up. And on the way up, we're gonna bite a kneecap off. Sooner or later, we'll be the last ones standing."

It's poetry. He's one of us—dismissed before he even begins. This is our new coach: Dan Campbell. He tells the world exactly who he is and what he will do. The world laughs. Campbell speaks about unity, competition, and culture but goes unheard. All anyone talks about is biting kneecaps.

Sheila Ford Hamp comprehends owner responsibilities. It's not running a football team, it's supporting a region's emotional state. She does the work, looks in the mirror, and diagnoses the root of systemic losing: ourselves.

Sheila promises to do things right. Battalions of yes-men are jettisoned.

Chris Spielman, thumping linebacker from the good ol' days, is brought in to advise. He's known what's best since telling this autograph-seeking kid outside the Silverdome to "go home."

Brad Holmes, another outsider, is hired as general manager. The former Enterprise Rent-A-Car clerk worked his way up the Rams front office, learning how to build a winner.[1] His hiring is fairly well received.

The same cannot be said for Dan Campbell. The lovable hunk previously held an interim head coaching job for half a season in Miami but he's not hired for experience. He's hired to change culture.

Campbell approached the temporary position with a mind toward lasting relationships. Two weeks into his Miami tenure, he brings the team together and promises, "I would do *anything* for you guys." It's genuine authenticity in a coaching industry full of social climbers.

Dan Campbell starts his day with two Venti Starbucks red eyes and still his enthusiasm dwarfs caffeine levels. He's not excited about coaching a team, he's excited about coaching *this* team: the poisoned locker room that never wins. Everything Campbell needs to know about Detroit he learned playing on 2008's winless squad. Winning in this place will be different. Attending the Met Gala hits different when you take the subway there.

Dan builds his coaching staff around former players and reaches out to veteran players to ask what worked. Two particular assistants—Ben Johnson and Hank Fraley—are championed and thus retained. Dan's first instinct is asking what his troops want. True servant leadership.

---

1. Drafting Aaron Donald.

We cannot create a new identity without severing the old one. Stafford only has a few good years left. Not wanting to spend them in another rebuild, he requests a trade.

He's not just the star player. Stafford's my totem, a substitute for paternal guidance. I've never met the man but project my bullshit on his career, making him life's navigational guide. Ultimate victory eludes us but we fight like hell in shitty circumstances. That's a win.

I would rather give away my social security number than admit this, but I sob when Stafford gets traded.[2] I don't weep over a player. I cry for how meaningful parasocial relationships became.

Stafford goes to the Rams for a bounty of picks. Thrown into the deal is Jared Goff, a former first overall pick now serving as cap filler. Goff led his Rams to the Super Bowl but got exposed on the big stage, held to a measly three points by Bill Belichick's Patriots. Coach Sean McVay makes him a pariah, ruining his confidence and reputation. Goff's overpaid. Goff's soft. Goff isn't a starter. His presence under center is an anthropomorphized white flag of surrender.

Goff doesn't come to Detroit because he's good. He comes because he's unwanted.

It's about reframing the facts. Being *somewhere* because you failed *elsewhere* isn't a bad place to be.

★ ★ ★

Feeling discarded like Goff, I arrive at the Phoenix House—a recovery center on the bustling border of Crown Heights and Bed-Stuy. I ring the buzzer, hoping no one will answer. A few seconds waiting is enough time to imagine the rest of my life.

I'll go home and continue using, telling myself I tried but excusing myself because "no one answered the door." Trying and failing to attend a

2. 901-05-3317.

meeting is better than nothing. I wasn't the one who failed to address my addictions. It was the receptionist.

Someone answers. I trade a perfect September afternoon for the fluorescent din of a windowless room. It's the best place I'll ever be.

My journey begins by telling a therapist, "I need to get sober." My only caveat is no 12-Step programs. They were the family religion, dished out as a childhood punishment worse than beatings or having my glasses confiscated.[3] They helped my dad not drink and my mom stop bulimically bingeing but it's hard to argue they served us. Meetings were a household pillar but the household was miserable.

Also, I dread someone asking about my higher power and watching eyes roll when I bring up Barry Sanders.

My program needs to belong to me, not my family. My therapist recommends an alternative: SMART Recovery.

Self Management And Recovery Training. Many programs revolve around an addict's powerlessness; SMART empowers. Individuals change behaviors by changing their thinking. This process is borrowed from cognitive behavioral therapy and is strengthened by self-inventory. You don't need to take steps or submit. You need to look inward and truthfully answer. I need to change the way I perceive—something I've practiced with my team for a lifetime.

Bryan, a tattooed man wearing jorts and a skullet, facilitates the meeting. He punches in for direct conversations and leads exercises on a whiteboard provided he finds a working marker. These are his tasks but his job is fostering buy-in. Even when the task is daunting. Even when constituents have only ever failed.

The preamble is read. I hate it. Structure revolves around individual shares followed by cross talk and exercises. I'm planning to leave but conversation turns to me before I can escape.

Something happens. I share. Everything. The stories of this book went untold until I tell them on this day, albeit with less expletives directed

---

3. This one sucked. I would stumble into cabinets for hours.

toward Matt Millen. Check-ins usually last a couple minutes. I expound for a half hour with blunt honesty that grinds the meeting to a halt. The room is windowless but part of me finally sees the sun.

The cliche that "a weight has been lifted" is wrong. Speaking about addiction makes me feel every ounce. Every aspect of life carries it.

My unique, earth-shattering epiphany is old hat to the group. They get to work. An exercise called ABC illustrates connections between thoughts and behaviors.

Activating events leverage underlying **B**eliefs about ourselves and the world, bringing unwanted **C**onsequences. Much of my perception is an excuse to use. What was cool and productive and fun is really just damage and low self-worth.

I get tools. From a scientific perspective an urge isn't cumbersome but a notion averaging roughly 20 minutes. I'm told to purchase the SMART handbook and do the exercises, organizing thoughts into "rational" versus "irrational." The procedure's cold logic doesn't bring the typical shame but the *same old* optimism.

I leave the meeting. I'm not a brand-new man but entertain the idea that one might exist.

The new regime begins.

2021 NFL DRAFT: APRIL 29–MAY 1

Dan, Brad, and Sheila enter their first draft on the same page. Cohesive decision-making structures look different than consensus.

It's a historically good draft headlined by quarterback prospects. The fan base clamors to replace Goff but—for once—the brain trust knows better. A gem falls into our lap.

Penei Sewell is more than the draft's best offensive tackle. He's the best prospect at the position in decades.[4] Sewell is franchise defining, bursting with character, and unlike anyone we've ever had. The Lions employed

4. Anthony Muñoz taken by the Bengals in 1980.

miracle makers by necessity because the offensive line could simply never execute. That changes now.

The Lions take Penei. The pick is boring, prudent, and absolutely correct. I attend the draft as press as part of NFL Fan Therapy, a footballcentric comedy troupe, violating professionalism by becoming the first person to celebrate an O-lineman pick by dancing on a table. The teardown begins by acquiring a wrecking ball.

The draft wears on. Sheila grows concerned, asking Brad if he's ever going to get a pass catcher. Despite it being his first rodeo, Brad Holmes remains confident, assuring his new boss he has it covered.

Amon-Ra St. Brown, a USC standout, tumbles in the draft. He has hands, tools, and work ethic but is undervalued due to occasionally lining up in the slot. I love the pick but overrate every USC alumnus. If the Lions took O. J. Simpson I'd call him a "player with mild character concerns."

Despite his ex–Mr. Universe father overseeing his training,[5] Amon-Ra does not possess eye-popping physical traits. However, he has something often overlooked but far more important: He's a great receiver.

Great receivers are always a bit crazy. St. Brown's no exception. He's the seventeenth player selected at his position and memorizes those picked before him, repeating their names like a mantra.

Picks are maligned. Brad and Dan are dismissed. The *Same Old Lions* will never get it right. The unknown factor is that these aren't the Same Old Lions. The new regime operates with the same approach as SMART Recovery: acknowledging necessary change and addressing it with actionable steps:

1. Set a goal.
2. Make a plan.
3. Acquire the tools to get there.

---

5. And giving him a fun name. John Brown calls his son "Amon-Ra" and adds "St." because it sounds cool.

WEEK 3: SEPTEMBER 26, 2021.
BALTIMORE RAVENS (1-1) v DETROIT LIONS (0-2).
FORD FIELD, DETROIT, MI.

WEEK 5: OCTOBER 10, 2021.
DETROIT LIONS (0-4) v MINNESOTA VIKINGS (1-3).
U. S. BANK STADIUM, MINNEAPOLIS, MN.

WEEK 7: OCTOBER 24, 2021.
DETROIT LIONS (0-6) v LOS ANGELES RAMS (5-1).
SOFI STADIUM, LOS ANGELES, CA.

Dan Campbell navigates the league's worst roster through a schedule stacked with contenders. The only triumphs are establishing identity: a ravenous hunger for victory that'll come—for better or worse—to define them. We suck but we're bought in.

Baltimore's a model organization. Someone could wake from a 20-year coma to see the Ravens sitting atop the AFC North playing the same style of football they remember. Winning is never certain, but Baltimore's methodology secures favorable bounces on the Plinko board of outcomes. They're what we want to be.

Goff struggles, seemingly stifled by his task's enormity. Replacing Stafford is a tall order. This transition would go better if some grandmotherly figure pulled all parties aside to warmly whisper, "You loved the last one like no one before and Goff's taking over a bad team. It'll be an adjustment for you both."

Fourth Quarter, 5:33; Ravens 16, Lions 14

An interception provides a path to victory. Suddenly raised stakes free Goff to showcase abilities, hitting tight ends over the middle and wide receivers in stride. We outplay Baltimore all afternoon. A go-ahead field goal allows the scoreboard to momentarily reflect that reality.

Fourth Quarter, 0:35; Lions 17, Ravens 16

A Lamar Jackson sack puts Baltimore at fourth and 19 with no timeouts. Dan Campbell's first win is upon us.

The Ravens convert. That's okay. Baltimore doesn't have enough time. Referees miss a delay of game as Justin Tucker sprints toward midfield like a vulnerable masseuse works there.

NFL history contains tens of thousands of field goal attempts. This 66-yarder is the longest. Tucker strikes the ball. It flutters toward the goalpost, bangs the crossbar, and hangs in stasis before drifting past the threshold of a perfect loss.

Dan Campbell winces in pained disbelief, one of us—too familiar with losing in this town. A win will not christen one a Detroit Lions coach but a loss like this will.

★ ★ ★

I attend SMART each week, learning to organize thoughts as rational versus irrational. I reflect on internal expectations. I expect myself to be happy, productive, and in flow state at all times. It's irrational. No one can do this. Why have I spent a lifetime trying?

I resume my studies, pursuing my master's degree without the assistance of my beloved Adderall, which I dropped between semesters like a too-taxing course. Learning isn't pointing consciousness at a topic and letting speed take over. I must explore ideas until genuine curiosity begins.

I'm damned near middle-aged but finally consider how my brain works. The Whiner spent decades repeatedly spinning a singular thought like a Top 40 DJ: *"You aren't good enough unless you use."*

SMART Recovery pipes up to ask the pragmatic question, "Um. Have you even *tried* accomplishing anything sober?"

Life-altering lessons begin with smaller, actionable learnings. If expectations are unrealistic, most outcomes will disappoint.

Fourth Quarter, 1:51; Vikings 16, Lions 9

Ace utility piece Jalen Reeves-Maybin wrestles the ball from a Viking. Irrational thought takes over. *The Lions will win a game.* Rational thought rebuts. *The team is years away. Focus on Penei and Amon-Ra's development.* Expecting wins is down payment on future disappointment.

We find the end zone. A normal coach would kick the extra point for overtime but Dan Campbell isn't a normal coach. He knows Detroit wins are precious. The desire for his team's triumph aligns with his trust in them.

Campbell goes for two. Goff isn't asked to be a hero, only to do what he's good at. A play action fake grants him a window, and he threads it to his receiver.

Fourth Quarter, 0:18; Lions 17, Vikings 16

Rational perspective deems a comeback impossible. Minnesota throws three straight completions against zero resistance. They boot the ball through the uprights as time expires, seizing victory by the thinnest of margins. Irrationality rules once more.

Football coaches are notorious for not saying anything to the media. Leaders of men must be taciturn and emotionless.

Dan Campbell meets with the media, fresh off the heroic comeback that wasn't. His eyes are puffy and voice sniffles. Dan Campbell is crying.

"When you see your players give all that they have and lose in that way? It's tough. You want it for them." The mountainous man quivers with emotion. Campbell's widely ridiculed for the display but real fans don't say a word. Someone finally gets it.

Dan promises the crucible will improve the team. I throw out rationality and believe. The man weeping behind the podium embodies what a winner looks like: someone who cares.

The embryonic team travels to Los Angeles to face Matthew Stafford. It's our Super Bowl but not the Rams'. They look forward to the real thing.

Changes have begun. Matt Patricia's hill—installed as a practice punishment—is now voluntarily sprinted. Players recognize what Dan's building and align their desires.

True meritocracies are rare. An established offensive coordinator is replaced by Ben Johnson, an untested assistant. St. Brown believes, espousing praise for the detailed explanation powering play installations. The coordinator Amon-Ra advocates for what will help him become an All-Pro.[6]

Playing the Rams is like running into an ex who decidedly won the breakup.[7] Stafford's marriage with Sean McVay turns Los Angeles into the league's best team, making it clear the only thing Matt needed to overcome was being attached to us.

We weren't Los Angeles. We never gave Matt an offensive genius or brilliant system. Like Barry or Calvin, Stafford *was* the system, walking into a bad situation and doing his damnedest. It's hard to consider the best way to help someone when you need them to save you. Jesus's disciples never asked what aquifers best transformed into wine or massaged his legs after walking on water. Slack-jawed amazement makes one not just believe in miracles but rely on them. Both Stafford and Jesus found the right supporting cast and got the job done at age 33.

Bob and I attend a high school friend's wedding, arranging travel to watch the game together. A group reconvenes in a different time, place, and dynamic. Children are adults and adults are children. The only consistency is the team remaining dogshit.

Dan Campbell coaches like a lifelong Detroiter, pulling out every trick. You can move on to greener pastures, but we'll do whatever it takes to be better—even if only for an afternoon.

A first-quarter Goff touchdown is chased with an onside kick attempt that ignores win probability metrics in favor of how badly we need this.

---

6. In addition to hatred for the 16 receivers taken before him.

7. I used a similar version of this analogy earlier. Forgive the repetition, the author's romantic life has been through it.

Balls to the wall is the only way to coach the Breakup Bowl. We recover the kick and stall but convert a daring fake punt, doing everything we can to delay the sight of Matthew in a Rams jersey.

Our inspiring afternoon ends once Stafford touches the ball. He dices the defense with long connections dissonantly viewed as happiness's harbinger. The Rams are better but we bite kneecaps, converting fourth-quarter fake punts as a harm-reductive way to watch the world burn.

Matthew wins. He was right to move on but so were we. Doing so made us lose our leader and every game but these losses taught us who we are.

I bitch about the outcome. Banjo Bob isn't having it, insisting the team showed character. He reframes the situation but I'm sick of moral victories.

"I'm proud of them. I like Dan Campbell." He soothes in a tone reminiscent of early childhood.

"You have Stockholm syndrome. You'll go your entire life without a Super Bowl, convinced that's enough."

"I'm not waiting for a Super Bowl. I'm spending the afternoon with my son." He excuses himself for a cigarette, punctuating his accidental mic-drop moment. The loss blurs with decades of others encompassing our relationship. We bridge our chasms on Sundays.

The goal of SMART Recovery is for participants to "live a balanced life." For that, participants must first decide what type of life they desire. There's a road map: the SMART Recovery handbook. My copy proclaims it's "new and improved" alongside an eight-year-old copyright and contains curriculum of cognitive behavioral therapy exercises.

Work varies from logging urges to analyzing triggers. People join the group to address addictions only to learn they're just symptoms. Sobriety doesn't provide happiness. The gift of recovery is ourselves. True to the program's rational nature, in order to fix ourselves we must first figure out who we are.

There's a working marker for the whiteboard. Bryan leads a group exercise called "hierarchy of values," asking us to rank the things we care about.

This process clarifies priorities, sparking reflection on how choices align with true desires.

We go around the windowless room, listing passions that pinpoint our hypocrisy. The group's a miasma of hipsters, outpatient emergencies, and savvy seniors. Despite surface-level differences we maintain similar interior lives. We use, we cope, stuck in a cycle by trauma we never properly processed.

Everyone lists their top value as "family" until it's my turn.

"Sundays."

"Sundays?"

"Sundays."

My answer is so absurd it turns the thought exercise into a monster truck commercial.

"As long as there's a Sunday I can get through the other days. I'll see the Lions, my people, and that's enough."

It's a humiliating answer. I care about Banjo Bob and Julion, but in order to be the person they need, a carrot must be dangled. That's the Lions—positioned in my life to make the losing team more than they are. Can the losing man be transformed in similar fashion?

Christmas reveals no shortage of bad memories. Arrested for stealing Baby Jesuses, screaming around the table over meals procured by dumpster diving. I attempt the same thinking back on Thanksgivings. No bad memories are found. Barry munching a turkey leg, dropped keys interrupting Aretha, reliving coin flips gone awry outside the Silverdome. My family peaked when the team was part of it.

SMART deals with potential disruption by proactively making a plan. Social events are loaded with triggers and impulses that rarely conjure our best selves. Navigating these situations requires acknowledging the pressure and arming ourselves with a strategy. Weddings, personal wins, devastation. All can derail and, as such, require a plan.

Sharing defeats the siloed existence of most addicts. Isolating with our worst tendencies fosters the erroneous belief that we're alone and uniquely bad. Sharing them affirms humanity and connects us.

If a member offers "cause for concern" about their recovery, the group swoops in with insights. Specifics don't matter but effort does. A plan, distraction, something else to focus on.

WEEK 13: DECEMBER 5, 2021. MINNESOTA VIKINGS (5-6) v DETROIT LIONS (0-10-1). FORD FIELD, DETROIT, MI.

Dan Campbell's team is 0–11. As bad as we've ever been. Reframe it.

The hierarchy of values is apparent. It isn't anything extraordinary. Campbell believes, letting that trait flow through every interaction like a bonding agent, incrementally building brotherhood.

Campbell calls Goff into his office. Jared thinks he's going to be thrown out again. Campbell tells him it's his team. Goff shows it on this day, putting Detroit up 20–6.

Three months of letdowns make any lead precarious, even double-digit ones. Sure enough, the Lions squander it.

Fourth Quarter, 8:41; Lions 23, Vikings 21

Dan Campbell believes. Goff throws to secure the win. *Interception!*

Fourth Quarter, 4:08; Lions 23, Vikings 21

Fourth and 1. Dan Campbell still believes. Goff drops back and gets stripped. Minnesota takes the lead.

Fourth Quarter, 1:50; Vikings 27, Lions 23

Unwavering belief offers additional shots at redemption. Goff has another chance but doesn't have much to work with. Just a fourth-round receiver, the seventeenth-best player in his positional draft class but Amon-Ra keeps getting open. The Island of Misfit Toys bring us to the Vikings' 12.

Fourth Quarter, 0:04; Vikings 27, Lions 23

One snap for the game. Goff isn't asked to be a hero, just to make his reads. Amon-Ra creates space and Goff finds him. *Touchdown Lions!* Horns blare. Goff runs over and hugs Dan Campbell.

Back in September, I purchased a cigar to celebrate Dan Campbell's first victory. In December, I dust it off and smoke on a victorious walk, puffing tobacco like my father.

The team grows stronger throughout December. The season's a wash but there's plenty to be happy about. A core has been unearthed and empowered.

SUPER BOWL LVI, FEBRUARY 13, 2022

Matthew shows the world who he is, first outdueling Tom Brady and then a strong 49ers team to put the Rams in the Super Bowl against Cincinnati. Michigan is awash in "Detroit Rams" T-shirts, sacrificing affiliations to root on our guy. Stafford throws the go-ahead touchdown and Aaron Donald ices it with a quarterback hit. Awful suspicion confirmed—we held him back.

Don't let the Lombardi Trophy fool you. Stafford doesn't become a champion on this day. That happened a decade earlier, shrugging off a dislocated shoulder to beat Cleveland. It just takes a Super Bowl win for the rest of the world to see him the way Detroit does.

I think I'll fail out of school without Adderall, without flow states. Life's reimagined to support education. I work as the night manager of a bowling alley, reviewing flash cards with drunks. The best way to understand a concept is having to explain it to a lush at 3 AM. I post a 4.0 GPA and earn my MBA.

The bowling alley fires me for crashing a lane cleaner.[8] It doesn't matter. I get a remote job at General Motors, fulfilling the wholesome Michigan life I fled without considering.

8. Also, whenever someone asks "Do you like bowling?" I reply, "No. I like real sports."

I walk for graduation in Michigan so Julion can watch. He's smart and good at school but these traits aren't valued in rural Michigan. If he sees me celebrated for these traits he'll know they're worthwhile.

Julion tries on the cap and gown.

"Was it hard?"

"Harder than you can imagine."

I explain our similar wiring, giving him the warnings I never received and pointing out the gifts. I finish my fake Dad talk and continue by taking him to lift weights and play basketball.

I roll into Target for ankle tape. Aidan Hutchinson, Michigan's favorite son and the previous day's draft pick, walks past. I stop the man near the frozen food, ask him to improve the team, and likely give him the creeps.

I drive to Bloomington, Indiana, imagining Bob's congratulations. A reminder of life's default setting awaits.

I knock on the shack door. No one answers. I find Banjo Bob motionless in a darkened room. He says he hasn't gotten up in months, "except to smoke." Piss bottles surround the bed but this ghastly sight is nothing compared to the birdseed.

Every inch of the shack is covered in birdseed. Bob doesn't like birds but a good hoarder doesn't pass up a bargain, in this case industrial-sized feed bags stored in a front closet until discovered by mice and spread throughout the shack until they cover every crevice. It's horrifying but not to Bob.

"I'm comfortable."

Getting sober, getting a master's, getting a job. These actions were intended to reach across generations, letting ancestors know everything worked out. The demons of the past in my father's shack retort in the form of piss bottles and birdseed.

The scary part isn't the house. It's knowing it mirrors the mind of its occupant.

An additional benefit of recovery is hopefully another Bob conversation topic. I imagine hushed, reverent convos about family dynamics. The abyss beckons instead. My payoff for getting clean is cleaning his shack.

Knowing they'll steal, I hire methheads to help. Joke's on them. Stealing from a hoarder is doing him a favor.

The man won't keep himself alive so I utilize SMART, hoping to alter my inconvenient reality by making a plan. Banjo Bob agrees to a set of conditions: 40 daily cigarettes, circadian check-ins, new levels of effort.

He doesn't follow through. Health is lied about. Promises are ignored. An 812 area code hitting my caller ID means flying to Indiana to care for him. Rebuilds are long on heartache.

WEEK 4: OCTOBER 2, 2022. SEATTLE SEAHAWKS (1-2) V DETROIT LIONS (1-2). FORD FIELD, DETROIT, MI.

SMART changes my outlook. The family I struggle with and the addiction that owned me become manageable tasks. Bryan's leaving. Someone needs to take over. Substances no longer drag me down. I can show others.

I sit in the chair, leading the meeting, using my flaws to punch in on other's interior lives. It's the best choice I've ever made. Nothing helps you stay sober like others looking to you, waiting to hear how it's done. A fellow member even purchases new markers.

I'm asked to leverage new sobriety competencies and lead a sensitive conversation with a friend. I sit down with Pablo, my USC urinal pal, to discuss his drinking. I talk about change coming in stages, emphasizing the importance of the precontemplation. I don't ask him to stop drinking. I ask that he think about *thinking about* changing. It doesn't happen that day but it does; he stops. Full-circle moments make my drinking buddy my brother.

A new culture's apparent.

Dan Campbell gleefully describes his process as, "Hey, man. There's no turds here." It's not a bad policy.

The Lions take a star turn as subjects of HBO's *Hard Knocks* documentary series. Cameras follow the team's training camp, capturing Campbell's locker room built around authenticity and competitiveness.[9] He doesn't bark like Patricia. Sure, Dan screams, but it's about how much he thinks about them, how much he cares.

Dan's empowering nature is further exhibited by the offense reconfiguring around Jared Goff's specifications. They aren't asking him to perform in a system; they're building the system around Goff's abilities. One SMART Recovery tool asks participants to schedule weeks around sobriety. Everything orienting around a specific goal makes big-picture success realistic.

I marry the wrong woman. Banjo Bob is willing to kill himself trying to make the wedding. He nearly does. He blows a tire, misses a flight, and nearly careens his car off a cliff. He does all these things but still comes through.

He beams throughout the weekend, looking resplendent with a gold Lion-headed cane and Detroit-themed socks. Switchblades are handed out and banjos are strummed. At one point he trips on a rock and hits his head. The blood pouring from his skull won't stop his soul flowing through his fingers. He shows me his love in the best way he can, becoming the man sobriety took away for an entire weekend. It's great to meet him.

There's a casual hang on the Sunday after the wedding. We grill meat, float in a river in inflatable tubes, and watch the Lions as Banjo Bob holds court.

Of course, the Lions disappoint. My entire community gathers to watch my team but we cannot stop Seattle.

I walk away and find Julion near the river, scolding him to share his inner tube. He does.

The Walkowskis taught a siloed existence. I avoided this fate but did not simply transcend it. Smaller decisions did. Connecting with others, shutting down defense mechanisms, being willing to change. These small factors, done after *finally* considering my well-being, were what did.

---

9. They also capture Aidan Hutchinson dancing to Michael Jackson's "Billie Jean."

I'm a new man. It won't be enough for some, but all I ever needed to be was "just a guy." I walk alongside the riverbed with Julion. I never fixed the Walkowskis but connected the generations, cobbled together my own existence, and brought the best parts along.

Shouts drift from the party. The Lions have made it close.

"Uncle Joel. You wanna go watch?"

"No."

I ignore the team to be present with loved ones. I no longer need the Lions to show me who I am.

Detroit loses, and loses, and loses, starting the season 1-6. Dan Campbell's job is in jeopardy.

GAME 16

GRIT

• 2022-2023 •

One Revitalization, One Division Title

2022	2023
9-8	12-5

There's only been one outcome. Imagining otherwise would be irrational. SMART teaches that balanced lives stand on rational foundations.

Losses unfold as I sagely nod along, concentrating on relationships this team improved. Why be results oriented? Football's just another addiction. Happiness must be found in each Sunday's unhappiness. *This* is rational, aligned with the only way it's ever been.

Dan can't coach, Goff's a bum, the Fords bungle. Anyone can love a winner. Loving *this* builds character.

Banjo Bob picked the perfect stand-in. I resign myself to permanent letdowns when it happens.

WHAM! The Detroit Lions become good.

Aidan Hutchinson single-handedly beats Green Bay, an inspiring comeback torpedoes Chicago, a decent Giants team gets throttled. It's not a fluke.

Talent's there, complemented by Campbell cajoling his players into frenzies. They step on the field, keenly aware they want it more. Detroit no longer hopes to win. They expect to.

A slow start likely removes the team from postseason contention but having no reward reframes the goal.

All we have to be is *our* best. The team from the town winning forgot will not be champions. *What else is new?* We settle on biting kneecaps and making life hell for freshly overmatched opponents. Campbell gives us an identity and we thrive.

WEEK 15: DECEMBER 18, 2022.
DETROIT LIONS (6-7) V NEW YORK JETS (7-6).
METLIFE STADIUM, EAST RUTHERFORD, NJ.

It's no different than Sasquatch sightings. I won't believe it until I see it myself. Bundled in Honolulu Blue, I make the hajj to New Jersey on a cold, bright day that makes everything look brittle. Except us.

Fourth Quarter, 2:00; Lions 19, Jets 17

Fourth and inches decides the game. Goff fakes the run, fakes the pass, and finds the backup tight end alone in the flat. He rumbles miles to the end zone, ushering in an era where Detroit's the one doling out back-breaking plays.

Outcomes improve once we know who we are.

★ ★ ★

SMART's Lifestyle Balance Pie exercise begins with drawing a pizza. Once finished, avoid drawing Italian caricatures and label slices with aspects important to your life. Different elements are then ranked, charted on a scale of 1–10, with dots connected. This exercise pinpoints where values reside. External environments tell us who to be and what to care about. It's important to ask ourselves what matters *to us*.

I know what I want to be: recovered. Knowing my priorities keeps me on the path. The pie makes me protective of energy and attention; speed made me lock in on whatever was in front of me. I protect my thoughts, my pie. Triggers and stressors don't get a slice.

I know who I am because I finally stopped to ask.

WEEK 18: JANUARY 8, 2023. DETROIT LIONS [8-8] V GREEN BAY PACKERS [8-8]. LAMBEAU FIELD, GREEN BAY, WI.

News spreads in the locker room while waiting to take the field. Tiebreakers set by a Seahawks-Rams match seal our fate and eliminate Detroit from playoff contention, but there's still a game to play. A big one.

Rodgers in Lambeau, flexed into prime time so the world can watch Green Bay punch their postseason ticket. All they have to do is beat the team they always do.

Knowing something won't yield success or impact trajectory stokes an instinct to shut down. I once wore a cap and gown to work after giving a previous employer my two weeks' notice. Surely the mighty Packers will best the sad-sack Lions. It's natural order.

There's just one problem. Detroit wants the win. The Packers try closing the door with a fourth-and-1 trick play on the goal line but we sniff it out. Goff lets loose, putting us on top with the best throw of his career—a cross-body shot to Kalif Raymond. Green Bay answers, then forces a three and out. A heroic defeat brews. *I've seen this one already.*

The defense holds. Our offensive line plows down the field, regaining control and the lead . . . *Gulp!* Now, with stakes at their highest, Aaron Rodgers has a chance to answer. Green Bay is confident. They've been coming through in this spot since 1993.

We send the blitz. Rodgers beats it, lofting the ball toward an uncovered receiver. Rodgers's preternatural gifts forge an unflappable confidence that crosses into hubris if only for a single play.[1] Kerby Joseph, beloved playmaking safety, sprints over and nets the ball. *Interception!*

We must kill the clock. Goff finds St. Brown. Normally reliable hands drop the ball, but he catches it between his legs. *This might be our day.*

Then again it might not be. Green Bay backs us up to second and 17, knowing we must run. We pass. Amon-Ra catches a short route. Tacklers swarm. Complaints about the play call are already leaving my lips as Amon-Ra pitches it to a trailing running back for a gain of 12. What looks like schoolyard improvisation is guts of the highest order.

Fourth Quarter, 1:15; Lions 20, Packers 16; Fourth and 1

A FG would boost the lead to a TD but gives Rodgers time to tie it. Campbell responds to pressure with emotion, trusting the quarterback no one wanted, and goes for it on fourth down. Goff finds his man. We take victory formation, ending Green Bay's season before their fair-weather fans.

This wasn't supposed to happen. Announcers say the Lions have nothing to play for. This is patently false. Dan Campbell intertwined macho posturing with genuine care, giving his team ultimate motivation: each other.

This is the lesson. Our best isn't obtained striving for external validation. The peak's found when efforts are dedicated to brethren. By virtue of being called the "Lions," the term "pride" is associated with this team. That term finally feels applicable.

★ ★ ★

Banjo Bob keeps dying.

---

1. And every podcast appearance.

His heart stops once a month, throttled back to function by defibrillator charges. He repeatedly passes away and returns, living the same character arc as *South Park*'s Kenny. It's grueling, exhausting, and our second-biggest problem.

The biggest is he hides it from me. Banjo Bob only updates me on the Lions. He'll answer the phone if we beat Green Bay on national TV or shock the world by drafting Jahmyr Gibbs and Sam LaPorta, but that's it. An updated Walkowski family crest would feature two nerds ignoring their problems to study depth charts.

The same isn't true for his health. I discover his hospitalizations when an 812 area code flashes across my caller ID, an exasperated doctor on the other end—"812" becomes shorthand for "there's a health scare no one told me about." This repeated occurrence turns me into a taskmaster.

"You need to tell me what's going on."

"I don't want to bother you."

"It's not a bother."

"You have a lot going on."

"This is more important."

Bob thinks my life is dynamic and interesting. So much so that he doesn't warrant a place in it. I fly to Indiana every six weeks. The burden becomes worthwhile when I enter his shack, watching his eyes flash with delight.

I beg for transparency, pleading to help. He brushes me off, repeatedly citing my life's importance.

April 2022

"You had school."

"You're more important."

August 2022

"You're getting married."

"Weddings are about family. You're my family."

March 2023

"You have work."

"I get time off for this situation."

July 2023

"You have a lot going on."

"You have more."

Every conversation ends the same way. I hold his hand, make the type of eye contact he hates, and confirm new protocols.

"You need to tell me when you're in the hospital."

He never tells me. It's strategic—his way of controlling the narrative. He says he's in good health, that his heart works, that diabetes isn't bad, that cigarettes are actually good for you.

Doctors tell a different story. The question, "How's my dad doing?" is answered by sighs and shitty outlooks. He doesn't lie to hurt me. He lies for legacy. After a lifetime spent deflecting tough conversations he'll be damned if he starts having them now.

I fly Julion to New York to see the life that being good at school can build. Nice apartment, good career, bustling friend groups, and a routine of chasing weightlifting and pickup hoops with tacos. There are lessons to share.

We're walking out of LaGuardia when that damned 812 area code flashes on my caller ID. I don't need to answer.

Bob flatlined in his hovel, waking to EMTs crouching past banjos to put defibrillator paddles to his chest.

Someone must hold his hand through the end. That someone's me. Instinct says "run to him," but I'm already doting on another generation.

Choosing between my dad and godson is a brutal choice but SMART has tools. I perform a cold-hearted cost-benefit analysis.

If I go to my father:

- His situation won't improve.
- My deeds will vanish from Earth within a couple months.

If I stay with Julion:

- His situation *might* improve.
- My deeds will be remembered for the rest of his life and might make him pay it forward.

The boy wins. I hide my anguish, giving him the best week of his life and the lessons.

"I'm just like you," at Yankee Stadium.

"You can find your way out," during a Broadway intermission.

"The trail's blazed. Just follow," as he boards the plane home.

I stay at LaGuardia, grabbing an armful of NFL preview magazines from Hudson News. Experts finally predict the Lions to win. I board the next flight to Indiana.

An isolated lump sits in a darkened room, surrounded by animal pelts and sports memorabilia. I rouse him awake, requesting updates on his condition. He shows off his leatherwork. He made his own football.

This is what he wants. To run from life and isolate, ignoring potential improvements. True desire was becoming this. Metamorphosis complete.

The only way he can be loved is to fall into such disrepair that I must drop everything and come to his side. I always do.

"Are you scared of dying?"

He offers no rebuttal but shows off his collection of gorilla masks, lovingly describing each one.

I make a plan for him to stay in this world even though he'll continue acting like he bet the under on his lifespan.

He adopts a serious expression, tells me he has reasons to live, and opens a drawer. It's filled with headpieces making it look like an arrow has gone through someone's head a la Steve Martin.

I can't stop what's coming but can make him more comfortable with it. A hospice nurse provides a list of helpful end-of-life questions. What do you ask a man who never asked himself anything?

Everything. I ask his proudest moment, his happiest times, building to the impactful query, "Do you have any regrets?"

"Of course not." He laughs, shaking his head at my absurdity. "I own seventeen banjos."

"Do you ever think about how different choices might have made this chapter easier on me?"

"Do you need to see the banjos again?"

He knows what he likes and concentrates energy in those places.

The questionnaire is for my benefit. Interrogation gets too difficult, too direct. He unearths his animalian grumble, shooing away unwanted queries with literal hisses.

I sit by his side for weeks, annoying the hell out of him. I know each time together could be our last and ask his thoughts on this.

"So what?"

There's only one way to reach him: the team.

I start writing this book, laying down beside my old dog, scratching together a handwritten history of the issues I inherited and how the team he gave me helped navigate them.

I take him out to dinner on his last birthday. He wears a shirt reading "I'm Not Dead Yet" and orders a hot dog with no condiments. I gift him my notebooks. He devours them like a bland hot dog, reading the entirety in one sitting.

"Did you like the book?"

"I did."

"What were your favorite parts?"

"The parts about you being an addict."

"Did you know I was an addict?"

"No. You never told me."

"I was a kid. I didn't realize."

"I didn't do a good job on that one."

"That's okay . . . This could be the last time we see each other."

"So what?"

I dig deeper. "How does that make you feel?"

"Sad."

I've been anticipating the big event for decades. How will I deal with it when it finally happens? Every thought revolves around its arrival. It's actually two things, forever connected. You can't love a parent without wondering what it's like to lose them. You can't love a losing team without wondering if they'll ever win.

WEEK 1: SEPTEMBER 7, 2023. DETROIT LIONS (0-0) V KANSAS CITY CHIEFS (0-0). ARROWHEAD STADIUM, KANSAS CITY, MO.

NFL seasons begin the Thursday after Labor Day with the champion playing a handpicked darling. The NFL chooses the Lions, the little rebuild that could, to face Patrick Mahomes and the dynastic Chiefs.

Surely we'll get killed. Kansas City raises their banner. Military jets swoop overhead and the anthem crescendos. Midnight for Cinderella has arrived.

Three and out on the first drive. Nine months considering Goff's redemption net eight measly yards. The season's first possession sets the tone for all that follows, but it's reckless to go all in on the first hand.

Dan makes the call. Statements weigh more than win-probability metrics. Frank Ragnow snaps the ball directly to a special teamer who attaches himself to Ragnow's rear end, falling forward for the first. It's a dumb decision for a football coach but brilliant for a leader. One single play lets the entire roster know who they'll be for the next five months.

Brad Holmes is maligned for overinvesting in running backs. Analysts cry it's an "*overvalued position*," but free-agent-signing David Montgomery's bruising style alternating with Jahmyr Gibbs's perimeter excellence is unstoppable. Kansas City reconfigures chess pieces to mitigate the run and Goff starts slinging.

The Chiefs are great. A methodical third-quarter drive will end us, but a deflected pass flutters into the solitary, extended hand of rookie safety Brian Branch. He's halfway to the end zone before anyone realizes. Tie game.

KC tacks on a couple field goals for a 20–14 lead. Goff conducts the winning touchdown drive. It is not otherworldly like Barry or Calvin. Goff's methodical effectiveness embodies quiet greatness, the football equivalent of Jesse Plemons's acting.

We beat the champs in their house. We're on their level.

Being hopeless is flamboyant and interesting. The most delicious meals of my life were devoured penniless inside a grocery store, rationalizing that eating inside the store isn't technically shoplifting.

Being good's different. It's a sober Saturday night, predictable and planned without dopamine roller coasters.

The Lions enjoy the same sustainable stability. We impose our will with the ground game, then put it away with the passing attack, bolstering chances with aggressive decision-making. The approach works—but because it's an organic offshoot of identity. Locker room trust increases the likelihood of calculated risks working.

A good team romps through the season. We bury the Packers in Green Bay. Amon-Ra emulates the Lambeau Leap, jumping into the stands, receiving a beer baptism by a low-character Wisconsinite. We beat the Panthers, best the Buccaneers, then destroy the Raiders.

This book depends on emotional authenticity. I'd be remiss if I didn't mention my dog dying right after the Raiders game. It feels like the only bad thing to ever happen. All my emotions went into that dog. With her gone, what happens to my feelings?

Banjo Bob is decimated by the dog's passing, not realizing his feelings are about himself. Grief is a running back finding daylight. Navigate obstacles, force yourself to keep going, find yourself alone with the void before you.

Greatness is helping others. Broader team chemistry is apparent by the intensity of skill-position players blocking downfield. Our most celebrated highlights are not stunning skills but impassioned blocks.

One play illustrates evolution. Montgomery gets the ball on a broken play, traversing disarray to find a running lane. Defenders pursue, but Jameson uses rare speed to take out multiple men and assist the 75-yard score. It's not planned. It's instinct. We're all in.[2]

We're 9–3. A lifetime's spent watching other teams spurt to success, wondering how that must feel. What's been longed for finally arrives. It's glorious.

However, life has room for all things. SMART Recovery's goal is a balanced life. It's only right that my two most anticipated events occur simultaneously.

An 812 area code flashes across my phone.

"I need help."

He's followed protocol.

Packing for a couple days isn't enough. I'll never come back. At least not in the same form. Banjo Bob's actively dying. He's scared. He needs me.

Bob lies on the bed, fetal in the familiar crevice that's cradled him for years. He's awake, reading a 1988 Detroit Lions Media Guide and wearing an arrow through his pate. I reposition the arrow to kiss his bald head.

"How are you?"

"I've got a splitting headache."

He gathers remaining strength and gestures at the arrow. "Don't cut off an archer in traffic." I politely laugh so conversation can move on to planning his death.

Death's so much effort. Work streams start up with the rapidity of popups on illegal streaming sites. I fix oxygen, call doctors, and change clothes. He just wants me to be happy, sharing esotericism to the end. "Do you want to shoot a BB gun in the backyard?"

---

2. Also warranting mention is a block against Tampa by Craig Reynolds that sends the target into the netherworld and Amon-Ra into the end zone.

He rummages through clutter for a bag of garbage. Inside is another bag of garbage. Inside that is a Detroit Lions game ball, awarded to a past defensive coordinator for overseeing a shutout. It's a beautiful gesture.

"You can't afford this."

My hands caress the ball's contours, tracing an elongated piece of leather jutting out.

"I'll take care of that for you." He rifles through tools, finds the right one, and snips off the offending piece. It's not much but takes everything he has. He admires his handiwork.

A plan's formed. I'll pack up his house and find a facility in the Detroit area.

"How do you feel about coming back to Michigan?"

"Will the Lions be on TV?"

"Yes."

"I'll do it."

He proudly announces that he's serious about his health. "I quit smoking." I don't have the heart to tell him it's too late. Doctors say his heart is functioning at 10% capacity. Mine feels the same.

WEEK 14: DECEMBER 10, 2023.
DETROIT LIONS (9-3) V CHICAGO BEARS (4-8).
SOLDIER FIELD, CHICAGO, IL.

Banjo Bob's thrilled the Bears game will be broadcast on local TV. We play a horrific first half but claw back to lead 13–10 at the break.

"I'd like an Asiago cheese bagel," is his only request. I'd go to the ends of the earth for him—and arguably have by being in Indiana—but all he wants is a crappy bagel. The New Yorker in me dies a little.

I'm in town buying bagels when an 812 number flashes across my phone.

"I'm scared, Slick."

"I'll be back in ten minutes."

"I'm scared now."

The combination of COPD and heart disease reduces oxygen to the brain, causing panic attacks. These maladies will cause death but the panic attacks are killing him, starting the moment he's alone with his thoughts. Feeling his feelings is too much. They must become someone else's problem.

Local EMTs know him well. One checks vitals while another plucks a banjo.

"He's dying but it's not necessarily an emergency."

EMTs try leaving but Bob won't let them go. He grabs one of their arms. "I'm scared."

"People don't go to the emergency room because they're scared."

"I'm dying."

"Not today."

The TV flickers in the background. I tell him to take deep breaths and watch the game. The Same Old Lions return to say goodbye. It's illogical for the team to play this poorly but makes perfect sense. If Bob's life flashes before his eyes, he should see the team playing like shit.

EMTs try escaping but the hoard blocks their path, trapping them in a darkened room with a pleading man.

"Take me to the hospital."

"Your condition hasn't changed."

"I'm more scared."

A lifetime's worth of repressed emotions start flowing. Bob's histrionics work. EMTs load him into an ambulance and hastily exit. The shack quiets quickly. The drone of a classic loss is all there is, all there's ever been.

The hospital won't take him. A cavalry of Midwestern health-care workers parade past Bob, saying the same thing. "There's no medical reason to keep you."

Banjo Bob continues displaying emotions.

He throws himself to the floor, attempting to injure himself enough to be admitted for just one more night. I pick him up, return him to the chair, and cradle him in my arms, but he won't stop. Again and again, he *thuds* to the floor. I sit on his lap, dusting off a childhood pose to stop my dad's self-harm.

He sticks his finger down his throat, vomiting on me.

"Doctor! I'm sick."

Nothing works. He ups the stakes with threats of suicide. Nurses continue discharge procedures, eager to rid themselves of this burden.

Loving my father makes me a bad person. "They'll only keep you if you say how you're gonna do it."

"I'LL SMOKE NEXT TO MY OXYGEN TANK AND BLOW MYSELF UP!"

Nurses sigh. The magic words. A specific threat legally requires action. Annoyed workers pass the buck, admitting him to a psychiatric hospital across the state. Helping my dad die has another hurdle. I must secure his release from the looney bin.

I can't see him. He's only reachable by phone a half hour each day. I isolate myself in his world, figuring out what to do with it.

I find a spot near family in Taylor, Michigan. In the evening, when calls are allowed, I wait fifteen rings for someone to answer. I wait another 10 minutes for him to pick up the phone and tell me, "Whatever you think."

"We're gonna pack your clothes and your instruments. Anything else we should bring?"

"The Bobby Layne autograph."

He softens during this stage, telling me he's grateful and proud. I appreciate the words but notice they aren't given in response to achievement. They're said to keep me in place, picking up the pieces after he responds to death's specter by faking clinical insanity.

WEEK 15: DECEMBER 16, 2023.
DENVER BRONCOS (7-6) v DETROIT LIONS (9-4).
FORD FIELD, DETROIT, MI.

The worst task is dealing with the volume of belongings. A forgotten fish tank sits in the corner. I can't fathom dumping it, ending minnows' lives. They did nothing wrong.

A Craigslist ad brings a teenage girl to claim it. Her brother and grandfather come with, eyeing some fishing gear.

"Take it. You're doing me a favor."

The old man breaks into tears and shrinks into my arms.

"You don't understand. This is Christmas," I clarify, toying with an epiphany to rid myself of the familial horde once and for all.

I have a game plan. Hoarding exists due to imaginary valuations. This perspective binds Walkowskis in debris-laden tombs. A dumpster gets parked in the driveway. My best friend, John, drives down from Detroit. We shield ourselves with hazmat masks and ready the burn bucket.

I'm getting rid of this family. All that shall remain is what I decide to bring along. The dumpster will be filled with our baggage. The burn bucket will cleanse us of trauma. I find written proof of my grandmother and her terrible actions. I watch it burn. The bad things we carried become ash and embers, wafting upward, vanishing in the night.

We post on social media about a "Free Estate Sale." Any item worth taking is yours. Locals claim familial remnants, sorting through our past until nothing remains.

Several individuals, incredulous that all this can be given away, offer money. They don't realize I'm the one getting the deal of a lifetime.

"What do you want for this?"

"Nothing."

"Is there anything I can do?"

"The Lions play at eight PM. Root for them."

We make the Lions the most popular team in rural Indiana. The last of Bob's belongings are taken. The shack is empty. I'm free. We drive to Buffalo Wild Wings and eat the worst chicken of our lives.

LaPorta. Gibbs. St. Brown. Young stars dominate Denver. The outcome's secured when Amon-Ra catches a slant in the red zone. He ascends over obstacles, flipping over a defender, contorting himself into being unstoppable. *Touchdown Lions!*

Our youth movement produces six touchdowns. The Same Old Lions are gone. They're in a dumpster next to hundreds of whoopee cushions.

My voice is hoarse from inhaled mold and multiple renditions of "Gridiron Heroes" but I need to speak. This story must be told. It's not a new beginning. It's the same story passed down except I'm the one telling it.

WEEK 16: DECEMBER 24, 2023. DETROIT LIONS (10-4) V MINNESOTA VIKINGS (7-7). U.S. BANK STADIUM, MINNEAPOLIS, MN.

I expertly guide the U-Haul into the mental hospital's circle drive. The car trailer is more stubborn, flattening rosebushes.

Everyone there knows me. I've called enough to develop rapport. No one mentions the rosebushes.

The ward door swings open. I expect a feeble man. Banjo Bob bounds out, refreshed. A stint in the state-run mental hospital was the vacation he always needed.[3]

I load him into the U-Haul, securing him like one of his beloved banjos. We pull away from Indiana, never to return. We're Detroiters.

We drive past a Cabela's.

"Cabela's has a great fish tank."

"I never want to hear you mention a fish tank."

"What if I want one for my room?"

"You tried that."

"Oh, yeah."

We pull into the American House assisted living center. Cousins chip in to make it a home.

Banjo Bob has a clean bed, a dresser, and pictures hung on the wall. We put up a Lions jersey. The number is "1." The nameplate reads "Before I Die."

Bob's roommate is Terrence, a 400-pound man doubling as the facility's preacher. He's good at two things: 1) asking me to improve my relationship with Jesus and 2) slipping off his walker and requesting I pick him up.

---

3. He protests the lack of transparency in asylum protocols about TV watching like he's Randle P. McMurphy.

Visitors—proud switchblade recipients—surround Bob with music, reminding him that he's loved. A lifetime playing guitar at every function pays deathbed dividends.

I spent most holidays hating my dad. I'd hear the phone endlessly ring, knowing he was there but too depressed to answer. He has a merry Christmas.

Banjo Bob shuffles to the common area. Balloons are hung and others gather, excited to watch the kitties. It's heaven.

The quarterback who wasn't good enough starts with the ball and leads a touchdown drive. Gibbs adds to the lead. Our feeble pass defense falters, allowing Minnesota to take a third-quarter lead.

This is when we cave to the pressure. Not anymore. We are the pressure.

St. Brown moves the chains, LaPorta makes clutch grabs, and Gibbs breaks out the best juke seen since #20. We take the lead and don't give it back. Things were unacceptable for too long. All we needed to do was hand the reins to the next generation.

Minnesota threatens. We muff a fumble and Justin Jefferson converts a third and 27. Did I pack *Same Old Lions* by mistake?

The Vikings go for the win. The route is jumped. *Interception!*

The Detroit Lions have won the division. This hasn't happened since 1993, a veritable lifetime ago, when Banjo Bob was the parent and I was the child. He lives to see it. More importantly, he gets to be in Detroit and feel it. Manifestation hangs above Bob's bed: "1 Before I Die." Maybe we picked the right nameplate for Bob's jersey after all.

GAME 17

THERE IS NO END

• 2024 •

Two Playoff Wins, Two Losses

Postseason
2-1

We sit outside the dining hall with the only notary available on short notice. A line of seniors gathered for supper snakes around our table. Banjo Bob fixates on the notary's rubber stamp. I get Bob's attention and slide paperwork across the table. DO NOT RESUSCITATE.

"There are implications. No lifesaving measures will be taken. Any questions?"

"How do you change the date on the rubber stamp?" The spectrum spares us one more uncomfortable conversation.

Life revolves around the senior center. Best hours are spent watching Banjo Bob gobble orange sherbet and guzzle Vernors ginger ale. Occasionally, I'll mention his diabetes. He passive-aggressively eats more, grumbling refill requests.

My favorite SMART Recovery tool asks participants to schedule life, packing calendars to avoid urges. This exercise is vital. Each hour's meticulously allocated to making Bob's death a happy one.

Banjo Bob is not at peace. We have the right conversations and medications but instincts don't change. The ambulance gets called whenever he gets scared—which is any time he's alone.

Like a parent to a colicky newborn, I exist to resolve disruption in another part of the bloodline. My cell phone ringer stays at full blast. I stay ready to placate fears, purchase sugary snacks, or correctly inform some doctor Bob lied to. There's always some urgent task.

Sundays remain unchanged, stubbornly dedicated to joy after all these years. Bob wouldn't have it any other way.

Bob's dying but that's not why he's depressed. Becoming Bob's caretaker has deprived him of his favorite activity. He can't vicariously live through me when my life sucks.

I follow every order except one: "Enjoy your life."

I remember 17 banjos that need rehoming and years of ignored car payments that need fronting. "I can't."

"Enjoy. Your. Life." We make a deal. With the postseason near, my most sacred duty is to bear witness and report back.

WEEK 18: JANUARY 7, 2024.
MINNESOTA VIKINGS (7-9) V DETROIT LIONS (11-5).
FORD FIELD, DETROIT, MI.

It's meaningless in a new way. The playoffs are locked up, but despite the perfunctory matchup, there's no chance Campbell lets up.

Ford Field feels like the entire stadium just attended their first meeting. Everyone's happy, surfing on gratitude, ignoring the hell we experienced to get here.

Except the team. Those boys kick ass.

An unknown number rings my phone. I know what that means.

"Your father's on life support."

I break the cardinal rule, Banjo Bob's only filial requirement. He won't like it—even under these circumstances—but I do it anyway.

I leave the game early.

No thinking, just adrenaline. I sprint to a cab, shrieking "take me to a hospital" in a desperate tone that tells the cabbie to rip me off. Three hundred dollars later, I sprint into the ICU. Seeing my father tethered to life-extending machines sparks the obvious question: *Why is a man wearing a DO NOT RESUSCITATE wristband on life support?*

WILD CARD: JANUARY 14, 2024. LOS ANGELES RAMS (10-7) V DETROIT LIONS (12-5). FORD FIELD, DETROIT, MI.

Night turns to morning and the playoff picture becomes clear. I stay by Banjo Bob's side, whispering sweet nothings into semiconscious ears. "We host the Rams on Sunday night. Ford Field's first playoff opponent is . . . Matthew. If you reach the other side and find something besides blackness . . . help us win."[1]

He's extubated. I wait for him to slip away but breathing stabilizes. He opens his eyes and blinks at me.

"We host the Rams on Sunday night . . ."

He gestures at the tube still down his throat. Doctors advise that it should remain in place, but Bob won't stop gesturing. He needs it removed like he's never needed anything. The staff reluctantly performs the kindness. He sips water and clears his throat. I lean close, eager for secrets from the beyond.

"Bring . . . me . . . my . . . arrow." The man who lived through gags is determined to die through them.

His body forgets how to walk. He relearns by leaning on a walker and lapping the nursing home while I bark encouragement. It's our salad days.

---

1. I also ask him to walk my dead dog. He remembers this statement and starts referring to death as "getting a dog."

We take up shuffleboard and host a string of visitors, each showing up with fond memories and orange sherbet.

Remaining hours are spent dissecting the game. Lions versus Stafford, Goff facing his old team, every storyline is getting wrapped up simultaneously.

"I'd like to watch it here with you."

"No. Report. Back."

The most expensive tickets in franchise history are a drop in the bucket. I buy two and fail at convincing him to go. "If your heart stops at the game it'd be fitting to ruin the Lions' day for once."

"RE. PORT. BACK."

We watch early games, barely talking but feeling everything. I take his custom jersey off the wall, squeeze it around his torso, and head to Ford Field with my mother.

It's the coldest day of the year. Every seat's filled an hour before kickoff but not because of temperature. There's nowhere else worth being. Sixty-five thousand sit in prayer, a ritual designed to shoo away the other shoe once and for all.

Matthew jogs out of the tunnel. We boo our beloved as negativity evolves into a spontaneous chant. *JA-RED GOFF! JA-RED GOFF!* Every Detroiter knows what it's like to be rejected, the sting of watching Matthew take home the crown with another. Chanting is our way of saying: "We're fine without you."

Campbell starts with the same message. We open with a grinding drive demonstrating Goff's support system. David Montgomery plunges for a score.

Second Quarter, 7:16; Lions 20, Rams 10; Fourth Down

Detroit can't quite pull away. Everyone knows Campbell's next move. Going for the jugular isn't a decision. It's an identity. Goff gets the defense to bite on a play-action fake. A window opens and a perfect throw finds Sam LaPorta for seven.

Fourth Quarter, 4:07; Lions 24, Rams 23

Matthew won't quit, repeatedly nipping our heels. We get the ball knowing we can't let him touch it again. The weight of not winning a playoff game since 1991 is palpable. Coming through now changes us forever.

We put the ball in Jared's hands. He finds Monty for a first. *Tick . . . tick . . . tick* . . . The clock runs but Goff passes. Amon-Ra grabs one in traffic, diving for a first down as the game enters the two-minute warning.

We've won but no one realizes.[2] Knowledge ripples through the building until victory formation ignites true euphoria. The Detroit Lions have won a playoff game.

Campbell gathers his men, hands Jared the game ball, and tells the world, "Jared Goff. You're good enough for Detroit." The throwaway is now the leader.

Jared and Dan and Sheila and Brad and Penei and Amon-Ra and others took on a problem they did not cause but accepted that solving it was their job. Exorcism complete.

Joy is hard earned. It isn't conjured with chemicals or quick fixes. The links between team and self are clear. We changed in September 2021 and are never going back.

My mother and I dance through the stadium, exiting into subzero Michigan weather that can't touch us. We're kept warm, cocooned by jubilant car-horn cacophony and *JA-RED GOFF* chants.

Banjo Bob's awake and waiting. I gift him every Ford Field knick-knack. Others filled a dumpster. We start anew with these.

I share it all. Explaining how the team represents me to the only one capable of understanding. I soliloquy for hours, receiving a single-word response, repeated en masse with different punctuations.

---

2. There are two minutes left and the Rams have a timeout, but everyone's too hyped to do math.

"Wonderful. Wonderful. Wonderful."

I remove the arrow from his head and send him off to sleep. Our shared dream came true in waking hours.

DIVISIONAL ROUND: JANUARY 21, 2024. TAMPA BAY BUCCANEERS (10-8) V DETROIT LIONS (13-5). FORD FIELD, DETROIT, MI.

A life lived at the foot of my father's deathbed pays off. He improves in every capacity, even convincing me to have his catheter removed.

They take it out.

I sit on the floor, quietly transcribing these journals. Banjo Bob rises from bed, urinating on both me and this book.[3] I dry off the urine, put Bob in his jersey, and adorn him with his arrow. Once it's in place like his personal halo, I drive to Ford Field.

Our downtrodden fan base steps up, becoming the sport's best home-field advantage. There are thousands like me, learning faults from the team that put the "lovable" in "lovable losers." We protested in the streets but always filled the seats. Only family can annually ruin Thanksgiving but still get invited.

Tampa ekes out a halftime tie. Even worse, the Bucs start the third quarter with the ball. On a key third down, Aidan Hutchinson bulls into the backfield to snuff out the threat. Our hometown hero comes through.

Third Quarter, 3:51; Lions 16, Buccaneers 10; Fourth and Goal

Campbell trusts the entire roster. The game's biggest carry goes to third-string running back Craig Reynolds. *Touchdown!*

Tampa won't simply let us have our day. We'll have to win it. Gibbs cuts outside, squirts past a defender, and throws another to the ground with

3. You can hate this book but will never take the mantle of worst review. The subject literally pissed on the author for writing a second draft.

a vicious stiff arm. *Touchdown!* It takes 25 years but someone finally fills Barry's shoes.

A Goff–St. Brown connection provides a 14-point lead with five minutes remaining. It should be safe, but Tampa throws a long touchdown on fourth and 10. A one-possession game with plenty of time left.

The cycle of devastating losses plays in my mind. Hail Marys, muffed extra points, a shack filled with whoopee cushions. I consider these thoughts and how to classify them: irrational.

A Tampa receiver breaks free across the middle. Derrick Barnes reaches for the ball, skying as high as a linebacker can sky, falling to Earth with possession. We roar like never before.

There are no right words so I settle on screaming. If my best days came sadly trudging out of the Silverdome, what does it mean to dance out of Ford Field like an overserved wedding guest?

Banjo Bob awaits, wide-eyed and agog. Conversation doesn't extend far beyond "Forward down the field" but satisfaction comes from mere proximity. The dying man and the son who resents him are a happy family.

NFC CHAMPIONSHIP: JANUARY 28, 2024. DETROIT LIONS (14-5) V SAN FRANCISCO 49ERS (13-5). LEVI'S STADIUM, SANTA CLARA, CA.

I need to be there with him but he needs me across the country. He argues that the bloodline that bought season tickets in 1934 warrants representation but that ain't it. Banjo Bob's addicted to living vicariously and needs one last fix.

Journalistic standards matter. Banjo Bob wants a firsthand recollection. I head to the NFC Championship.

The nursing home is five minutes from the airport. I stay too long, hoping he'll change his mind. He doesn't. He wants me gone.

Lions fans buy flights and hotels and tickets in droves, draining relatively humble bank accounts, but money doesn't matter. The fan base spares no expense to fill Frisco's house with Honolulu Blue.

California's perfect. Clear skies and no expectations. San Francisco has great personnel and previous playoff failures as motivation. They're better.

"Are you nervous?" my seatmate asks.

"No. I'm just happy to be here."

The anthem plays. Thoughts turn to what Dan and Brad have built, how it has provided something to focus on during my darkest days. Swollen with gratitude, I bawl my fucking eyes out. The sadness I power through isn't felt until this moment, weeping in the bleachers. Military jets screech overhead but I can't hear them over my cries.

We start with a home-run swing. Jamo takes the reverse. No hole awaits but raw speed creates one, positively dusting those dudes. All they can grab is a handful of undershirt that cartoonishly extends like cheese in a pizza commercial, snapping as he scores. It's the happiest moment of my life.

I rationalize the Niners' quality. They advance down the field, get held to a field goal attempt, and *CLANG* it off the upright, wasting a possession.

A lifetime of bad luck is undone in a single half. Montgomery spears into the end zone: *14–0 Lions!* This cannot be happening.

I expect every Niner possession to turn the tide but it doesn't. Fan-favorite Malcolm Rodriguez picks off Brock Purdy. We cannot be stopped. Gibbs goes into the end zone untouched. We tack on a field goal and jog to the locker room.

It's halftime of the NFC Championship. Detroit leads by 17 points. Holy shit. Holy fucking shit.

I let myself think the forbidden thought: *The Detroit Lions are going to the Super Bowl.*

I make sure Banjo Bob is not controlling the game from beyond. He finally answers the phone.

"Can you believe this?"

"Nope."

"Me neither."

Journey is introduced as the halftime performer and plays "Don't Stop Believing." I never did. I settle into prayer and meditation.

This cannot be happening.

It doesn't.

Third Quarter, 7:05; Lions 24, Niners 10; Fourth and 2

Up two touchdowns, Dan Campbell goes for the jugular because that's who he is. A normal coach would take the field goal. Then again, a normal coach doesn't save this franchise. Goff finds his receiver with a perfect pass . . . *dropped!*

It begins.

Grasping at straws, San Francisco buys a scratch-off lotto ticket and takes a shot over the top. A Lions defender circles underneath, waiting to secure the Super Bowl.

Bonk! The ball clanks off the defender's face, wobbling into the waiting arms of a Niner for a gain of 51. If I die and go to hell the devil won't be waiting for me. This play will be. God abandons us the moment ball grazes face mask. Niners score.

We answer by handing the ball to Jahmyr, our perfect back. *Fumble!* San Francisco pounces on it and scores in four plays. Tie game. Another opportunity to respond. Facing third and 9, Goff finds the open man but, again, the pass is dropped.

San Francisco takes the lead. I rationalize it's just a field goal. We can bounce back.

Fourth Quarter, 7:38; Niners 27, Lions 24; Fourth and 3

Goff leads a healthy drive, advancing the ball to the Niner 30. A normal coach would take the field goal and tie. Then again, a normal coach wouldn't inspire me to quit pills after 25 years.

We fail. Niner ball. It's over.

Momentum is real. The way things have gone will be the way things go until they're changed. The defense steps onto the field with the trepidation I have entering Banjo Bob's hoarder shack. SMART taught me what comes next.

An **A**ctivating event catalyzes existing **B**eliefs to create unwanted **C**onsequences. It was substance abuse in my life but—in this instance—it's the Niners' clinching touchdown. A ball bouncing off a face mask brought back the Same Old Lions. It sucks but I had my moment—the singular second where I got to think *the Lions are going to the Super Bowl.* It was nice but I didn't need it. Not like I did the losses.

The only thing pulling me out of loss-induced dissociation is observing Niners fans barely smiling. *Why aren't they happier?* They have so much that the grandest conquest is just another pleasant afternoon. I'll take euphoria from close calls over satisfaction from the ultimate prize every time.

I'll never see the Lions in the Super Bowl. I'll never save Banjo Bob. It could be disheartening. It should be. But it's been enough to sustain me.

I loved him the only way he let me. Trauma and mental health developed habits he couldn't change. He had no motivation to do better. It was his way to connect. He knew I'd be there to clean up his mess. It made him feel loved.

I can't stop imagining that maybe he'll get better. Not just shrug off death but finally see his child and show him the way. That's what every kid wants.

That's not what every kid gets. Sometimes you get a dad who only talks about football. The only available win is figuring out how to love him. It's taxing and imperfect but it's yours. You did it, so enjoy it. Don't be like those pleased-as-punch San Franciscans. Every win warrants celebration—even half measures and compromises.

Banjo Bob waits for me. I expect mirrored disappointment. The thing he waited a lifetime for will not occur, but he wears a smile—and a fake arrow.

"They fucking blew it," I ruefully declare.

"They had a great season," Bob clarifies.

"A Super Bowl literally slipped through our fingers."

"I like being a fan."

"You're going to die and got teased in your last game. It's cruel."

I collapse in his chair. The exhaustion I've been running from hits me the millisecond ass meets cigarette-burnt fabric.

"So . . . how was the game?"

"Traumatic. I'll be figuring out how it damaged me for the rest of my days, eternally wondering how it could've been different. I fucking loved it."

Clarity crosses his face as he absorbs the facts. He is the team and has been the entire time. He pisses in a Gatorade bottle.

★ ★ ★

Julion unsheaths Banjo Bob's cane to reveal a sword. *Surprise and delight!* Banjo Bob's an imperfect father but an exceptional distant relative.

We circle the senior center. Walking between my withered father and Paul Bunyanesque godson makes us look like a chart explaining evolution. That's not far off.

We rest on couches in the lobby, long abandoned by 7 PM. Julion and Banjo Bob have an impassioned discussion on what makes a good knife. One of them mentions a knife, describes it in detail, as the other concludes, "that's a good knife."

I ask for a photo to preserve the moment. We pull in props and silly poses, filling the frame with gags. The final shot features me seated, holding Bob's gold-headed Lion cane. Julion and Bob stand behind me with arms crossed, looking like my protectors. They are. I didn't know how to care for myself until they needed me.

Banjo Bob announces "I'm going to bed" in the emphatic fashion reserved for children and the elderly. "Tonight was perfect." I take off the arrow, kiss my father's head, and turn off the light. "Good night, Banjo Bob."

He dies in his sleep. It's the storybook ending we longed for but we don't get those, not in Detroit. There's always a way for a loss to hurt worse. Our job is finding it.

He's mistakenly revived. Again. Doctors ignore the signs, paperwork, and bracelet, shocking him back to this mortal coil for another round of goodbyes. I rush to the ICU to find Banjo Bob wearing a confused expression and his trademark arrow.[4]

I enter my mother's kitchen on a peaceful, sunny morning. *Beat.* I go apeshit. Cups are broken and expletives unleashed in a torrent reserved for third-down failures. I throw a shitty little tantrum.

My only source of pride is keeping it together. Everything has been "fine" even though it's been hell. Not acknowledging these emotions saves them for later, setting up a fireworks display in my mother's kitchen.

I tried conquering the generations and my own emotions. I fail. Banjo Bob defeats me. My chest heaves and eyes water. Julion watches the entire thing. I fail him.

Julion's mom, Kayleigh, also watches. I detect a flicker of disappointment in her eyes because I look for it.

"I'm sorry your son saw that." She refuses the apology, telling me I deserve to feel my feelings. That I expressed emotions in a safe manner, around those who make me feel secure. I consider my worthiness to feel, fingering shards of what used to be an espresso cup.

A key component of being a good man is knowing how to be mad or sad or bad. Kayleigh lets me know that even my worst moments did right by her son.

I take Julion to the gym. "We're not working out. We're working through emotions." He follows me around, learning to love what I do, confident he can keep up, and begging to be pushed. *I get it, kid.*

He does more for me than I do for him. It's the power of being needed. The same is true for my dad.

He never told me what the lessons were. I had to find wins where there weren't any. That process became my worldview. He didn't parent me but I

---

4. The arrow's presence in this work is repetitive. It's not an attempt at literary device but an honest recollection. Every time something goes wrong he puts on the arrow.

got kindness, humor, and far too many switchblades. Blazing my own path always led me back to him, bringing a bit more of the world each time.

Banjo Bob loses mobility. No more leather sewn or banjos plucked.

Banjo Bob loses verbal ability. I'll never find out what makes a good knife for the thousandth time.

With nothing else to lose, he gains peace.

I'm alone with him, sitting on the foot of his bed, soaking in the vision. I've defined him many ways but here, where it matters most, he's just my old man.

Boys talk football with their fathers.

Knowing he can hear me, I break down the roster. Like the city they represent, the team's beautiful once again. The impossible has happened. The Detroit Lions are good. They can be trusted. I tell him how good it is and how good it will be.

"Campbell's the coach. I see my values in his efforts. There's talent. Penei and Jared and Saint. Sam and Gibbs and Monty. Even sweet Jameson's coming along. We were worried about him but he got there. Finally, the Lions contain every wonderful thing a football team can contain. This hasn't been true since you entered this world."

I wax poetic, expounding about my team to an audience of one. The Lions define this chapter—not because they're good or my dad's dying, but because they've defined every chapter. That's how it goes for boys and their teams.

"A city creates a way to be a fan. A family makes a boy rudderless; the same thing happens to his squad. They lose and lose. Another boy enters. He falls in love with Barry because that's what happens when one watches Barry Sanders. Hope's chased by losing and more losing. We waste a chance at salvation, lose some more, and hubris sends us to rock bottom. We figure out what's wrong, pinpoint inherited errors, and rebuild the right way. It works.

"Sports are not life or death. They're life. Few teams win the Super Bowl and fewer people live out their dreams. The only way to guarantee victory is to define it yourself. I'm sober, tending my wounds by telling my story."

I state my piece and pause for response. He has nothing to say.

Banjo Bob is dead. We got our storybook ending after all.

We listen to bluegrass until the coroner arrives. He brings a stretcher, loads my father into a body bag, and offers a last look.

"Wait."

I grab a garment and unzip the body bag. I squeeze a jersey around his already stiffening torso. The number is 1. The nameplate reads, "Before I Die." It's a tribute to something that almost came true. That's okay. It's more than most people get.

The coroner closes the body bag and wheels my father away. That's what he thinks anyway. It's just the body. Important parts stay behind. I tell them to Julion. They're with me as I write this. I use them when I need a silver lining. Or when I need to know what a good knife is.

I weep but not as hard as expected. If Banjo Bob taught me anything it's how to take a loss.

Thanks, Dad.

APRIL 25, 2024

I have two errands downtown. It's a zoo. Once again, Detroit is the center of the world.

Errand #1

I park illegally outside Ford Field and enter the empty stadium. I do not savor the sight of my favorite place. I sprint through the corridor, enter the pro shop, and drop $200 on an Amon-Ra jersey. I needed to replace one.

Errand #2

They tell me, "Park by the dumpster," so I do. A woman hands me a clipboard and asks me to sign, so I do. I accept Bob's remains, wrap them in

Amon-Ra's jersey, and drive back to my job at an automaker. I don't think about the hard parts. I dwell on the positives. Uh, there's no traffic?

Over three days, Detroit hosts the NFL draft and 775,000 fans. Detroit's clean and happy and impressive, reverting to its natural state: a football town. The original football town.

I'm not back for Detroit. I'm back for me. I can't let scar tissue take hold. I don't want to remember Detroit as death's backdrop. I need it to stay my home.

Julion, now a blossoming young man, skips a track meet to visit. We make a deal. I'll take him to the draft and a ball game, but he owes me a practice. We wear our running shoes and promise to push each other.

The draft and game tick away. A warm spring day becomes a cool, welcoming evening. It's perfect ball-game weather but he just wants it to end. He's a great young runner, piloting his fledgling body to six-minute miles. He needs me to know how strong his stamina is, how much he can endure. *I've known for years. We're the same.*

The game ends. We take off, weaving through hot-dog-stuffed masses. We break from the crowd and into a sprint. He's faster than me. I cultivated his masculine bravado for it to someday tell me I'm old. We pass the draft and the glistening waterfront. He lets me lead even though I don't know where I'm going. The practice hasn't led him astray yet.

It's nice to be pubescent, waking up each day as a better version of yourself. He needs me to see his speed. *I've found something. I'm good at it.* He thinks he's just gotten an ability. He doesn't see the confidence and character that comes with it. I do.

Julion tries dusting me. The old dog won't let him. I can endure too. We push each other. Harder, faster, farther.

Onlookers notice. Pedestrians offer fist pounds and high fives. Beer drinkers shout encouragement from pleasant patios.

"Are they cheering for me?" Julion asks.

"Yeah. You're great at this."

"Cool."

Sharing something he loves with someone he loves makes the world take notice. I'm proud of him but that doesn't matter. He's proud of himself. We've traveled so far from the baseball stadium, much farther from the funeral home parking lot.

Feet pound pavement as the city cheers us on. We cut onto Brush Street, beginning the next lap. Sprint, sweat, nothing but our efforts and bond. We slip into the shadows of Ford Field, disappearing into the good Detroit night, knowing we can keep going.

Forward Down the Field!

ACKNOWLEDGMENTS

There are so many thank-yous, a staggering abundance of gratitude.

Thank you to . . .

This book. Your existence helped me navigate many difficult times. I don't know what I would've done without you waiting, demanding my best.

My mother, Collette Cullen. Reading this aloud to you was my favorite life experience.

Rachel Kearney. Your support, friendship, and copy edits made the last two years way easier.

Scott Kauffman. My agent, my champion, my friend. You're in for Sunday, pal.

Nick Olah for picking me up off the floor, John Scaramucci for always coming to my rescue.

Chau Tu, genius, bulldog, bestie. Sorry I didn't know the right em dash formatting.

Matt Holt, Katie Dickman, Kerri Stebbins, and everyone at the Matt Holt imprint for their enthusiasm and partnership. Scott Stratten is also the man.

My marketing/PR help. Diana Hussein for a lifetime in my corner. Kate Bryan for demonstrating what the good side of a family can be.

Thursday crew. My heroes. I'll shut up about this now. Special shout-out to Bryan Clark for leading the pack.

Dr. Liam Harris for telling me to keep going.

Appu Goundan for taking me to the water park.

Cate & Isfi for keeping me alive in Vallejo.

Dr. Nikita for promising to help and then not.

Brielle Farmer, Ben Zurawski & Nikki Vargas for invaluable contributions to the proposal. Y'all helped this come to life.

Jeff LaPenna for always believing this could happen. John Capogna for eating.

Paul Myers . . . "HEY!"

Bryan Hood for giving me Ray Carver in 2008.

James Hamilton for early feedback, Jeff Cerulli for rides to hoops and an assist on early feedback—his first!

Great friends and early reads: Kathryn Berk, Nate Myers, Richie Tolway, Bozo, Hoopster Jurich, Donnie Sengstack, Taylor Slifko, Kira Frabutt, Chris Daniels, Peter Bryan, Jeff Wesselschmidt, Anthony DeVito, Chris Waelti, Nate Fridson, Carl Sonnefeld, Ethan SP, Brendan Gibbons, John Rosenberger, Elias DiSabato, Matt Benjamin, Turkey's Nest/Fan Therapy Crew, Brock Alter, Josh Gondelman, Joseph Roberts, Heidi Knappenberger, Nandini Vijayakumar, Adam Nollen, Alex Feldhaus, Diana Gold (although it was *pretty early* for an acknowledgment), and many more.

Big thanks to Clay Rodriguez for my author photo and Erin Klema for the cover photography.

My professor, Dr. Todd Boyd.

Uncle Russ Gibb.

Gabe, Billy, Genevive, Esther, Elliot, Jen, Thomas x2 <3 Liam <3.

Julion and Kayleigh Cullen for trusting me with this story and supporting along the way.

Tilly. We finished, baby.

Banjo Bob. You were always a character. I'm honored to help you formally become one.

Absolutely no thanks to:

Matt Millen

Matt Patricia

BIBLIOGRAPHY

GAME 2

van der Kolk, Bessel. *The Body Keeps the Score: Brain, Mind, and Body in the Healing of Trauma*. Penguin Books, 2014.

Bak, Richard. *When Lions Were Kings*. Taylor Publishing Company, 1997.

"Scapegoat." Wikipedia. https://www.en.wikipedia.org/wiki/Scapegoat.

"A History of the Detroit Lions Franchise Ownership." *Lions Wire*. June 24, 2020. https://www.lionswire.usatoday.com/2020/06/24/a-history-of-the-detroit-lions-franchise-ownership/.

"Here's why the Lions always play on Thanksgiving, explained." *Sporting News*, accessed November 12, 2025. https://www.sportingnews.com/us/nfl/news/detroit-lions-thanksgiving-explained/5ym3h65v3d3m16ev64nuk5kfj.

GAME 3

Leavitt, Theodore. "Marketing Myopia." *Harvard Business Review*, July–August 1960.

Plimpton, George. *Paper Lion: Confessions of a Last-String Quarterback*. Harper Perennial, 1966.

"William Clay Ford Sr.: The Right Owner for the Detroit Lions?" *Bleacher Report*. https://www.bleacherreport.com/articles/181471-william-clay-ford-sr-the-right-owner-for-the-detroit-lions.

"Highlight: 3 Minutes in 1976—Lions Owner." Reddit. https://www.reddit.com/r/nfl/comments/g8e9zy/oc_highlight_3_minutes_in_1976_lions_owner/.

"20 Years Ago: Russ Thomas Had One Last Contract Squabble." *Bleacher Report*. https://www.bleacherreport.com/articles/217081-20-years-ago-russ-thomas-had-one-last-contract-squabble.

"Alex Karras NFL Gambling Suspension." *Fornology*. https://www.fornology.blogspot.com/2020/09/alex-karras-nfl-gambling-suspension.html.

"Pro Football: Bush-League Scandal." *Time*. https://www.time.com/archive/6626391/pro-football-bush-league-scandal/.

"Russ Thomas & William Clay Ford." DetroitYES Forums. https://www.detroityes.com/mb/showthread.php?24416-Russ-Thomas-amp-William-Clay-Ford.

GAME 4

Reedy, Joe. "Popular Documentary 'Bye Bye Barry' Sheds New Light on Sanders' Decision to Retire from Lions." AP News. December 8, 2023. https://www.apnews.com/article/detroit-lions-barry-sanders-documentary-amazon-prime-5d893b81b0c937423ce39deddccf3f27.

Bye Bye Barry. Directed by Ken Rodgers and Angela Ellis. NFL Films, 2023.

"William Sanders Ignores Son Barry in Hall Introduction." *The Oklahoman*. https://www.oklahoman.com/story/news/2004/08/09/william-sanders-ignores-son-barry-in-hall-introduction/61979184007/.

Kensler, Tom. "OSU Going To Japan: Pokes Play Tech in '88." *The Oklahoman*. https://www.oklahoman.com/story/news/1987/10/27/osu-going-to-japan-pokes-play-tech-in-tokyo-in-88/62673434007/?gnt-cfr=1&gca-cat=p&gca-uir=true&gca-epti=z113423d00----v113423b0038xxd003865&gca-ft=162&gca-ds=sophi.

Murphy, Austin. "A Lamb Among Lions." *Sports Illustrated Vault*. https://www.vault.si.com/vault/1990/09/10/a-lamb-among-lions-a-gentle-soul-off-the-field-barry-sanders-runs-up-a-storm-for-detroit.

Brandt, Gil. "Hall Recall: Barry Sanders." Pro Football Hall of Fame. https://www.profootballhof.com/news/2004/07/news-hall-recall-barry-sanders/.

"Yes, Virginia, Detroit Once Had a More-Hated GM Than Matt Millen." *Bleacher Report.* https://www.bleacherreport.com/articles/1937425.

"Barry Sanders Signs $9.5-Million Contract." *Los Angeles Times*, Sept. 8, 1989. https://www.latimes.com/archives/la-xpm-1989-09-08-sp-1886-story.html.

"Great Migration: Definition, Causes & Impact." History.com. https://www.history.com/articles/great-migration.

"Schmidt Named New Lions General Manager." UPI archives. https://www.upi.com/Archives/1989/12/27/Schmidt-named-new-Lions-general-manager/4155630738000/.

"What Happened To Andre Ware?" Pro Football History. https://www.profootballhistory.com/what-happened-to-andre-ware/.

"Detroit Lions Lineman Mike Utley Is Paralyzed in Game." *ClickOnDetroit.* https://www.clickondetroit.com/video/sports/2021/11/15/nov-17-1991-footage-detroit-lions-lineman-mike-utley-is-paralyzed-in-game-against-la-rams/.

de la Rosa, Poch. "What Happened to Eric Andolsek?" Pro Football History. https://www.profootballhistory.com/eric-andolsek/.

St. Germain, Brent. "Not Forgotten: Promising NFL Player Looms Large in Memory." *Houma Today.* https://www.houmatoday.com/story/news/2007/06/23/not-forgotten-promising-nfl-player-looms-large-in-memory-of-those-who-knew-him/26934503007/#:~:text=who%20knew%20him-,NOT%20FORGOTTEN%3A%20Promising%20NFL%20player%20looms%20large%20in,of%20those%20who%20knew%20him&text=THIBODAUX%20%E2%80%93%20Eric%20Andolsek%20of%20Thibodaux,the%20Detroit%20Lions%20offensive%20line.

Rogers, Justin. "'There Was No Question:' In 1989, Lions Were Locked on Barry Sanders at No. 3 in NFL Draft." *The Detroit News*, April 22, 2019.

https://www.detroitnews.com/story/sports/nfl/lions/2019/04/22/1989-detroit-lions-locked-barry-sanders-no-3-nfl-draft/3538675002/.

GAME 5

"The History of NFL Free Agency: A Journey Through Time." Front Office NFL. https://www.operations.nfl.com/inside-football-ops/nfl-operations/2025-nfl-free-agency/the-history-of-nfl-free-agency/.

DeArdo, Bryan. "Former Lions Coach Says Joe Montana Wanted to Team Up with Barry Sanders in Detroit." CBS Sports, March 30, 2023. https://www.cbssports.com/nfl/news/former-lions-coach-says-joe-montana-wanted-to-team-up-with-barry-sanders-in-detroit/.

Clear, James. "Delayed Gratification and Its Impact on Success." *James Clear*. https://www.jamesclear.com/delayed-gratification.

"Heavy Day of Trading at NFL Draft." UPI archives. April 25, 1993. https://www.upi.com/Archives/1993/04/25/Heavy-day-of-trading-at-NFL-draft/1495735710400/.

GAME 6

"Bobby Ross." Wikipedia. https://www.en.wikipedia.org/wiki/Bobby_Ross.

"Did Ray Lewis-Led Ravens Defense Nudge Barry Sanders Into Early Retirement?" Baltimore Ravens. https://www.baltimoreravens.com/news/did-ray-lewis-led-ravens-defense-nudge-barry-sanders-into-early-retirement-18705354.

Schwab, Frank. "Barry Sanders Will Tell Story About His Shocking Retirement in New Documentary." Yahoo Sports. https://www.sports.yahoo.com/barry-sanders-will-tell-story-about-his-shocking-retirement-in-new-documentary-180041838.html?guccounter=1&guce_referrer=aHR0cHM6Ly93d3cuZ29vZ2xlLmNvbS8&guce_referrer_sig=AQAAAEzjF79Rh06bwnn5NApIOLR84IXOqYEiCThVTJ4c8-NVBV_lDXWj_tg8Z9AtQpBVNAumA_in8sxmliuxEI-PYHzBj2Y72kVPXlxQ6xHJnMaXCXDJx738XhBPl0pBb0nWIeO3j-aGlU16qnFESszcWQsvsJ7oY4OcGlWkVulMoZkM.

Litsky, Frank. "Moeller Resigns as Michigan Coach." *New York Times*, May 5, 1995. https://www.nytimes.com/1995/05/05/sports/college-football-moeller-resigns-as-michigan-coach.html.

Gill, Joe. "Barry Sanders: Incredible and Selfless." *Bleacher Report,* September 12, 2209. https://www.bleacherreport.com/articles/253055-barry-sanders-incredible-and-selfless.

Davenport, Gary. "Barry Sanders and Other Top NFL Players Who Retired Too Early." *Bleacher Report,* July 16, 2019. https://www.bleacherreport.com/articles/2845172-barry-sanders-and-other-top-nfl-players-who-retired-too-early.

GAME 7

Rosenberg, Michael "The Seven-Year Glitch." *Sports Illustrated Vault,* December 2, 2013. https://www.vault.si.com/vault/2013/12/02/the-sevenyear-glitch.

Silver, Michael. "Detroit's Darling: Rookie Joey Harrington Has All the Tools—the Talent, the Toughness and the Moxie—to Bring Real Hope to the Fans of the Long-Lost Lions." *Sports Illustrated*, November 11, 2002. https://www.vault.si.com/vault/2002/11/11/detroits-darling-rookie-joey-harrington-has-all-the-toolsthe-talent-the-toughness-and-the-moxieto-bring-real-hope-to-the-fans-of-the-longlost-lion.

Jahnke, James. "Harrington: 4 Years with Detroit Lions 'Absolutely Crushed Me.'" *Detroit Free Press*, December 21, 2015. https://www.freep.com/story/sports/nfl/lions/2015/12/21/joey-harrington-detroit-lions/77712416/.

"Joey Harrington Looks Back Fondly on NFL Career." NFL.com, December 22, 2015. https://www.nfl.com/news/joey-harrington-looks-back-fondly-on-nfl-career-0ap3000000607173.

"Morton Invited to Appear on Tonight Show." 247Sports. https://www.247sports.com/nfl/detroit-lions/Article/Morton-Invited-To-Appear-on-Tonight-Show-104031762/.

Meinke, Kyle. "5 Days That Defined William Clay Ford." MLive. https://www.mlive.com/lions/2014/03/5_days_that_defined_william_cl.html.

King, Peter. "When There's a Job to Do, Former Linebacker Matt Millen Doesn't Hesitate to Jump In and Get His Hands Dirty, But This Novice NFL Executive Has His Work Cut Out for Him in Trying to Turn the Detroit Lions into Champions." *Sports Illustrated Vault*, July 16, 2001. https://www.vault.si.com/vault/2001/07/16/when-theres-a-job-to-do-former-linebacker-matt-millen-doesnt-hesitate-to-jump-in-and-get-his-hands-dirty-but-this-novice-nfl-executive-has-his-work-cut-out-for-him-in-trying-to-turn-the-detroit-lions-into-champions.

GAME 8

Graff, Gary. "Russ Gibb, Detroit Rock Concert Pioneer & Man Behind 'Paul Is Dead' Rumors, Dead at 87." *Billboard*, May 1, 2019. https://www.billboard.com/music/rock/russ-gibb-detroit-grande-paul-is-dead-8509569/.

"The NFL Fines the Detroit Lions Over 'Rooney Rule' Violation." African American Registry. https://www.aaregistry.org/story/nfl-levies-fine-over-rooney-rule/.

Baumgardner, Nick. "There Was Only One Charles Rogers, the Athlete 'Who Could Do Anything.'" *The Athletic*, November 11, 2019. https://www.nytimes.com/athletic/1369069/2019/11/11/there-was-only-one-charles-rogers-the-athlete-who-could-do-anything/.

Tucker, Cody J. "Ex-Football Star Charles Rogers Tries to Repair Life in Fort Myers." *News-Press*. https://www.news-press.com/story/sports/2017/04/20/ex-football-star-charles-rogers-tries-repair-life-fort-myers/100691344/.

Zeigler, Cyd. "Matt Millen Once Called a Player the Worst-of-All Gay Slurs as Detroit Lions GM." *Outsports*, November 3, 2024. https://www.outsports.com/2024/11/3/4010160/matt-millen-calls-player-a-faggot/.

Bien, Louis. "Charles Rogers' Tragic Decline and Lasting Legacy." *SB Nation*, November 12, 2019. https://www.sbnation.com/2019/11/12/20959376/charles-rogers-death-lions-michigan-state-career-criticism.

GAME 9

Wilson, Ryan. "Even Matt Millen Warned Al Davis Not to Draft JaMarcus Russell." *CBS Sports*, February 23, 2015. Accessed October 9, 2025. https://www.cbssports.com/nfl/news/even-matt-millen-warned-al-davis-not-to-draft-jamarcus-russell/.

Associated Press. "Kitnas' Halloween Costumes Scare Up Negative Response." *The Spokesman-Review*, November 1, 2007. Accessed October 9, 2025. https://www.spokesman.com/stories/2007/nov/01/kitnas-halloween-costumes-scare-up-negative/.

Associated Press. "Lions Assistant Suspended after Arrests." *NewsOn6*, December 19, 2006. Accessed October 9, 2025. https://www.newson6.com/story/5e3689d72f69d76f620a06f9/lions-assistant-suspended-after-arrests.

Yuille, Sean. "Roy Williams: Wide Receiver Turned Pizza Hut Delivery Man." Pride of Detroit. Accessed April 14, 2025. https://www.prideofdetroit.com/2007/10/17/202814/05.

Weixlmann, Ben. "Tatum Bell Tries to Pull Fast One, Gets Caught Stealing Rudi's Baggage." *Bleacher Report*, September 8, 2008. https://www.bleacherreport.com/articles/53702-tatum-bell-tries-to-pull-fast-one-gets-caught-stealing-rudis-baggage.

Dow, Bill. "How the Detroit Lions drove Joey Harrington into depression; Thanksgiving revenge memories." *Detroit Free Press*, November 24, 2020. https://www.freep.com/story/sports/nfl/lions/2020/11/24/detroit-lions-joey-harrington-depression-thanksgiving-steve-mariucci/6374734002/.

GAME 10

Burke, Chris. "The Day Detroit Turned to Matthew Stafford." *The Athletic*, September 4, 2018. https://www.nytimes.com/athletic/456673/2018/09/04/the-day-detroit-turned-to-matthew-stafford.

Yusuf, Farouk. "The NFL Rookie Wage Scale: A Game-Changer for the League." *Sportskeeda*, March 21, 2023. Accessed October 9, 2025. https://www.sportskeeda.com/nfl/the-nfl-rookie-wage-scale-a-game-changer-league.

"2011 NFL Team Salary Cap Tracker." Spotrac. Accessed April 14, 2025. https://www.spotrac.com/nfl/cap/2011.

Laird, Sam. "Concussions Ended His Promising NFL Career, So He Became an Olympian Instead." Mashable. Accessed April 14, 2025. https://www.mashable.com/article/jahvid-best-nfl-olympics.

McKelvie, Eric. "Detroit Lions: A Look at Jahvid Best's Concussion-Filled Career." *Bleacher Report*, January 27, 2013. Accessed April 10, 2025. https://www.bleacherreport.com/articles/1503000-detroit-lions-a-look-at-jahvid-bests-concussion-filled-career.

GAME 11

Rivera, Joe. "What is the Madden Curse? A Complete History of NFL Stars Who Experienced Cover Jinx." *The Sporting News*, accessed April 14, 2025. https://www.sportingnews.com/uk/nfl/news/madden-curse-cover-list-history/rfohxki52h57l5vmd9umn2a1.

Yuille, Sean. "Inside the Numbers on Lions' Arrests." *Pride of Detroit*, May 28, 2012. Accessed April 14, 2025. https://www.prideofdetroit.com/2012/5/28/3047577/detroit-lions-arrests-numbers-nfl.

Florio, Mike. "Lions Ban Titus Young from OTAs for Sucker-Punching Louis Delmas." *NBC Sports*, May 21, 2012. Accessed April 14, 2025. https://www.nbcsports.com/nfl/profootballtalk/rumor-mill/news/lions-ban-titus-young-from-otas-for-sucker-punching-louis-delmas.

Magary, Drew. "Titus Young Will Take a Nap in Your AT&T Store." *Deadspin*, May 8, 2013. Accessed October 9, 2025. https://deadspin.com/titus-young-will-take-a-nap-in-your-at-t-store-496122722/.

Skiver, Kevin. "Ex-NFL Player Titus Young Writes from Jail about Hearing Voices to Commit Crimes," *CBS Sports*, January 30, 2018. https://www.cbssports.com/nfl/news/ex-nfl-player-titus-young-writes-from-jail-about-hearing-voices-to-commit-crimes/.

"Lions Benched Titus Young for Sabotaging Their Passing Offense." NBC Sports. https://www.nbcsports.com/nfl/profootballtalk/rumor-mill/news/lions-benched-titus-young-for-sabotaging-their-passing-offense.

Fenno, Nathan. "Mental Illness or Brain Injury? Driven by Voices to Commit Crime, Titus Young Is in Prison but Still Believes He Could Play in the NFL." *Los Angeles Times*, January 29, 2018. https://www.latimes.com/sports/nfl/la-sp-nfl-young-mental-health-20180128-htmlstory.html.

GAMES 13-14

Mathews, Ryan. "5 Takeaways: Matt Patricia Detroit Lions Introductory Press Conference." *Pride of Detroit*, February 7, 2018. Accessed October 9, 2025. https://www.prideofdetroit.com/2018/2/7/16987374/5-takeaways-matt-patricia-detroit-lions-introductory-press-conference.

"Leadership Styles to Know for Dynamics of Leading Organizations." *Fiveable*. Accessed October 9, 2025. https://www.fiveable.me/lists/leadership-styles.

Snell, Robert. "Lions' Patricia Indicted, Not Tried in '96 Sex Assault." *The Detroit News*, May 9, 2018. Accessed October 9, 2025. https://www.detroitnews.com/story/sports/nfl/lions/2018/05/09/matt-patricia-indicted-sex-assault/34742627/.

Murphy, Bryan. "What Did Matt Patricia Say to Darius Slay? Revisiting the Lions Feud and 'Cordial' Eagles Reunion." *The Sporting News*, January 15, 2024. Accessed October 9, 2025. 10-9-2025 https://www.sportingnews.com/us/nfl/news/matt-patricia-darius-slay-lions-feud-eagles-reunion/ad3d4b0dcc39a74f1d03efe3.

Wagner-McGough, Sean. "Lions Coach Matt Patricia Scolds a Reporter for His Posture, Tells Him to 'Respect' the Process." *CBS Sports*, October 31, 2018. Accessed October 9, 2025. https://www.cbssports.com/nfl/news/lions-coach-matt-patricia-scolds-a-reporter-for-his-posture-tells-him-to-respect-the-process/.

Williams, Charean. "Quandre Diggs Has Gotten Bitter Feelings about Trade from Detroit." *NBC Sports*, September 28, 2022. Accessed October

9, 2025. https://www.nbcsports.com/nfl/profootballtalk/rumor-mill/news/quandre-diggs-has-gotten-bitter-feelings-about-trade-from-detroit.

GAMES 15-16

Birkett, Dave. "Detroit Lions Hire Brad Holmes as General Manager from L.A. Rams." *Detroit Free Press*, January 14, 2021. https://www.freep.com/story/sports/nfl/lions/2021/01/14/detroit-lions-brad-holmes-general-manager-la-rams/4144977001/.

Woodyard, Eric. "Filled with Former NFL Players, Detroit Lions Coaching Staff Knows What It Takes to Win." ESPN, July 9, 2021. https://www.espn.com/blog/detroit-lions/post/_/id/37846/filled-with-former-nfl-players-detroit-lions-coaching-staff-knows-what-it-takes-to-win.

Woodyard, Eric. "'The Rise' of Detroit Lions OC Ben Johnson." ESPN, September 28, 2023. https://www.espn.com/nfl/story/_/id/38508867/the-rise-detroit-lions-oc-ben-johnson.

SMART Recovery Handbook. https://www.smartrecovery.org.

"Dry Drunk." *American Addiction Centers*. https://www.americanaddictioncenters.org/blog/dry-drunk.

Payton, Mike. "Tracking the 16 Receivers Taken Before Amon-Ra St. Brown." *AtoZSports*, October 9, 2025. https://www.atozsports.com/detroit/lions-tracking-the-16-receivers-taken-before-amon-ra-st-brown/.

ABOUT THE AUTHOR

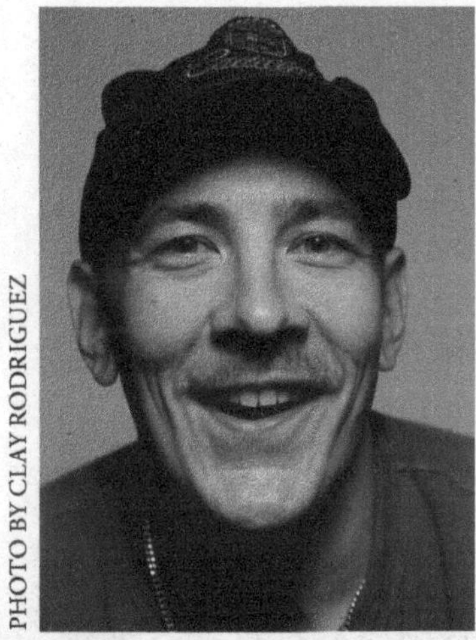
PHOTO BY CLAY RODRIGUEZ

Joel's a nationally touring comedian, award-winning roast battler, and second-funniest cast member on the popular NFL Fan Therapy web series. His writing has appeared in *The New York Times,* Comedy Central, and got him banned from Major League Baseball.

His nonprofit, "Big Walkowski," raises money for organ donation with a basketball tournament (that he usually wins).

Most importantly, Joel Walkowski runs a SMART Recovery meeting Thursdays at 6:30 PM at the Phoenix House in Brooklyn, NY. Come through if compelled.

More books coming . . .

More information available at BigWalkowski.com